When Things Get Back to Normal

Illinois State University/Fiction Collective Series

Curtis White, Series Editor

Also available in the series

PLANE GEOMETRY AND OTHER AFFAIRS OF THE HEART

by R. M. Berry

*

WHEN

THINGS

GET BACK

TO NORMAL

*

AND OTHER STORIES BY CONSTANCE PIERCE

ILLINOIS STATE UNIVERSITY
NORMAL

FICTION COLLECTIVE
NEW YORK · BOULDER

Copyright © 1986 by Constance Pierce
All rights reserved.
First Edition
First Printing, 1986
Library of Congress Cataloging in Publication Data

Pierce, Constance
  When things get back to normal.

I. Illinois State University/Fiction Collective (U.S.) II. Title.
PS3566.I3817W4 1986 813.'54   86-27870
ISBN 0-932511-00-7
ISBN 0-932511-10-5 (pbk.)

This publication is the 1985 winner of the Illinois State
University/Fiction Collective Award, jointly sponsored by the Illinois
State University Fine Arts Festival and the Fiction Collective.

Published by Illinois State University/Fiction Collective with support
from Illinois State University Foundation, the National Endowment
for the Arts, and the New York State Council on the Arts, and with
the cooperation of Brooklyn College and Teachers & Writers
Collaborative.

Grateful acknowledgment is made to the following publications in
which these stories first appeared: Alaska Quarterly Review for "The
Gourmand" and "Woman Waiting for Train at Dusk" and The
Pikestaff Forum for "When Things Get Back to Normal."

Grateful acknowledgment is also made to the Graduate School, the
School of Arts and Sciences, and the President's Fund of the
University of Colorado, Boulder.

Some of the stories in this collection were written with the help of a
fellowship from The National Endowment for the Arts.

Typeset by Fisher Composition, Inc.
Manufactured in the United States of America.
Designed by Abe Lerner

CONTENTS

When Things Get Back to Normal

The Gourmand

*

MONSIEUR MAURICE RAMBEAU, the self-styled connoisseur from Poitiers, was having a heart attack.

He had been walking along the street of an obscure village in the Touraine after a very unsatisfactory lunch in a bistro that had been especially recommended to him by the best wine merchant in Tours several days earlier. The lunch had turned out to be ordinary in every detail and in no way worth the extravagant excursion to this place of no distinction, he'd been thinking, when suddenly he had felt his steps slow to a shuffle. He had sagged against the piebald trunk of a sycamore whose limbs had been amputated to a dozen stumps, thinking it was the heat that was doing him in, cursing the primitive village habit of lopping off the natural leaves and branches that might have provided charm to an otherwise charmless spot, camouflage of a depressing emptiness—at least, some relief from the sun. Then a great pain had run through his own substantial trunk, down his own stubby limbs, and he had understood.

Just as his knees were collapsing, he dragged himself onto a mound of grass leading up to a copse, a small park where red canna lilies were growing in a raucous profusion in front of the thick shade of trees that were mercifully untrimmed. But here he sank down, still in the sun. The trees above the mound were just out of his reach, like a distant heaven. He lay silent and livid, staring up at the horrible blue of a too-close sky.

Soon a crowd gathered. Someone tucked a white-papered parcel of laundry under his head, someone else ran for the doctor. A covey of pigeons, that had been huddled among the lilies until the assault of Rambeau on their territory, moved out and began to walk around, eyeing the little man. He could see them pecking at the air, traversing the outline of his body, their neck-feathers undulating in a slow iridescence. Even in his delirium, all he could think of was that he would like to wring their spastic necks, one by one.

It wasn't clear to him why he was so angry at these birds, and he didn't trouble himself to wonder, tangled as he was in his desire to kill them and the secondary matter of the heart attack and all it might come to mean. But the violence of this emotion was profound and eventually obsessive, distracting him from everything else that was going on within him, and much that was going on outside, as the strange villagers moved up and stood very near, their legs seeming a kind of a fence between him and the trees, before he lost sight of everything in his fever for the birds.

Yes, he could see these birds: headless, plucked and trussed, lying all in a row in a huge roasting pan. The breasts would be plumping up, the skin pale and naked even of pin-feathers. Then there would be their succulent well-turned legs, bound together, but one would know about the dark mysterious caverns underneath. . . .

Suddenly, the little man was blazing with passion. He lay half-paralyzed, mouth agape, the eyes loose and rolling out of his control, but there was an unmistakable commotion deep in his baggy trousers. Far away, he was sure he heard a woman titter.

Quickly, with an extraordinary surge of will under the circumstances, he moved his mind along, produced the corpses slathered innocently in honey, sputtering in their

10

own grease. A tumble of raisins now obscured the caverns that had provoked him, crossing some internal wires. Bringing on him the mortifying laughter of a faceless woman that he would give ten years, if he had ten left, to thrash and throttle. Yes, yes—out of the oven and onto a platter of cress, he thought, burning in his haze.

All in a row, all in a row, there: brown and steaming, a spray of fresh orange slices to the side. And between the carcasses, what? Carrots? No, too much like oranges—something more. . . . Leeks! Oh, leeks! Piles and piles of baby, buttery leeks separating the miserable creatures, all on a bed of nice rice, a little fennel dusted over. . . .

This *tour de force* was broken into by some shuffling in the crowd at the arrival of the doctor, a cherubic man in black with very red cheeks. He knelt and began to fumble with M. Rambeau's shirt front, the nervous fingers freezing the patient's will, serving him up to his fury and terror at last.

A few moments later, there was an ambulance, a wild race through the streets, the alarms honking like geese. Inside the vehicle, alone and finally out of the sun, M. Rambeau had an *aperçu* of what the meal had cost him. Outside, a little like a ceremonial guard on either side, the pigeons flew, banking and rolling in a playful formation.

THE TENANTS AT AUXILLAC

The Tenants at Auxillac

*

1. The Big House and the little house

As THE impoverished new Master of a dubious patrimony, an old estate that was poorly maintained and
dismantling, Edouard had much on his mind. For one
thing, "Auxillac" was in the Lot River Valley, several
hours remote from his beloved Paris. He was lonely, and
far from the center of the universe. For another, he knew
with a dread that compounded day by day that he had
made a great mistake in renting out the little house on his
property, in spite of the welcome revenue.

The tenants, a young couple who had at first seemed
merely odd, had proven to be worse than even a landlord's
worst nightmare. In a few short weeks they had already,
in some profound way, managed to threaten everything he
cherished. Secretly, he had even felt some threat to his
life, though this came and went.

It was a life, now that he thought about it, that could
very well have been doomed from the start. Yes, sometimes it all seemed to add up to forty years of travail on
an earth that had been unreasonably grudging and unsym-
pathetic, perhaps even diabolical and hostile to him from
the beginning.

More and more, since the arrival of the tenants, he was
convinced this was the case. He was crossing the apex of
life's narrow stile, one foot even now being drawn to the
downward side, and sometimes he almost knew that

things must have been slipping out from under him all along. How else to account for such a miserable state of affairs?

But whatever the mystery, whatever the case fate had constructed against him, whatever the methods used to compute his on-going punishment, he knew that unless he was very, very careful, he would fall utterly and reach the end in a humiliating tumble, everything got away from him.

What, exactly, the tenants contributed to this foreboding, he wasn't sure. But they seemed implicated far out of the expected proportion. Yes, it had been a great, great mistake to rent out his little house.

The little house, though in bad repair, nevertheless had three storys and fifteen rooms, but Edouard always called it "the little house." Some architectural wit or madman had had a joke along the way, at someone else's expense, he often thought, boiling. Though the little house was not particularly old, it sometimes gave the impression of being an oversized cottage in a forest arranged by the Brothers Grimm. Coming upon it from another angle, Edouard would be struck by another eccentricity: a bit of *Bauhaus*, with a touch of the Swiss chalet. The phrase "the little house" could make such an outrage seem amusing (though one was not in the least amused!), as if one felt affection (when one felt crazed with loathing that such liberties had been taken with one's taste in advance!). But most of all, such a phrase would underscore discreetly, but unmistakably, that there was also . . . a Big House.

The manor house at Auxillac, drafty and wobbling on a hill overlooking the river, could be called "The Big House," but there were many times when the Master preferred to let drop a reference to his "15th-Century Chateau." For what was a "chateau" but a very big house?

Auxillac had that indeed. And if it hadn't been entirely constructed in the 15th century, what of it? What, truly, were centuries in the great scheme of things? A tiny portion of the Big House *had* been constructed in the 15th century, and the fact was properly recorded in the proper records, irrefutable. If there were embellishments from the 16th, 17th, 18th, 19th, and even his own unfortunate century, Well? So? Time marched on, more was the pity.

Yes, time marched on, one managed as one could, but reminders of the facts were relentless. Day after tenuous day, he caught the proof of things as he glimpsed himself, billowing like a small whale in the half-silvered oceans of his mirrors. He had needs.

In winter and early spring especially, when the river valley, so pleasant in summer, became a fearful and wretched place, he felt his worst despair. Then he was confined to his bedroom, his outpost, the only room he could afford to heat. The room reproached him, cramped and badly appointed by anyone's standards. Its large vicious mirror loomed on the wall, drawing the whole room into it, no place to hide. He confronted himself in thin sunlight and gloom, swathed in a plush smoking jacket that had belonged to his late father. It told the tale. Though the velvet fortunately revealed only the most minute evidence of decline, no more than two or three ravages of moths and mildew, he himself had a hungry look. In spite of the jacket, in spite of being more than well-enough padded. The mirror proved beyond a doubt that he was ragged around the edges. Oh, yes, anyone could see it, he often thought, scrutinizing his form and his room in firelight and moonlight. Anyone could see that he had needs, needs far beyond his fiscal measure.

In that tenebrous parade of minutes and hours, when warmth and visitors alike were scarce as pocket money, he had lost his better judgment. Then had he (temporarily deranged, he was now convinced) put his little house up for grabs. With consequences to be suffered in a sunnier season.

Well? So? Didn't the flesh itself attest to an *incorrigible* penchant for the richest meats and cheeses? The most buttery sweets, copious liqueurs? To be obtained at monstrous expense in the best of times, but now only at the sacrifice of everyday necessities? Didn't the background to his mirror's image expose an *overwhelming* appetite for the creature comforts, soft upholsteries, art objects? And the need, he thought in sinking defeat, for the extensive replacement and rehabilitation of same?

But: in what way could an appetite be one's own fault? Only in the prim philosophies of a prim era. No, he was not in the least inclined to blame himself for tastes and appetites and penchants. His responsibility was to address them, address the facts of the constraints and small satisfactions of his nature, by labor or scheme or whatever it took.

In the sere days of winter, he paced the worn rug of his seasonal quarters, preoccupied with the evidence and mentally tallying and retallying his financial ledgers, despair gathering like the ice at his windows. The rug itself was a rare *Bokhara*. That much was still evident! he never failed to note with pride. But then: Would its woof and warp one day be no more than bleached strings barely tethered? Like the unhappy tapestry that sagged along his wall? An Aubusson, it was true, but its birds and rabbits now impossible to distinguish from its dogs and goats? No, no—there would be no other solution but to rent out the little house.

Besides, summer brought its own problems, the guests stopping by, en route from Paris to the resorts of the Mediterranean and on the way back sometimes as well. Luminous guests, members of select social circles that he longed, deep in his being, to worm inside. Guests sure to note the state of his affairs, though so far apparently willing to give him the benefit of the doubt, to write off the usual signs of decline to an unusual confidence, to eccentricity or an enviable oblivion to the opinions of others. Guests sure to remark on that curiosity, the little house, though apparently hoodwinked so far by his feigned amusement. Guests he believed would agree with him on matters of his 15th-(documented!) Century Chateau, though he could never be more than 99% sure. Still, he thought he himself offered a proper model of the proper attitude. And of course the fact that such a Big House was in one's private possession alone nipped much in bud, didn't it?

Yes, he had made his peace with the architectural facts of the Big House, and with those of the little house too. If the latter was a cause for spiteful gossip, he had a narrative at the ready, a witty tale with enough charm to devastate the charming, enough to shift the monstrosity into the gentle light of historical eccentricity. And who cared about the charmless in any case, beyond the need to remain wary of them, to impede their influence in matters of one's own reputation, where it counted.

Oh, my, yes, he never failed to laugh, regaling those who counted with the tale of how the little house had come into being, at the whim of a 1920's painter of the avant-garde, whose vision had suddenly veered 180° just prior to the Second World War, resulting in the nostalgic scallops of balcony, bits of thatch on the roof, wood trim perforated in the shapes of hearts and flowers. *Never mind!* he never failed to exhort generously, with much physical evidence of having never minded something that he had always minded more than he could say: arms far-flung in expansiveness, a benevolent smile and beam of

17

eye, head cocked at just the right angle of amusement to
chide anyone who might be constructing a damaging
charge or reproof. *Never mind!* his tone brimming with a
proprietary charm of his own. Didn't the little house have
the drollest character? he would ask, beating them to the
punch. These amusing indiscretions happened with Vi-
sionaries, as everyone knew. Didn't the little house have
its special charm, after all?

Well, whatever his guests thought, he had made his
peace with architecture. But not with the encompassing
state of his patrimony, the cockeyed economy of his parents—who had not even had the cracked artist's excuse
for radical shifts in perspective. Almost hourly he had
cause to lament their lack of good sense near the end,
cause to lament that Auxillac had been their sole legacy,
the sole repository of all their hard-earned wealth, accu-
mulated slowly and at such sacrifice over a long lifetime.
How often he wished that he could have come to his
property in the normal way: received it into his hands
from a long line of finely shaped hands, each pair having
lovingly managed the upkeep of their charge, adding tastefully to its value, and then cheerfully relinquishing it in
an orderly and gracious fashion into the next set of capa-
ble hands, until it was passed like a perfectly polished
jewel into his own, at the end of the line.

Instead, his parents had begun with no tangible resources. After a lifetime of hard work, they had made the
annals of restaurateur fame in Paris and that was nothing
to sneeze at, a testament to native craft and the survival
instincts. But in the Circles of his dreams, nothing to
crow about either.

As they grew more substantial, his parents had taken to
leasing the awful little house at Auxillac for August vacation. And later, growing plump and rich, acquiring ever
more stars and forks in the tourist guides, they had leased

the Big House, and finally the whole estate, once the aged
avant-gardist had met with a freakish accident in a tarn at
the far end of the property, leaving everything to a niece
in America. On retirement, the old restaurateurs had approached the niece through the proper representatives and
made the deal. Auxillac and all it signified had been at-
tained. It was a logical end to things, Edouard could see,
after all their craft and sacrifice. But until the end of their
lives, they themselves regarded Auxillac as if it were out
of a magical fairy tale.

With great sentiment Edouard remembered the winking
and jabbing of elbows-to-ribs as the two old treasures had
guarded their "secret" until all the papers were in order.
Misty of eye and nostril, he recollected their tearful be-
stowal of a will that would make him Master of Auxillac
on their demise, passed to him by his father's broad hand,
growing unsteady even then. It was the culmination of
their life-long plan, to turn over to their son the Chateau,
a vast acreage, room for an eye to range and survey and
appropriate to itself a great river and great valley, as if the
owner were an eagle in an aerie. With these acquisitions,
he might achieve the proper confidence, and a social position that had been mysteriously just out of their reach,
even in the end, rich and famous restaurateurs or no.

Oh, he was—he was!—perfectly happy to be the owner
of a chateau. He was grateful for the serious thoughts of
his well-meaning parents on his future, as incomplete as
these thoughts had turned out to be. He was undeniably
fond of this land, he was! But the upkeep—

The upkeep, slowly but surely, was edging him toward
a precipice. The Big House needed a roof, slate, priced as
dearly as a vital organ. A master craftsman would have to
do the work and would extort a fortune for it. Most of his
furnishings wavered and threatened to collapse on contact. Such upholsteries as he had were hanging together

19

by threads. Paint peeled, tiles were chipping by the hour, the marble was scratched as if it had suffered a deliberate attack. Several of his outbuildings were little more than piles of stone. Someone would have to make a swipe at the grounds in summer when the guests were on him. There were weeds, as always, on the old tennis court. How could he ever hold on?

Or was that part of the plot? he never failed to wonder. That he should lose his grasp so that every private thing he owned could be subsumed into the public domain, Auxillac transformed from a well-loved ancestral estate into a perpetually open house that any riff-raff could wander through for a few francs on a Sunday afternoon, peering into closets, fingering the drapes, encouraging their brats to take a quick pee in a jardiniere or his sainted mother's bidet?

Now that the Pinks and Reds were in power, anything was possible. Sometimes he imagined the "President" himself, that scoundrel and lunatic, leading such a procession, skipping and dipping, piping a maddening tune as all the rodents of city and town danced through the Big House and the little house and all along his hills and meadows. That such a madman could have come to power in a free election, in an ancient civilized country, was truly the worst fact of all. If by some chance there was even one tiny star working in his behalf in the heavens, he thanked it daily that his parents had not lived to witness these new horrors.

After several weeks of nervously reworking his haphazard ledgers, shivering in front of a small stove in his bedroom, his shoulders huddled beneath a thick horseblanket that he had discovered by luck in a crumbling stable at the far end of his property, he managed a cranky acceptance of fate's disdain. Figuring and re-figuring the pitiful receipts from Auxillac's meager produce altered nothing.

And so the advertisement had gone out, offering his little house for rent. Gone out in the newspapers of several provincial cities, newspapers very unlikely to be read by anyone in the discerning Paris Circles.

Sometimes at dusk, while he enjoyed what were sure to be the last evenings of peace on his estate, he would sit at the window in one of his many rooms aloft and look out over the property before it disappeared into the night. The hills rolled darkly in the distance, and between them and his eye lay all that he owned. How few, how few indeed, could seek out such a vantage point, one that opened up a great sweep of the world, and proclaim oneself to be Master of all surveyed?

Sometimes his eye would dwell on a particularly dark spot in this vista—the treacherous tarn from whose dank regions the corpse of the old avant-gardist had never been retrieved. Oh, unhappy man! Edouard would sympathize. To have come to such a wretched fate: doomed to linger, untenable, in the vicinity of what had been one's own property, and yet to have that property indisputably in the possession of another. It was hard to imagine a more mortifying end to things.

As the region around the tarn, and then the entire view, disappeared into the black of night as though that unhappy lagoon were the source of darkness itself, the present Master of Auxillac felt a chill. The moon rose and settled into the heavens like a distant monocle, and Edouard felt himself suddenly under unbearable scrutiny. Oh, yes—he and the dead man had more in common than might meet the ordinary eye, that he could see. Once there were tenants, it would be impossible to say what was one's own, what not, to the watchful world beyond his gate.

He gazed up at the monocle in a silent offer to barter.

21

The monocle did not waver. Indeed: what had he, Edouard, to barter? What but the thing that he was already in the process of bartering? The source of his pride, the source of his shame.

2. *The Charmless Couple and Their Great Red Dog*

When the couple, the DuBonns, had first come, Edouard had been put off, immediately. Though he was one who suffered the prickly heat and chill of doubts every day of his life, he had an almost mystical faith in the first impression, and his first impression of this odd couple agitated his neck and back, his plump shoulders, and left them in cool gooseflesh. He had known sure as truth itself, that if he were an animal, hackles would be bristling. He would be on guard.

The young woman, with her longish black hair parted in the middle, would have been pretty to many, Edouard supposed. But she was certainly not to *his* taste, and even if her presence hadn't exuded some vague danger into the atmosphere, he felt sure that she would nevertheless have left a poor first impression on him. After all, there was something—how would he say it? Well, he didn't want to sound like a *snob*, even to himself, but there was something, if it *must* be said, *déclassé* about her: the ornate earrings like tiny snakes uncoiling onto her neck, their garnet eyes unwinking and rude. There were the too-bright clothes, their odd design . . . something gypsy-like about her, though she seemed clean and quiet enough, her wretched clothes in good repair.

Quite! Like a stone. She wandered here and there about the little house, vaguely curious, no more, as far as he could tell. Then she went back to the car and left the whole matter to her husband.

The husband was all-too-relaxed on another man's property to suit Edouard. The man was disconcerting in his appearance too, thin and angular. Already he had the beginnings of an egg-head, an uncongenial phrenology, the hair creeping far back from very dark and deepset eyes. Below, a frazzled beard was beginning to streak luridly with gray. Oh no—there was neither charm nor personality in this prospective tenant. This, one could see, in spite of the young man's primitive attempts at cordiality. His clothes, too, were a scandal. They looked like work-clothes, but the sort of thing unsavory students and politicos wore for show. And, oh: the *amused* air with which the scoundrel had strolled about the grounds! The *casual* air with which he had flung open doors within the little house, pounded mattresses, checking dust on the furnishings with an impudent forefinger: these were what half-convinced Edouard to turn the couple away and seek some other solution to his financial woes.

On the pretext of consulting Pablo, his ancient retainer, Edouard bought himself a moment to think. He excused himself from the couple's company with the extreme politeness he reserved for those for whom he felt absolute scorn, and then he withdrew, leaving them to murmur to each other through the lowered window of their *rented* automobile.

Now that was another thing: how could they think of living so far from town without a car, no public or private transportation? Would they presume to borrow his car? Oh, yes, he could see that if he were to let them have the little house, soon he wouldn't be able to lay claim to his own little Renault.

Pondering these horrors, Edouard stumbled along the winding route that led down the hill to the servants' hut. Pablo, whose father had come from Spain in the previous century to oversee the estate in its most lavish circum-

23

stances, had lived through several owners. Much to Edouard's dissatisfaction, the old man was impervious to any sort of threat or intimidation, no matter how cunningly wrought. Edouard tried to intimidate, dropping a hint that a person living on another's property might well count his blessings, help with the general maintenance without complaint, perform minor services graciously, when possible pay a bit of rent. None of this made the impression it was meant to, Pablo and his wife Miranda being secure in some mad arrangements his parents had made near the end. Sometimes he wished his parents were alive so that he could bring a suit in his interests, really! No, not possible to intimidate, not possible to get the mail brought up to the house promptly, not possible to get twigs and weeds rounded up except at the whim of the old man, not possible to get the laundry done except as a grudging favor, not possible to get a meal served for guests except by a humiliating wheedle or bray, not possible to get some item picked up in the village without the bastard's old truck being petrolled on one's account, not possible to get a shrub pruned unless it was hard on the hut itself. . . .

By the time Edouard reached the hut, he had worked himself into a lather of complaints. Sometimes he longed to burn down the hut, the two old Spaniards either crisped inside or standing out in the rain with a claim on nothing, both possibilities promising equal pleasure.

As he stepped into the hut, he could see Pablo sitting at the kitchen table, etching what looked like a doggish animal on a large stone. At the stove Miranda silently stirred a pungent stew that caused Edouard to wrinkle his nose, attempt a retreat. After all, he had nothing he wished to discuss with either of these primitives, who hadn't even the grace to scramble around and get him a chair, though

24

they were clearly aware of his presence. Yes, a retreat, thought Edouard, preparing to turn.

But as it often happened when he wandered into Pablo's *presumed* sphere of influence, he was stalled in his tracks by a commanding eye. Though it was an eye watering with the mists of the River Styx, he noted with some satisfaction. Still, against his will, he found himself staying, and then revealing much more than it was in his interests for the old vulture to know. He found himself relating all his troubles about the roof, the tile, the marble, the furniture, the grounds, ending up, to his horror, with a humiliating bleat on the need for someone to chop wood for the remaining cool weeks of spring.

Edouard related everything helplessly gritting his parsimonious teeth while the words rolled voluptuously through them, the mesmerizing eye working its spell, summoning all the details of private business from beyond his useless will. Even so, he practiced his special mode: spilling out his secrets with excessive solicitude, but undercoating every unctuous phrase with bile and scorn. Perhaps, he always hoped, he could undo his shameful revelations, in some way, by the parallel discourse, secret and obscene, running along the nether kinks of his brain. Perhaps, he always hoped, he could redeem this mysterious compulsion to betray himself, redeem his slack tongue, and all it hinted about a slack constitution and a sense of propriety that was somehow slack as well, all the usual tautness of its outside to the contrary.

Looking at Pablo's enormous steady eye, he could see these were vain hopes, good to swell an ego, but useless in the real moment at hand. He knew what the old gargoyle was thinking: Why didn't a man barely of middle age chop his own wood? Well, he did chop what he could!

25

Hadn't that all-seeing Cyclopean eye noted the Master of the property hewing and sawing, huffing and puffing in the nearer woods, like a peasant woodchopper in a fairy tale? One was no longer a spring calf. One did what one could do.

Boiling, Edouard spoke sweetly as a courtier, sputtering impotently to a stop only when the old peasant had lowered his eye to his carving again. Well, why not lower the eye? Edouard thought. Hasn't he learned all there is to know? Furious, yet smiling like an obedient son, Edouard waited for Pablo's pronouncement. That was how the old bastard did it. He *pronounced*, exploiting his age for the privilege of impudence! Behind his ingenious smile, Edouard entertained a delicious impulse as he watched the man's bent head and imagined the vulnerable mush lying just beneath the pate.

"Take it," Pablo pronounced, never looking up. "It's a dump. Count your blessings."

Distressed and unable to deny that the old man was partly right (though partly wrong: the little house was not in the best repair, not in the most pleasing architectural style, but it was hardly a dump! Shouldn't a lifelong gentleman's retainer have a bit more discretion and humility? Not to mention a more discriminating judgment?), Edouard brooded all the way back up the hill to where the couple waited in their rented car. Indeed there were only these two applicants. Perhaps he should count his blessings, he thought with a feeling of being singularly unblessed, of being perhaps the special target of all the malevolent fates in the universe. The old government had been big on talk about preserving the stately old places, but getting any money out of these communists would be like trying to get a drop of decent wine on his own property.

Quickly, Edouard squinted his eyes and pursed his lips,

26

pushing away that two-headed monster before it distracted him from the important business at hand. Along with his horror of the new regime, it was a persistent discontent that Pablo, on the grounds that he had planted the vineyards many years before from stock developed and passed along by his father, took such grapes as there were each year for himself and produced an almost respectable wine, leaving the owner of the property (the benefactor of the devil's old age!) to drink the vinegary swill that had been made and stored in the "Caveau" before the War.

Well, he would not get into that now, Edouard thought, turning toward the prospective tenants.

The woman was sitting at the wheel of the car, one thin arm strung with elaborate bracelets, crooked into a "V" and resting on the window. She was looking straight into Edouard's eyes with a thoroughly noncommital half-smile. Her husband's frizzed head was bent close to hers, as if they were conspiring, and he too was looking at the Master of Auxillac with a curious half-smile, neither friendly nor solicitous nor even quite amused. Though amusement seemed possible, Edouard thought, greatly irritated.

Well and so. What could he do? He advanced toward them, already extending the hand of agreement. Sometimes he couldn't help thinking that his parents had had it in for him all along, leaving this old place and not a cent to keep it up. Perhaps they had hated him in the cradle even, spent their lives conceiving a *coup de grâce* of such amazing subtlety that their best revenge on him, for whatever it was that had set them off, would be in knowing that he would never figure it out. Well, one was not so naive as one might have appeared as a child!

Then, sagging in the effort of containing this unfair thought, he shook the cool hands of first, the husband,

27

then the wife. Yes, he would rent out his monstrosity of a little house and be grateful that his parents had had the foresight to acquire a piece of property with such a resource for him. Still, it was tempting to think of selling it all off and being done with it.

But how could he, he thought as he made arrangements with these repulsive young people. What was he but the owner of an estate? If not that, then a middle-aged orphan with no profession, an unsuccessful student of economy, a man with no distinctions that would admit him even to the outer circumference of the social circles he craved, craved to swallow him up, if the truth must be said.

Besides, he thought, watching the heads of his new tenants dip toward each other as the car wound down his drive and away from him. Besides, Auxillac had been his childhood summer home. He saw a brief image of his robust young parents, spading about in their shorts and sandals, transplanting and puttering on their rented grounds. Suddenly they suspended their garden implements in the air, turned their benevolent adoring faces on him, as if he and he alone held all they had lived for, a delicate old dream that for the moment held together as if bright and sturdy in his charge. One false move and it would disintegrate, erase all their hard hours.

Suddenly, he felt heartened by this responsibility and by all the past sentiments that were swirling about as his sensory orifices took in the image, whiff, and rustle of an infant Spring. How his parents would have loved this spring at Auxillac. How they had talked in their few moments of leisure among the busy hours at the restaurant, talked of the gardens and how the fruit trees would flower in spring, how the place would be set ablaze with tulips and daffodils—

Well, his ambitions in the garden so far were lagging, but Auxillac had been what Auxillac had been for the old

28

folks. That counted for something. He would rent out the little house, yes. Before all was said and done, perhaps he would evict the old Spaniards and rent out the hut down the hill, rent out the stables and the vineyard too.

But he would never, never sell Auxillac.

The couple moved in early one Sunday morning. They came in a rented van, bringing several suitcases, some boxes, a very deep chair on rockers, and a large blood-colored dog, something like a mastiff. They had not told Edouard about the animal, and the way they moved it in right under his nose—the nose being poised at the time on an upstairs window sill of the Big House, the owner of the nose spying on the activity below—had irritated him so much that he had spent the entire afternoon painting the kitchen, a belated attempt to cut expenses through his own labor and not leave himself vulnerable to renters and whatever other horrors he might be asked to adapt himself to further down the line.

All afternoon as he painted, he glanced out the window toward the little house with amazement. Though people were moving in, there was no activity of moving in. No windows were open to air things out (not that anything needed airing out in his little house!). There were no sounds of furniture being moved about (not that any permission had been given for moving any furniture about!). The windows and doors were tightly sealed, the environs silent as a tomb. If not for the presence of the rented van, he would have thought that the new tenants had gone to the village on an errand, or—wistfully, wistfully—that they had been only a terrible hallucination and his little house was still clearly under his jurisdiction, no question as to who was Lord and Master of every inch of Auxillac.

In the cruel response to this daydream, the tenants' monster dog put in an appearance toward evening, coming

29

out of the shadows of the trees like an omen and settling onto the slab of stonework in front of the door to the little house like a pool of blood. It was a most unusual color for a dog, Edouard observed. In fact, he felt sure that he had never seen such a hue in that species. The beast was by no stretch of the imagination brown, not even "chestnut" nor the redder shades of "golden." By earlier daylight it had seemed unnaturally red, more the color of a fresh wound. But as dusk crept in and the creature remained puddling on the stone in front of the little house, it looked more the color of dried blood, the remains of a crime. As Edouard cleaned his paintbrushes and eyed the sleeping animal and the utterly dark and silent little house, he could not help but think that this hound of hell had placed itself very presumptuously indeed at that doorstep: as if guarding private property for the DuBonns. The thought caused his fingers to go momentarily limp. A paintbrush dripping with turpentine fell to the floor, leaving a haphazard trail on his trousers from hip to shin, and he spent several minutes attending to the damage to his clothing and his kitchen floor. When he had all his painting gear more or less clean and shoved into a pantry, he returned to the window that looked out across the courtyard to the little house and was shocked to see that the great red dog of the tenants had risen up out of its sleep and settled imperially onto its large haunches, its wide breast thrust up and out, its head high and proudly assumptive: the Lion at the Gate! Its eyes were trained on the kitchen window of the Big House, and Edouard could feel them subsuming the Master of Auxillac into their yellow light. At the same time, they seemed to be warning him, of what he couldn't say, but one thing he knew: it wasn't a friendly warning. No, he thought, watching the animal disappear as dark took over. Not in the least friendly, and perhaps even a threat.

30

Well, he thought later that evening as he collapsed, exhausted, at his kitchen table with a very fine Amontillado that a Christmas guest had left three months before. Well, apparitions near evening were common enough when the body was fatigued and the spirit had suffered a humiliating defeat. He would put the ominous red dog out of his mind. Tomorrow was as always (what else?) a new day.

He sat for some time admiring the new paint, which he had had to apply in long stripes of varying colors, since his decision to paint had been an impetuous one requiring him to make use of what he had. A sudden noise, the scrape of a shoe on the steps perhaps, made him look up from his wine—straight into the face of the new tenant, standing at the kitchen door. It gave him a momentary shock. He was used to being alone on the place, except for Pablo and Miranda, who never ventured from their quarters after sundown, cherishing some eccentric Spanish folklore about the night air. The face on the other side of the door's glass was, well, how should he say it? It seemed at once amused and abstracted, and even after he'd managed to cover his surprise and beckon the man into the kitchen, DuBonn stood still for a moment, as though the gesture did not immediately register. Then he entered, wearing a light jacket over his "workclothes" and said that he had come to borrow a little wine for dinner, that he would replace it the next day when he would be returning the van to its agent.

With some irritation, Edouard took down the large key to the room his father had always called the "Caveau," though it was entirely above ground and certainly not a cellar; still, the Caveau it had been pronounced and the Caveau it would ever be, as long as Edouard was at the helm of things. Clutching the key he left the kitchen and began the uncomfortable trek across the bumpy courtyard to the room where his vinegary stock reposed in a gauze

31

of spider webs. It was a cold night for Spring, he noted with a sinking heart as he shuffled toward his destination. He would have to make a fire in the bedroom, a project that filled him with dread. More often than not the room would fill up with smoke and all the heat would disappear out the window that he, gasping, would have to fling open at the last moment, conceding yet another small defeat. If he had more money, he'd simply sell this dump and move back to Paris. His days in Paris, as a student, had been the best of his life. He had had a tiny room in a building of tiny rooms, full of other students, everyone on an equal footing. There had been beautiful girls willing to come to his tiny room, after a nice dinner at his parents' stellar restaurant. He had had great companions, a comfortable life, wine of distinction, for his parents always saved him the quarter-bottles and half-bottles left unfinished by their extravagant clientele. He had ranged them all in an open cupboard in his room, the labels and vintages visible to all the friends and girl friends who climbed the picturesque stairs to his lair.

Struggling to keep his balance and body warmth, he thought with a bitter gall of his selections of wines in the Caveau. All the fine bottles his parents had left had been consumed by guests the first summer that Auxillac had been under his dominion. And though it was not often that he criticized the Circles, he had since thought from time to time that a guest of real distinction would have replenished his stock more substantially than had been the case. Occasionally someone brought a nice bottle of this or that, but more often it was some local produce passed off as "quaint" or "droll." Very nice!

Yes, he'd like to move back to Paris, get a cozy little set of rooms, heated, an almost-fashionable address, a library, a dining room for the *carefully* selected guests of real distinction.

32

But he was dreaming. Paris had been the seat of his failure too, the site of his dismal career as an economic consultant, a field his well-meaning parrents had steered him toward and for which he hadn't had a mote of talent. And what guests would come if he were to sell the chateau and take those rooms, however fashionable the address? The Circles he yearned for, the Circles that he could sometimes slip almost within—would they seek out a middle-aged nobody with a set of rooms? No, he would have to stay here, in the primitive valley of the Lot, with only Cahors, a boring city, nearby. He would have to count on Auxillac to draw such luminaries as it might. One needed brilliant friends—people with charm, personality, discretion, wit, erudition—that had been the lesson, the only lesson, of his aspiring father. How he wished that the old man could have found some way to leave him money as well.

Such were his thoughts as he passed across the courtyard under the still, bare trees, their twigs like fragments of net against the sky. The moon was full, with a mere wisp of bluish cloud over it, but otherwise the night was almost as clear as day.

Inside the Caveau, he grabbed a random bottle and blew the dust and cobwebs from it, and filled it from the tap of a moldy cask. Then he headed back to the kitchen, after locking up his wine, entering to find his guest bent over a stack of mail and well-worn ledgers which were piled among the lemons and potatoes on the work table near the sink. Glancing up at his landlord, DuBonn appeared entirely at his ease, not in the least embarrassed at having been caught snooping about—in fact, he reached out his hand and gave the ledgers a solid pat, as though to indicate that they were in order! Was this to be the price of a new slate roof? To be snooped upon and treated so casually by one's *tenant!*

33

Edouard moved into the room and placed the bottle of wine on a shelf at waist height, to his right, far from the tenant, and stood facing the man down. One would soon see what was what. Suddenly, the man's smile widened enormously, and he became the portrait of amicability, telling a rapid and charming little story of the move, chatting, working his way toward the wine, taking hold of the bottle at the very instant that his free hand fell to Edouard's shoulder in a clasp of comradely warmth. Before the landlord knew it, the man was out of the Big House and Edouard was left standing bemused in the center of the kitchen.

After a simple meal of salad and potatoes, Edouard—still very much disconcerted—took a basket and filled it with kindling from the large box behind the cook-stove and then went upstairs to work on his bedroom fire. After some sputtering failures, he finally got the fire burning cosily, but the room, as usual, was full of smoke. Edouard moved to the large window overlooking the little house and opened it to let in the air. The little house was dark, which gave him heart. At least these tenants would retire at a decent hour and not disturb his sleep. That was something.

He was just turning back into the room when something in the side yard caught his eye: there was movement behind a piece of shrubbery. And although the twigs and branches were bare, they created a grid that did not allow him to see much beyond it. All he could tell was that there was bulk and there was movement. He leaned further into the night and peered at the scene, straining his eyes. The moon that had shone so clearly earlier was suddenly clouded by an obstructive fluff, and though he knew that something was going on below, he had no idea what it was. Well, what could it be? Maybe the dog. The thought caused him to fume for an instant, but he was cold, the room was free of smoke, and his bed as inviting as a mistress. He closed the window and turned out the light. It had indeed been a mistake, renting the house. That he knew. But tomorrow, as always, would be a new day, if the fates were with him.

3. An Encounter in the Garden

Several days went by before Edouard spoke to DuBonn again. During that time he noted that (1) the van had been returned to wherever it needed to go, (2) a taxi with an unfamiliar logo had deposited the male tenant back in the courtyard separating the Big House from the little house, and (3) the wine had *not* been replaced. Very well. He would have to keep such details in mind.

But there were other disturbing facts. On several occasions Edouard had seen the DuBonns conversing openly and very amicably with the old peasants, Pablo and Miranda. Sometimes the four had stood at the edge of the hill that obscured the hut below, sometimes in an intimate configuration among the shrubs of his gardens. The two men appeared to argue good-naturedly, laughing and making points about who-knew-what with a convivial thump of forefinger to the chest of the opponent. Even the gnome-like Pablo, so often bent or bowed, seemed to swell up and out, rising to the challenge. It was curious behavior from the stony old goat, Edouard noted, and then noted again. Pablo had never met his benefactor with such approbation and good humor!

Edouard noted also that the women would talk with animated faces and hands, earrings agitating as their heads nodded and confirmed some unfathomable something, the heads similarly wrapped in bandannas or babushkas or

35

whatever, the two sets of shoulders enfolded in rough shawls. The face of Miranda, so glum and grudging as the woman went about the minimal housekeeping chores that Edouard could extract for the Big House, was suddenly round and roseate, twinkling of eye, lips busily working on grins, grimaces and whispers, revealing several gaps between the teeth with no apology, whereas with her employer she ever contrived to keep these losses from view, never more than mumbling through lips barely parted. This doomed little ruse, so appropriately contrite and humble, had never failed to touch Edouard. For what was a toothless creature but one whose every meal was precarious? One for whom life itself depended on the kindnesses of others whose fangs could still procure the necessary? Yes, contrition and humility and a modest arrangement of lip was the proper mode for such a tenuous circumstance. Miranda's sudden abandon was most unfit, most unfit.

The female tenant, too, was transformed in these encounters: the cryptic half-smile she reserved for her landlord suddenly widening into a crescent, the usual closed expression of the face jimmied loose by something in these exchanges with his old burdens, though who could imagine what?

Watching from the edge of a window at the Big House or peering from the camouflage of a nearby thicket, Edouard would be struck by a curious fact: that while images of these enthusiastic quadrilogues conveyed themselves to the eye readily enough, neither phoneme nor morpheme reached the ear. He had turned that organ this way and that, cupped a hand to it, risked discovery by flexing it near a hole in his cover, and had heard nothing.

Then, most disturbing of all, some days went by when he did not see the tenants at all, nor catch any stir within or about his little house, neither hair nor hide of their

36

hideous dog, nor any evidence of the thoroughly necessary putting-outside of the dog, a stirring one would have thought very pressing indeed. Sometimes during those preternaturally still days, when—curiously—Pablo and Miranda were often scarce as well, Edouard had an almost certain feeling that he, and he alone, was the only *living* presence on the property. Odd as some might have found this, it produced in Edouard a flare of joy.

Before giving way to his customary chill, a feeling never far away. Why was it, he wondered, that even the most natural pleasures were always being undercut by unnatural dread? As if nature itself conspired with black forces, somewhere? It made it hard to live a life.

After several days, during which the landlord's blood traversed an unsteady route between the two extremes of this familiar thermometer, days when he imagined himself in gloomy relation to a dead cat that he had observed out in his stable early one spring, the cat thawing out by noon only to freeze up again at night, dismantling and reconstituting itself some way or other day to day, against the day when everything would get away from it—after some time of this, Edouard again saw the male tenant.

The man was working the soil around a bed of tulip bulbs, long since exhausted, near some shrubbery in the side yard. Edouard decided to accost DuBonn there, more out of curiosity about the man's nature (which he was 99% sure to be very dull, in spite of his elusive behavior) than from any desire to cultivate good will or neighborly relations. For in what sense were they neighbors? "Neighbors," a fine word, but not one that needed to countenance interlopers, intruders, foreign bodies, or squatters, after all. "Neighbors," by everything he had ever understood, meant whose who held deeds to what was near, persons one lived in proximity to over a span of years.

Testing this definition in his mind as he descended

37

from his bedroom where he had been putting DuBonn under careful scrutiny, then stepping out the kitchen door and walking around the Big House so that he could come up on the man undetected from behind, thereby putting him at a disadvantage, Edouard shuffled to a stop near the cool wall of his dwelling and leaned pensively against it. There was something in this definition of "neighbors" that needed revising, he felt sure. While he had lived "in proximity" to Pablo and Miranda for some time, and would do so until they rolled into their graves, they were hardly "neighbors." Though there was some question about the "deed" to the hut: though some freethinkers might say that for the moment, at least, Pablo and Miranda "owned" some property near (or on!) his property: still, he couldn't think of them as "neighbors." His parents had specified in their will, in a moment of sentimental madness, that the hut was to be provisionally in the hands of the old people until they passed along to their tiny lots in the churchyard, but this was a gesture of charity, nothing about it meant to put the two old oddities on an equal footing with the major heir. Besides, soon enough those churchyard lots were on the agenda, no doubt of it.

Those lots were provisional too, Edouard thought, forgetting his tenant and his mission as he sagged harder against the cool masonry of his house and rested an inclement brow there, in hope of relief. Yes, even the grave, though it might be deeded property, purchased and paid for in full, could be guaranteed only so long. Memories were short. Even a person who had prudently arranged heirs to pass things along to, in the hope that such scoundrels might now and then check out the graveyard to make sure vandals hadn't come in the night to do their work, even such prudent souls as these couldn't count on much. Likely as not, heirs would sell things off and move to another continent, squandering centuries of ancestral sacrifice on intangibles, pleasures of the moment. Even the most responsible hands one might deliver things into—hands that would groom the small mound religiously, weeding, pruning, maintaining the monument and the symbolic low fence one envisioned, all this providing a stern imperative to any subsequent heirs as to what was expected—even these hands could manage only so much.

Weak from the ghastly midday sun, though he still leaned onto his shady house, Edouard realized that his eyes were swimming with tiny glass-like circles. They distorted things, so that for several moments he felt himself prey to visions. Yes, yes, one could see archaeologists digging around one's final domain, some future species of children tossing one's skull back and forth in a game, future dogs lifting a bit of humerus or tibia and trotting off to bury it in the common ground of a park. . . .

As he began to come around, among the tracings of skulls and dogs and children, he could make out pieces of a hedge of forsythia just beginning to leaf along the edge of the hill—a hedge planted by his mother, Edouard thought, fuming. A woman whose maternal and national feelings were such that she had put two Spanish nobodies before the interests of her own French child! He endured still another apparition as that unnatural woman rose before him, smiling and fingering the sharp edges of her trowel.

Suddenly these glassy visions of life-after-death gave way to the unmistakable presence of the DuBonns' real-life dog, who had seized the opportunity to creep up dangerously close while the landlord had been travelling elsewhere. Edouard was so taken by surprise that he reeled near a faint. What in the world was happening, when the stuff of the worst metaphysical daydreams could

39

without warning metamorphose into a threatening physical reality? In the relative safety of one's own yard?

The red animal had sat down square in front of
Edouard, its large toes digging into the earth for support of
its body. A huge foamy tongue lolled out the side of an
enormous mouth, which ruffled with a loose black lip and
displayed two sabre-teeth of prehistoric dimension jutting
from the lower gum.

Take it, Edouard suddenly thought, surrendering. Take
it all. He was tired. Everything was just too much of a
struggle. What did he care if this monster ran all over the
countryside with his bones in its chops? As long as it
didn't bury them on another man's property, what did he
care what happened to him? Life was hardly worth living.
Sometimes he felt like diving into the tarn with the old
artist after all, never to be recovered. Let them have it all.

Of course there was no way they could have it all, could
they, if he lingered in the tarn—Edouard thought, rally-
ing, just in time to see the haunches of the dog disappear
near the weed-filled tennis court. No, in the tarn he might
ever assert a kind of spiritual ownership, perhaps even
casting effects not unlike the unpleasant spookiness that
overtook him at weak moments when his sympathies for
the dead avant-gardist gave way to something far more
troublesome.

Feeling himself reviving in the best of spirits, Edouard
relinquished this whole unfortunate interlude and
bounded away from the tomblike chill of the masonry and
out into the warm sunshine of this sterling day. He had a
mission, after all, he thought, positioning himself to come
up behind the male tenant, whom he could see thoroughly absorbed in the tulip bed, his unsuspecting back as
inviting as a nymph sleeping in the woods of an afternoon. Breathing deeply with the pleasure of his prospects,
Edouard looked fondly on his mother's forsythia and even

40

on his father's disastrous project, the tennis court, built by his father and Pablo in more agile days, undulant and cracking from the first, but a tennis court nonetheless. His proud father had cagily broken up old bricks and rubbed the powdered clay onto the court's surface and told his less-than-brilliant guests that it was an early *longue paume*. Not in the best repair, Edouard could still hear the old man say, as he gave his visitors a tour. No, not in the best repair, but then, history—well, one made certain exchanges, this for that.

Closing in on DuBonn's back, Edouard had mixed feelings when DuBonn started and whipped his head around, giving Edouard an unambiguous look, full of irritation and bad will. What a jumpy fellow, Edouard thought, satisfied to see that something of the effect he was after was, for once, what he had got. On the other hand, he felt offended. How he resented the tenant's looking resentful! After all, in whose side yard were they? His own irritation must have been transparent, releasing DuBonn's elaborate social manner, because just as suddenly a smiling DuBonn moved conspiratorially toward him, drawing Edouard's shoulder into a comradely embrace, gesturing with good (too-good!) nature, moving the garden implement through the air for emphasis, making quite elegant small talk, actually, on the tulips. Oh, he was a sly one, all right! Edouard thought.

At some point in this little dance, it occurred to Edouard that they were standing near the very tree that had shielded the commotion of whatever it was that had intrigued him some nights earlier and that it was now at that very tree that DuBonn was exhorting the tulips bulbs. He waited for the proper transition to present itself and then very coyly inquired if his neighbor had found occasion to enjoy the yard by night, explaining that he himself much appreciated a stroll among the plants and shrubs, especially under a full moon and especially on the kind of brisk night they had been having of late, and in fact had taken just such a constitutional only a few nights before and, indeed, *hadn't* he seen his neighbor enjoying the same kind of outing that very night?

The tenant, who followed this winding discourse with an amused look, laughed warmly when it was over, a paradigm of cordiality, assuring the landlord that indeed he might have seen him on such a walk, though it was highly unlikely, he not being fond of such excursions, preferring instead to spend an evening with a book by the fire or to go to bed early, should firewood run low (he said this last with just a hint—no more—of accusation, which caused Edouard's own casual smile to knot like a dried fig). But, the man added, it was possible that Edouard had seen him in the yard, because occasionally he was given to sleepwalking, particularly on the nights when a bright moon disturbed his rest, but on the whole he thought that if Monsieur had noted some activity in the yard on that said night, chances were good that it had been the dog, Sangrito.

Undaunted, and delighted that his tenant had been so careless as to give him the last righteous word, Edouard replied that no doubt it had been the dog, for a dog was wont to go out at night, though this must be a very un-doggy dog indeed if it could wander out into the yard on such a night as the one under discussion and resist—oh, at who knew what price to its nature—the impulse to bay at the moon, for that was indeed the nature of dogs, or so he had thought; but then, after all, he did not have a dog himself—in fact, he had made it a point never to have a dog, since he did not like their noises and the mess they made around the property, not to mention that when one had guests in the summer, as he himself invariably did, many of them the children of good friends, one did not

42

particularly want to have a dog around, not only for the mess in the yard that would no doubt be tracked in upon one's floors, but also because a dog, especially a large dog, might be careless and hurt one of the children, in which case one would very likely face medical bills, and if the parent were not a particularly close friend—more of a relative *stranger* (he paused for emphasis and eyed DuBonn sharply), perhaps one would be met with a lawsuit. For his own part, he preferred not to have a dog. And given that Monsieur's nature *seemed* so congenial to one's own, indeed it was a surprise that his most esteemed new *tenant* did not share some of the property-owner's own reservations about the beasts, which anyone could see were indisputably filthy and destructive interlopers into a civilized environment.

On that note, Edouard, who had been backing out of the yard of the little house and toward his own definite territory, threw the man a little salute and twirled out of sight around the corner of the Big House.

Edouard was slow to go about his lunch. Though he had a fresh-enough fish, four days old at the most, and had thought earlier in the morning of poaching it and having a nice lunch of fish and fish-broth, the conversation in the yard had taken away his appetite, never mind his triumph at the end. He didn't like that fellow, that's all there was to it. There was something odder than he'd thought at first about him. That he'd pried into one's ledgers, well, that wasn't pleasant, but was really nothing in and of itself. That was the way of the country. Edouard never received a letter but that it had been opened and scanned by who knew how many curious eyes in the village. Old Pablo, whom Edouard felt sure could barely read, looked at all mail coming to the Big House as a matter of course and eavesdropped on every telephone conversation, and

43

no doubt had instructed Miranda to do the same in his absence. It was not pleasant, but these were rustics who did not appreciate the pleasures of privacy and Edouard had grown used to their ways. But that DuBonn did not show the least embarrassment—! And that he was irritated to find the *Master* of the property going about his Masterly business of traversing the land. Well, that was very odd indeed. And DuBonn had bolted like an untrained horse when he, Edouard, had come up behind him. Why so guilty about coaxing tulip bulbs? It was a waste of time, certainly, but hardly a crime. And who did he think he was, moving in a dog the size of that monster without so much as a by-your-leave? It was infuriating.

Unable to spend the day in the leisurely fashion he had planned on, once burdened with these distressing thoughts, Edouard puttered here and there about the chateau, wandering into the bedroom his dead parents had shared, musty as the grave with its old maroon drapes. Oh, well. His father had had good intentions. Why not leave a son a chateau? Even if it takes every sou?

Well, this was no time for sentiment. The parents, the hard-working, aspiring, acquisitive restaurateurs were gone. The Big House was a drain on him, true, but they had meant well. And what if they had sold the restaurant without consulting him?

He pushed that curious resentment aside before it got a hold. Though he had no desire, now or ever, for the restaurant, sometimes he could strangle his parents in their graves for selling it off without a word to him, no consultation, hint or explanation. Well, he couldn't get into that now. The problem at hand was serious. In a week, even, the first guests from Paris could be on him. It would be warm enough. Perhaps some luminaries from the literary world, a statesman-like journalist or an actress bound for the festival at Cannes, who knew? And he could see now what he had been looking away from for weeks: there would be difficulties. The dog, surely. They were not clean animals, and one so large. . . . His brain curdled with imagery. And there would be the beast's general rooting and uprooting, damage to the grounds that might prove costly. And the tenants themselves were sure to raise an eyebrow or two among the guests. These Du-Bonns were dull, he was sure, and there was their pathetically dated gypsy-proletariat garb. Not that he himself courted fashion in the frantic way of many of his countrymen—of a certain class, of course. His own wardrobe was meagre, but discreet and expensive, if not always in the best repair. A perfectly natural lack of coordination and absentmindedness had resulted in unfortunate rents and rips, indelible soilings and the like, and the meandering contours of his flesh brought on baggings and saggings that disrupted the lines of his garments, and even managed to divert his best intentions: shifting the tail of a shirt from his trousers, easing a button from its hole, edging an exquisite silk sock toward the gulley of a shoe.

But the tenants: their casual attitude about the actual ownership of the estate, his own privilege and authority. The dog, their own wandering around at all hours of the night, spading up the earth without permission—surely his guests could be forgiven if they should take such behavior amiss, and in that event, it would be at considerable cost to his own esteem.

It had occurred to him to try to pass the tenants off as a handyman and his wife. After all, the fellow looked like a handyman. And if it seemed that his own largess included giving Pablo a season of rest before the grave (the useless wretch!), so much the better. Or, another strategy: he had thought that if the tenants should, after a brief sojourn at Auxillac, suddenly acquire just the marginal suggestion of charm or elegance, he might say that they were his long-term guests, old friends that had fallen on hard times, needed a place to stop awhile, the use of one's vehicle. (His fear that the DuBonns would prevail upon him for his little Renault had come to pass. At least once a week they borrowed it for a trip to the village, or who-knew-where-else? How could anyone know? He would get the odometer fixed someday, but until then, he was at their mercy.)

Oh, the mortification of having the Circles discover that his own times had grown so hard that he had taken in renters! And more and more he could see that neither handyman nor extended-guest stratagem would fool anyone. As a handyman, DuBonn would appear careless, un-respectful of one's property, and as a friend, he would seem too bland, his wife too predictably odd. It was true that some members of the Circles, being creative beings, cultivated a kind of *de rigueur* oddness and eccentricity, but that was affectation and not a fact of nature and not predictable. Their poses had style, wit, intelligence. The DuBonns, these problematics, were without all these. And without charm and personality too: it was as simple, and as complex, as that.

4. *A Discreet Actress on Her Way to Cannes*

As Edouard expected, a few weeks' time did produce a guest from Paris. And much to his delight, but tempered by some nervousness about the tenants, it was an actress on her way to Cannes.

This actress was no emptyheaded starlet. This was a woman of considerable charm and personality, a sophisti-cate who wore her 45 years well, an artist who chose her scripts with the greatest discretion, having appeared in some half-dozen classics of the past two decades, a name not on the vulgar lips of the masses, but one whispered with awe among the *cognoscenti*. Edouard took some pride in the knowledge that her visits to Auxillac, if written up in the popular tabloids, would have meant nothing to the man on the street, but if detailed in whispers over lunches at certain select bistros in the fashionable quarters of Paris would have meant everything.

The actress arrived in time for lunch on a Sunday, planning to spend only the night and then to go on to Cannes with her driver. This had been her practice for several years. She hated airports, she told Edouard. And airplanes, trains and hotels. She was very pleased to have discovered Auxillac through their mutual friends, she often told him too, and to have discovered him, words he treasured.

On this particular Sunday, Edouard had pressed a grumbling Miranda into service, ordering a spread of cold meats, salads, cheese and sweets to be laid out on a nicely linened table in a copse near the tennis court where trees were sufficiently thick to obscure the condition of that unfortunate part of his property. When the actress arrived (Oh, how he admired the *class* of that woman: the beige hair in a perfectly discreet roll at the base of the neck, the subtlety of her make-up and dress, the *devastating* dips and crests of her adorable voice—like music!), he greeted her with his warmest manner—one that carefully did not betray the least passion: burying her dry, well-formed hand in both of his own, lightly, lightly; cooing a babble of complimentary phrases as he led her into the house and up the stairs to her room—her special room: the wallpaper in good repair (the same could not be said of all his rooms and he had to be very selective in housing his guests, saving the drabber appointments for the children and elderly relatives of the Circles), the fireplace in the best marble, crested with the logo of some forgotten baronet, properly regal for a queen of the serious cinema, the bed itself a triumph of the exquisite taste of its period, beautifully carved, and festooned with fresh drapery only that morning by his Spanish trollette. With some pride (well-hidden) he opened the bedroom's door for the actress and escorted her in, her driver following with her bags. It was the same room she always occupied, but he had made some improvements during his long winter. Nothing expensive, but little things he had been able to manage with a few francs—new paint on the mouldings, the addition of some quite handsome 18th-century sconces found in a box in the empty servants' dormitory on the fourth story, some lace pillows Miranda had fashioned in the slow season and sold to him too dearly. Of these he murmured to his guest, waving a hand toward a baggage stand for the driver's benefit, flinging open a window to the warm spring sunshine, all the time a delicate hand reposing dryly within his. The actress murmured appropriate pleasure, neither ebullient nor perfunctory, but some warmly neutral degree in between. And he, the *soul* of discretion (oh, he could match any one of them!), left her to make a brief toilette and accustom herself to her environs, taking his leave from a spot near the window to insure that she noted the majestic sweep of his property and the valley beyond, which was very charming now in its greenery; all this framed by a hearty vine blooming with delicate yellow flowers. He would wait for her in the trees near the tennis court.

"Tell me, Monsieur Edouard. . . ," the actress began, once they were seated at their table and had apportioned discreet mounds of the treats on their respective plates. Oh, that woman! Never, never had she showed him the encouragement of calling him simply "Edouard" or "Eddy" in the manner of some of the more familiar members of her circle. Her formality was exasperating! And yet the deprivation she implied: that, in itself, was an ex-cruciating pleasure!

"Tell me. . . ." So discreetly did that little sliver of ham disappear between her lips! She was the *quintessence* of subtlety!

". . . do you have guests other than myself?"

Edouard felt his elation drain away from surfaces and orifices, reconstituting itself as a bilgy mixture of doom and fear deep in his middle region. So.

And yet, she had lowered her eyes, as though the an-swer were of no importance whatsoever. Yes, clearly, she was giving him the chance to affirm or deny by design or whim. What a woman!

"I only ask . . .," she continued, abstractedly, totally ab-sorbed, she made it seem, in the forsythia that rolled away from her side in a swirl of yellow. ". . . because as I was breathing at my window . . . taking in some of your splendid country air . . . I thought I noticed some activity . . . at your little house. . . ?"

With such finesse had the question finally been put be-tween them, delivered in among the main business, she made it seem, of admiring the flowers, taking a bite of salad, a nibble of bread, a sip of wine, that though his heart still lurched about in his chest from so early a dis-covery of the tenants, her manner (spreading itself out like a *mistress* for his deception!), her manner and her *tact* gave him courage.

"Yes, yes," he inserted finally into a blather of general gossip about his plans for the season, yes, he had guests of sorts, well, not really guests, but sort of perpetual hangers-on—she did know, did she not, that he was ex-pecting Monsieur Roland Lassalle, the writer, early in June? Yes, yes—and his wife—well, not hangers-on in the exploitative sense, no, no—and did she know that

49

Madame Gustavson, wife of the Scandinavian director, one of her colleagues, would be coming—yes, with the children, on her way to the South, yes—well, yes, it *was* hard to find amusements for the children so far in the country, but yes, they did make their own society after a time and there was always a little museum of natural history in the village—yes, yes, one *did* have to be grateful for the government's determination to educate the provinces, didn't one? Well, actually, if he had to put a name to them—it was odd, wasn't it, how *everything*, even the most intimate things, required a name? Oh, she *did* object to "star?" Well, that was mostly Americans, no? Yes, yes, weren't they? Yes, . . . well, if they had to have a name, he supposed they would have to be called . . . well, "tenants," he guessed would. . . .

There. It was out.

And she: oh, the *soul* of discretion! the *pinnacle* of civilization! Diplomatically she spread her bread with a little pill of butter, offering—no, insisting!—that she butter a piece for him too . . . after all, he was her host. The least *she* could do would be to offer these minor ministrations. And had he procured this beautiful butter in the neighborhood? It had a wonderful flavor . . . and what of the ham? So often cured ham was just a touch rancid, no matter how fine the shop where one had bought it—but, yes, this was so sweet, a marvel, really—yes, and where did he get those beautiful pastries? Really? And did he think that one could call in and have a little basket prepared to take in the car, and yes, if housing was such a problem all over the country, as the periodicals led one to believe, then more and more . . . people would have to open up a bit . . . if everyone were to be housed . . . it was the only responsible thing. . . . And what of this firm little cheese? It reminded her of an English cheese she had had in Sussex once. Of course the English were hardly gourmets, but—

50

After this chatty repast, which put Edouard considerably more at ease with the troublesome fact of the tenants, the actress retired to her room where she said she must take care of some social correspondence, and so they had disbanded, agreeing to meet before sundown to plot an evening meal and perhaps take a stroll about the property before dark.

Edouard passed the intervening time with a quick trip to the village in the Renault for a few bottles of decent wine and more of the cheese that had found such favor, these being bought from a woman who would open her shop just for him, even on a Sunday. Such were the privileges of being Master at Auxillac! Once back at the chateau, he made some small, useless efforts to pile the bricks and stones of some of his crumbling out-buildings into orderly configurations that suggested construction rather than its telltale opposite.

Shortly before sundown the actress reappeared and collaborated on a make-do version of *ratatouille* that, once in the oven, could take care of itself, and then, when the sun was hovering on the horizon, washing the grounds (and even the evidence of his more dissolute property) in a most satisfactory apricot light, Edouard led his guest out on his arm and they strolled here and there, chatting amicably about nothing, admiring the light and the "vistas," as the actress called them, lisping the word softly.

It was almost dusk when they started back up the winding stone walk that led eventually to the courtyard, and Edouard had settled into a benevolent ease brought about by the company of so charming a female and by a momentary sense that perhaps his empire held together more firmly than he had imagined.

Suddenly, as the walk turned a corner of the Big House, they found themselves face to face with M. and Mme. Du-Bonn.

There was no choice but to introduce them. Edouard willed an ingenious tone into his voice, one calculated to speak (to the actress, whom he carefully faced) a benevolent egalitarianism, but one that, as it traveled over his shoulder to the ears of the DuBonns, he trusted would twist neatly to confirm that he was lord of the manor and not to be disturbed. Thus he made the introductions, careful to choose the most formal language and to reveal nothing significant about either party to the other.

To his surprise, the actress seemed strangely intrigued by the couple, and long after Edouard had deemed it fit that they should break off the episode and go to their respective quarters, she persisted in talking with the DuBonns about this and that, inquiring in her triumphantly discreet way about the particulars of their lives, why they had come to the Lot, how they were spending their time, etcetcete! Finally, livid with the whole invasion (he would speak with Monsieur tomorrow!), Edouard excused himself to check on the supper and went into the Big House.

The night was dark as bile and the ratatouille growing cool on the stove when the actress finally took her leave of the DuBonns and joined her host. Though her face was blushing attractively with the evening chill when she entered the kitchen, Edouard kept a stony reserve. After all, what did it say when so refined a person lapsed in so basic a way and caused a *host* such discommoding pique? For entirely too long had he been left brooding alone over his sparkling china—not his best, true—that would never have done for such a simple meal—but very nice china after all, and brought out and shined up especially for the pleasure of this guest, no one else. And the dinner had grown cold, the warmth of the oven had died away and left the kitchen cold as well—all this because the guest

52

had indulged some impetuous and selfish curiosity about an entirely insignificant couple of tenants.

As the actress took her place at the table amid a flurry of apology for dawdling so long, she began to attack her food with the energy of a peasant. Under ordinary circumstances the charm of this would have devastated Edouard. He would have taken it as proof that she had begun, at last, to view him as an intimate. But in his deep sulk, Edouard found her gusto unseemly, insult to injury. Between her hearty bites of the ratatouille and a rather savage breaking of bread, the bread being leftover from lunch and a little stale, she battered him with tidbits about the tenants. Did he know that the woman was an artist? Yes, yes, she had actually had quite a little success in a show somewhere in the provinces, Bordeaux, perhaps. She, the actress, had remembered reading something about it once the woman had mentioned it to her. And the man, did Monsieur know the identity of this unassuming tenant? (Edouard could not be sure, but he thought that he detected a hint of the tease in the way she said "tenant.") Well, didn't the name "DuBonn" mean anything? No? How amusing. Well, "DuBonn" was the name of a very, very old family—German originally, of course—Monsieur knew "Bonn," after the city?

Edouard's brood grew blacker with the condescension of this remark, and though the actress still stuffed herself with the cold ratatouille, he rose and began to take things from the table and store them away. He would not sit still for her insults!

Well, "DuBonn" was the name of a *very* old family, the actress chattered on. Yes, yes, quite old, lawyers and bankers, yes—provincials—from Lyons, she thought. Though the female DuBonn was from somewhere near his own region, a family of aristocrats, descending from one

53

of the famous barons of Prussia or some such. But the
DuBonns: yes, very old family, a Jewish banking family,
actually. Divested of everything by the Vichy the *instant*
the opportunity arose—well, those things happened. Oh,
no, it wasn't in the least an important family now, scat-
tered here, there, and everywhere—they were, after all,
divested, as just said. No, the man didn't seem particularly bitter, but then who could say? It had all happened a
long time ago, perhaps even before M. DuBonn had been
born—it *was* hard to tell how old he was, was it not? No,
no bitterness on the surface, at least. Something very
stoical about it, attractive, didn't M. Edouard think? Yes,
it was something, wasn't it? Fascinating! Of course, not a
sou now, but what *History.* . . .

The dip and crest of the voice during this recital was
less adorable than Edouard had found it earlier in the afternoon. What was this? So the wife was a little artist
who had had a "success" in Bordeaux? What of it? Bordeaux was a perfectly nice city, but it was hardly Paris.
The husband a "fascinating" orphan Jew? My, my, this
great actress had odd enthusiasms. None of this information had made the tenants any more attractive in his own
eyes. He still maintained, to himself, that they were odd
and dull. That he had fallen on such times, that they were
necessary to his economy, goaded him like a lance. And
who knew where it all would lead? They might settle in
with this rumored "history" and he might have a time of
it dislodging them, if by some miracle his fortunes should
improve.

So deep in a new funk that for a moment he had to turn
entirely away from this insufferable guest, Edouard suddenly found himself the recipient of a torrent of compli-
ments, interspersed with almost amusing pieces of gossip,
gossip having nothing to do with the tenants but with
several members within or only slightly without the Paris

Circles, some snippets about such and such an actor or director, or such and such a *bon vivant*. And then: elaborate appreciations of the ratatouille, the bedroom above, the beauty of Auxillac's grounds, and so forth—all so charmingly advanced that he began to feel his black mood disperse and soon he was chuckling at a *bon mot* here and there, relaxing finally into his former good humor.

No more was said about the tenants, and late into the night host and guest chatted, building a smoky fire against the evening's chill in the library and finishing off the bottle of Amontillado left by the Christmas visitor.

At some juncture in these festivities—deep into their fellowship where it could not have been linked with M. and Mme. DuBonn—the actress slipped her porcelain little hand into Edouard's and inquired if she might not spend another night as his guest. After all, the brouhaha at Cannes was several days away, and besides it was something of a bore, if the truth must be told—yes, yes— a spectacle without substance, really—and the utter *charm* of her present milieu—well, if the truth were to be told. . . .

5. The Awful Comradeship

Restored to his former state of enthrallment and well-soothed by the Amontillado, Edouard did not wake until very late the following morning. So late, that passing his guest's bedroom, he could see that Miranda had already dressed the bed and put the room in perfect order. An unusual punctuality and attention for Miranda, he remarked to himself on the way down his stairs.

In the kitchen, he found the old woman putting away the butter and jam from the actress's breakfast. Very nice! he thought, sitting down and dunking a bit of stale bread in the remains of the actress's coffee and slipping it into his furry mouth. Very nice: Miranda had never made such a punctual start on disposing of his own dribblings and crumbs. And wasn't that some of his mother's best Limoges? The actress could never have found that on her own. Miranda had been meddling again. But this was a different order of things, was it not? One's mother's best Limoges, and wasn't that the antique coffee server rumored to have been used at Versailles, a gift of a loyal client at the restaurant? Wasn't the napkin one of his mother's finest, perhaps the only one with no stain or ravelling? Oh, yes, a very different order of things. Could this be, somehow, the upshot of Miranda's rapport with the female tenant? What next?

Out in the courtyard he could see the actress's dark driver whistling as he waxed her Mercedes. It was a scene that restored him to his former good mood. A loyal employee going merrily and *unassumingly* about his work after passing a night in a small room off a kitchen, with no complaint, lovingly tending a car that was itself a tasteful six years old. Oh, everything about the actress was so right! he thought, forgiving her 100% for the previous evening. What was there to worry about? How could she possibly see anything in his tenants? What was there to see? Just because his two old peasants had been captivated and put up to who-knew-what-kind-of mischief, a testament to the primitive's judgment, there was no reason to think that his guest, a sophisticated woman of the world, would have any use for the tenants beyond the causal *divertissement,* something to relieve the initial depression of shifting from the center of the world to its outer limits. He understood that well enough.

Yes, all was forgiven, though he had to envy the training of her driver, he thought again, watching the young man shine the discreet chrome on the automobile as if

56

the car were his own, and yet there was no hint that he presumed ownership in any other way. Yes, much depended on such understandings for the world to twirl smoothly on its course; the world had need of persons who could be trusted to maintain the fine distinction between presuming an owner's interest and presuming the thing itself. With a quick dip of his barometer, he thought again of the tenants, who had by now metamorphosed in his mind as his employees. Yes, maintaining such fine distinctions was certainly a dying art.

Gnawing on a last hunk of bread dipped hastily in the actress's dregs just as glowering Miranda had whisked the coffee cup to the sink, Edouard wandered out in the late morning sun, allowing the old woman's swift critique *("Tête de cochon!")* to stall where it was, preferring to note neither the unbecoming remark nor the bold display of toothlessness. He had no intention of getting into anything with his serfs. Let them do as they would. He had other fish to fry.

It was a perfect day, he thought, exhilarating in the leisure of his late waking and the benevolent warmth and odors of his estate. A perfect day, he repeated to himself smugly, as if he'd engineered it himself. The air close to the ground was crisp and cool (reminding one, as earth might and should, that the grave was a certainty), but further up the air was warm and pleasant (asserting, as sunshine might and should, that one was not dead until dead). The light reflecting from the bluish swell of his noble fields and the tender green of the valley below, just visible above a hedge of tall flowers—all this was very reassuring. In such shades lay the promise of the actress's contentment. In such shades much soothing could occur, so that his guest would be compelled to favor him without reservation, and once back in Paris, to pass among the Circles the most flattering accounts of his hospitality.

57

Smiling widely at such a prospect, Edouard strolled out onto the lawn and began his search for his—might he not call her?—friend.

When he found her, he was less than happy, for it was among the profuse foliage of the copse where they had taken their fine midday meal the previous day, and she was now relaxed in one of the garden chairs there, hair loosened, a large flowered hat drifting on her lap, bright sunlight glaring from a huge hole in the shrubbery through which could be seen the ill-conceived tennis court, buckling with roots and lush with weeds. All around her on the ground lay the debris of this surgery, and Edouard noted that the flowers in her hat were the forsythia blossoms that only the day before had performed such a fortuitous camouflage. He was irritated that she had taken such liberties with his shrubbery, but this was nothing beside the abomination he discovered once fully within the copse. The actress was having her portrait painted by Mme. DuBonn.

Oh, how delightful to see him, the actress cooed, springing up (guiltily?) from her chair. Advancing, she put out her tepid fingers and took his wrist, leading him into his own trees as if he were her infrequent visitor. As for the "artist from Bordeaux" or wherever, she was silent as always in his presence, smiling (smirking?) with a hint of condescension, he thought he could safely surmise. Well, credit where it's due, at least she was walking off a few steps now, pretending to consult her palette in the light while his guest bade him a Judas's good morning, over-solicitous, unctuous, humiliating to them both, actually. Oh, he would find a way to be stern with her. She was, after all, still his guest.

Apparently undaunted by the square face he had turned on her in preparation for sternness, the actress disengaged her fingers to beckon the gypsy minx back into the shade.

58

Taking up her pose again, the model kept her eyes carefully on a spot over his shoulder and began a seranade of flattery and general prattle, as if he were a dolt and there were no limits to her charm, whereas he could clearly see that those charms had severe limitations. Would he please forgive her utter *butchery* of his most marvelous shrubbery? But she had felt sure, given his most *charming*, accommodating manner, that he would not have denied her the flowers for her bonnet nor Mme. DuBonn the light necessary for carrying out her work. He had noticed, hadn't he, that Mme. was being so kind as to paint her portrait? Yes, yes—what other miracles would be wrought by the *generous* host at Auxillac? One hardly expected, when coming for an overnight stay—that invitation itself being the *epitome* of generosity and unusual enough in this cool era—to be brought into contact with an accomplished artist like Mme. DuBonn who would agree, matching the matchless M. Edouard in her generosity, to paint one's portrait in a scene of such natural beauty as *only* Auxillac could proffer at this time of the year. And by the way, since the festival at Cannes, as she had told him on the previous evening—might she add the most *delightful* previous evening?—was several days off, and such a bore anyway—hadn't she told him it was a bore? Well, it most assuredly was—she had thought she might commission Jenny (Jenny!) to paint this portrait of her—she was sure that the work wouldn't take more than a couple of days, if he wouldn't mind putting up with her company yet another day or two—and she was fairly sure she could trust that he wouldn't mind, especially since she had often heard in Paris that he was a host of *exceptional* hospitality—which of course her own limited experience in his company had borne out in a *hundred* instances, as well—and besides, if the portrait were not finished by the time she must go to Cannes, then of

59

course it could be finished from a photograph, no? All the artists used photographs nowadays—after all, who had time to sit for weeks? In any case. . . .

As she chattered, Edouard kept his face unrelenting, even as he reassured her that, certainly, she might stay as long as she wished, treat the place as though it were her own (though he was very careful to indicate with a pointed look that the place was *not* her own!). And most assuredly Mme. DuBonn would paint a distinguished and *flattering* portrait (oh, how ingeniously he could cast doubt on flattery, even as he flattered!) of his guest, for how rare were the opportunities for such a provocative . . . subject . . . and such a charming little . . . talent . . . to meet? And that such a happy coincidence had taken place on his own property was a great source of delight, of course. And now if the ladies (his look did not include Mme. DuBonn) would excuse him. . . .

All afternoon, while the two women chatted merrily in the trees, Edouard lounged in a fit of gloom in the library of the Big House, pretending to read a book. The titters that drifted across the lawn and into his window were a great distraction from his thoughts, which were aligning and realigning furiously, trying to discover whether or not he was being duped, and if so, whether it would be worth the personal humiliation of the moment in the interest of a long-term payoff in rumors about his largess as a host. Had the actress perceived his vanity about that matter? (Had she or had she not glanced slyly at him as she made her remark about his hospitality being well-known in Paris?) And if so, would she pass along the information and an account of her sly flattery to an influential friend at lunch some afternoon? And would the tale then be passed along from friend to friend, until he eventually be-came some emperor without clothes to members of this

Circle and that? Would a horde of merrymakers swoop down on the Lot, putting in a few days at Auxillac merely to carry away tales about him and his vanity to brighten dull moments while taking the sun and whatnot, using him as a source of sport?

These were horrifying possibilities, and separating probabilities from less-probable fears was not made any easier by the titters emanating from the copse nor, later, by scenes framed in his window in the late afternoon sun: of the actress and *both* DuBonns, *and* the dog, setting off on a jaunt across his fields, and of the same group returning much later, the women's arms bursting with his wildflowers, the two of them giggling like girls, DuBonn talking low to them in his phony congeniality, the miserable cur running ahead, its huge toes ripping up sod that would have to be replaced by Edouard himself. It was abominable. Nor would these horrors be relieved by the disappearance still later of the actress into the little house, nor by the cozy scene later still, of the three taking bread and some wine that looked suspiciously like a bottle from his Caveau, in the side yard of the little house, very near where DuBonn's tulips—mysteriously restored to life— wagged like red gossipy tongues.

Never mind that in an afterthought half-way through this little feast alfresco DuBonn put in an appearance at the Big House and entreated (weakly, Edouard thought) his landlord to join them. Edouard declined, naturally, stressing plainly that he had prepared a small meal for himself *and* his guest somewhat earlier, at an appropriate hour. He would not be moved, though DuBonn lingered in the kitchen doorway, looking, to Edouard's eye, like a vagabond for hire. After a stream of banter (that had got DuBonn nowhere for once, Edouard thought, taking a little pleasure in that in spite of his anger), DuBonn shrugged and left, ambling easily toward the little house

61

to join the women, stopping to scratch the head of his dog and stopping again to regard the tulips—two emblems that Edouard noted from his window with a further discomfort.

In the few moments of daylight remaining, Edouard stood at his window, at an angle which wouldn't reveal him, and endured the trills of laughter and the low-pitched chitchat, not at all sure that he wasn't the butt of a joke that was being passed about his courtyard with a nudge of the elbow or roll of the eye. Finally, swirling in frustration and impotence, his balance affected, even his hair straining as if trying to escape a prickly scalp, Edouard tossed a few crusts of bread and a discolored wedge of cheese on the table for the actress, should she be expecting a sumptuous repast at the Big House after all, and stumbled up to his bed, where he lay in wide-eyed misery most of the night.

6. What Next?

The actress's plans to spend "another day or two" at Auxillac quickly stretched out to claim the rest of the week, and it seemed to Edouard that she spent every moment with the DuBonns, either the wife or the husband or both. Leisurely, but with much incomprensible chatter and giggling and snickering and tittering, the portrait took shape in the trees. Often, the threesome strolled his ancestral land as though it were their own, while the "master of Auxillac," as he now thought of himself, in lower-case within the skeptic's quotation, watched from a perch high in his Big House. Later, he would see them taking refreshments at an ugly table that had somehow materialized on his courtyard bricks. The actress's driver had been pressed into service. Edouard often saw him chauffering the three off to somewhere, the actress throwing decorum out the window and sitting up front so that her precious DuBonns might have her rear seat to themselves. And—in a thoroughly inappropriate use of one's driver—the man would be made to uncork bottles and slice up meats and cheese in the courtyard. Really, there were laws, Edouard felt sure, or at least boards of grievance for such violations. Several times, with a sinking heart, Edouard had noticed that the driver had even been invited to take a chair with his employer and her friends, a further impropriety. But nothing prepared him for a scene near sunset one day: the four of them assembled in the courtyard as usual, but then their number increasing by two—Pablo and Miranda shyly taking chairs at the edge of things, Pablo producing one of the disputed wines of Auxillac, a "gift" extended on only two previous occasions to one who was (arguably) the rightful owner.

Oh, the actress was always careful to invite her host to join these mob scenes, Edouard thought, seeing through her as if through glass. Careful to invite him to walk, to ride, to eat, tour the valley, regard the "vistas," as if such invitations were her natural province. She was careful to spend a little time with him each evening, though she took no further suppers in the Big House, but since he had nothing whatsoever he wished to discuss with her, these were awkward occasions. She jabbered on (nervously, he thought) about the DuBonns, while he brooded on how it would all come to bear on his dreams of the Circles. (Would they be out of his reach in the future, except as snickering house guests, tenants of sorts?)

He was always careful to yawn at these recitals, to turn up the music, to insist on reading out loud from a fascinating passage he claimed to have discovered in Proust only that afternoon while others had been *cavorting* about the wilds of his property.

63

Now, that was another thing. He had been forced into calling up Proust, whom he had most certainly not been reading (Proust wasn't *his* cup of tea at all), and on other occasions, such luminaries from the intellectual life as he could remember from his student days. All because the actress regaled him nightly with remnants of highbrow subjects discussed with the DuBonns. The one time he had put in an appearance in the courtyard, just to check things out, he had found their talk full of innuendo: cryptic, allusive, contorted, mystifying. It seemed to depend for substance, as far as he could tell, on the raised eyebrow. He couldn't make head nor heels of much of the language, and he had his doubts that the actress could either, or for that matter, the DuBonns themselves, the fakes. Thus excluded, and having no faith that any of them knew what they were talking about (there was much reference to "esthetics," politics, philosophy and worse), certainly not the actress, though it was her indistinct words that most often trilled and shrilled above the others, he began to wonder if this double-talk wasn't a discourse on himself, a sinister tactic whereby he was further made the gull. This mumbo-jumbo was something unnatural, portending something, whether his own humiliation or something smaller, he didn't know. It was always possible that the DuBonns had put some sort of spell on the weak-willed creature. Oh, well. One knew this kind of talk had a certain cachet, among certain groups, to each his own, but fortunately it wasn't the kind of thing that ever prevailed in the Circles, where wit and light banter ruled, the *bon mot* a science. And yet, there he was, night after night, insinuating Proust, or Rimbaud, or Cocteau, or Rousseau—all sounding alike, and what if he were asked to cough up something precise? Who knew what the DuBonns might put her up to?

Well, it hadn't happened yet. The actress was far too

busy telling him more than he'd ever wanted to know about his tenants, most of it unconvincing, all of it boring. After a couple of evenings, he began to relax a little about the woman's opinion: her own days within the Circle were numbered.

When the actress was not sitting for her portrait or otherwise involved with the DuBonns in the afternoons, Edouard noted that she often went upstairs to her room, and spying on her from must far enough back in some bushes to give him a full view of her window, he could see that she was sitting at his mother's exquisite Biedermeier desk, writing. Sometimes her hair would have been let down from its roll (well? Why pretend decorum and discretion in the minor matters of taste if the major were going to be thrown open to any experimentation?), sometimes the collar of her blouse undone, sleeves rolled up like the male DuBonn's, feet propped on sills, and more. Sometimes she appeared angry (once she threw a pen, no question of it). But catching her face in his father's scratched binoculars one afternoon, he was surprised to see that it looked almost as gentle as his own darling mother's. What was she up to?

Did Monsieur Edouard know, she would say in the evening (Oh, how the false regard punished him like nettle now!), did Monsieur know that Monsieur DuBonn had studied law, philosophy, poetry? Yes, yes, the major work done in England she believed, but then he had found colleagues everywhere, apparently, oh a major success or several, if she had understood, though some misreadings also, but oh yes, her understanding was that he was a quite well-regarded scholar, though somewhat controversial, if Jenny hadn't been too modest in her descriptions. Oh, Monsieur was not impressed with Jenny? Really? For oneself, one couldn't disagree more. One would even say,

65

in fact, that Jenny would have a chance in Paris, yes, a very good chance. Monsieur didn't care for her clothes? Truly? She herself found them charming, very originally unoriginal, irreverently dated, but that was the point: to mock the silly pendulum of fashion, no? Oh, it was quite an esthetic, quite a philosophy in its own right, as was Jenny's clever style of painting. Had Monsieur noticed? One couldn't help marking his absence at the "studio." Well, yes, it *seemed* to be the old Impressionism—of course: that was the point. Really? Monsieur couldn't see the point? How droll. Well, anyway, for oneself, the Du-Bonns certainly seemed at home at Auxillac, adding immensely to what Monsieur could offer his guests—oh, no, of course one didn't mean that good company and extraordinary amenities were lacking in the past, it was just that the DuBonns . . . well, they were unusual and very fascinating, by one's own lights. Monsieur really should see the *books* that now lined the walls of his little house. Oh, yes, many volumes. M. DuBonn was quite the intellect, quite the wit and raconteur also, and such history. Oh, one had discoursed earlier on the interesting history of Karl DuBonn? Well, surely there was much more to know, but if that was her host's feeling. . . . But Monsieur should certainly check out the DuBonns' library. One didn't mean to be impertinent, but they were perhaps a bit more extensive in their books, the DuBonns were, than was Monsieur himself, if what one now saw in his library were the extent of his books—and were they? Oh, they were? Well, in any case, the DuBonns' fascinating library. . . .

No longer fascinated with much at all, pleasured only briefly in his spying on the actress at her writing, as he would have enjoyed spying on any beautiful woman, as he enjoyed spying in general, Edouard felt the excruciating tightness of his life, never far away, in a new dimension.

66

As the week neared its end, his old swivel gave way to something else, chuggish, sluggish, depressing. Positive and negative poles, elation and dread—hard as the old mania and de-mania had been on him, they had always been broadly ranging, passionate and active, and—he flattered himself even yet—ingenious. Only once had something in them served him up to fate altogether: when he had faced the monster-dog in his yard.

But now, like a chicken on a spit, he turned slowly, passively, taking the heat of something mingled, ambiguous: a kind of hopeful hopelessness, a kind of hopeless hope, reflecting on what was, speculating on what might be, these also hard to distinguish. He began to see himself as Edouard the Pretender, misguided claimant of a truncated realm hardly worth the bother.

Do what you will, he said to no one special a dozen times each day, forgetting to keep an eye on the mélange that swarmed about Auxillac. Take it, take me, take over, what do I care?

As he had ponderd "neighbors"—but with such illumination and imagery!—now he dragged himself listlessly near "tenants" and "guests." It bored him, frankly, and though he felt a bit of the old flare as he dawdled near "host" (was the host an agent of hospitality or, as with certain bacteria and insects, no more than a kind of restaurant for a craftier and more powerful parasite?), he could see that he reflected and speculated without much wit or charm, though he thought the "restaurant" connection might be clever. Still, even it was an inside joke, further proof of his insular life.

At night he dreamed himself tumbling down through a black water, rolling, colliding with stones and mortar, odd bits of furniture, china, banging himself on shin and temple. Once, near a mysterious source of light, he was confronted by the grinning face of a man floating by in top hat and tails. Watching him float away, trailing bubbles, he knew it had been the old avant-gardist.

Strangely, this apparition brought him back to life, he couldn't have said why. What had he been thinking of, rolling over and playing dead like a lesser dog? he thought on waking Saturday morning. What had happened to family feeling, if nothing else? Didn't he owe the old folks something? He lay in his bed building energy, his eyes studying the remains of plaster laurels on his ceiling as if they were relics of the saints, revelations of destiny. Oh, destiny was a much happier word than fate! He would see what could be salvaged. He owed his parents that at least. He knew now what the actress was made of, and he believed he could sift and shake it more to his advantage. The Circles would find her out in time, but they had personages to engage them that were more amusing than this minor has-been of the minor "classics." They couldn't be everywhere at once, and until they had her number, she was a danger to him. He would have to work swiftly to reconvert her to himself before she headed off like a wayward missile, but it could be done, he had no doubt of it.

As for the tenants, he could see now that they were very dangerous. He had, after all, seen several films in which employees had taken over the control of things, where masters had become slaves to their own servants, even (he shuddered with the thought) the owners of rich and remote estates butchered by underlings who then proceeded to claim all the authority of the owners for themselves.

Now, with all morning and afternoon free to ponder as the actress and the unsuspecting DuBonns wandered here and there, unwittingly wandering ever nearer his web, he began to remember what it was that had bothered him about the tenants in the first place.

68

7. In the Afternoon, the Actress
Had Been Writing

Always the same letter. To a much younger actress named Inez Castillo, who had "aroused her sympathies" a few years earlier, she was fond of telling people who remarked on her interest, though she truly thought it was no one's business but her own. Yes, it had all happened when "the Spanish waif" had stepped in nude for her in a film by an important German director, now dead, and, yes, it was a tragedy, so young, yes, yes, etc.

The actress had long ago reassured herself that the scenes in question had been tastefully carried out. Yes, care had been taken that the more-public private parts alluded to the most private ones, no more than that, and with the death of the director, the film had become a Classic and earned a great deal of money in America. All this had given the anonymous nude body, even, a minor credential. One liked to think that (as mentor) one could have parlayed this into something long before now for Inez Castillo, if the young woman had not been so unruly. Occasionally "incorrigible" seemed the better word for it, the guest at Auxillac thought every afternoon when she took out her host's grotesque stationery box to extract several sheets of his inferior stationery. Sometimes "wanton" or even "stupid" seemed better words.

Still, she labored at her mission. By now, many matters of pride were involved. And as the time at Auxillac stretched out, holding off the hour of reckoning at Cannes and a reunion with her own mentor, now in a stew about many things, including some governmental meddling into the affairs of his Art, the correspondence became a relief, an escape from the persons below, one of them quite dreary. In fact, she was finding it harder and harder to stay

69

charming and delightful in anyone's company. She had much on her mind. Time was passing and opportunity with it, and who knew what horrors the ideologues now in power would come up with to thwart a goal or need? The whole country seemed in a state of siege or madness. Whole buildings blew up in the night, in the middle of Paris. These atmospherics took their toll, no question.

Even her own nature was becoming much less reliable, though whether this had to do with the politics of the moment or a dozen other dissatisfactions, she didn't know. On some days her personality and metabolism seemed to lurch from hour to hour, very frightening, actually.

She'd first become aware of these barometrics when she'd watched Inez Castillo walk onto the German's set and had suffered one of her special fits of vision that she called, privately, Terminally Lucid—rare then, but by now the order of the day.

That morning, observing how nervously the girl occupied the stark white scene, its absolute center, suddenly she had been struck Terminally Lucid by the vision of a plucked chicken, shuffling its feet this way and that, turning slightly and freezing in subtle attitudes at the German's incessant directions, offering its pathetic little defeathered nub up for viewing . . . excruciating—"Offering *itself* up for a meal," the actress had heard herself say to herself, in searing revelation.

And then, in a second flash: ". . . and then for the end . . . that is the meal's."

The whole cinematic enterprise was suddenly spread before her like an alimentary canal. The poor dumb chicken was tumbling through it, frame after frame, no exit, breaking down under many acids and biles, heading for its fate. The actress had felt herself weaken under the lacerating beams of truth cutting across truth: the

70

THE TENANTS AT AUXILLAC

chicken tumbling toward its fate, then transmogrified—
spreading itself out on a great white platter as if it were a
natural nest—the body stretching, displaying itself, relinquishing freely that which was most its own, turning its
private self into something for others to pick and nibble
on, and smiling all the time, no nervousness now. Oh, it
was something: lolling and rolling and posing with
trussed feet, offering up its chicken-smile. . . . And yet it
wasn't brown the way a roasted bird would be, but white
as the cadaver that, in truth, it was.

Weak with lucidity, her eyes telescope and kaleido-
scope at once, she had had to take a seat. And then, to her
mild horror, she'd turned ravenous, as it was nearing
lunch, and the little bird was something else again. Promise and portent were lurking, and it had been necessary to
sit this way and that way in her seat, trying to accommodate a raging hunger and minor nausea, the flashing heat
of her distress and a strange chill that was intermittently
in the air—perhaps brought in, she thought later, by the
cool Shade tarrying nearby, tapping his foot for the German.

It was a queer day, indeed. Her natural sensitivity to
images augmented, by something. Hard to comprehend.
She had seen a hundred naked walk-ons in her time, had
been Terminally Lucid often enough to keep her wits
about her, maintain an equilibrium. In the end, she had
felt herself sinking into a mysterious poignancy, devastating. This, or something else, or a dozen things in cahoots
had settled in, and growing inside her was an uncharac-
teristic sense of duty: she must protect and guide the girl.

Finally Lucid gave way to Insipid, as her twirling eyes
slowed down and closed on a kind of marquee: *Poule/
Poulet*, a childhood joke. She had dozed a few minutes
and then gone for a gargantuan lunch to recover.

But she had not recovered, and she had not been able to

forget little, terrible Inez, the agent of insight, so innocent of so much that she would need and want to know, though she herself had never felt the need of protégées before. Mysterious. Though she had recovered from the general seizure, the idea that Inez was a duty had remained, like a low-grade fever.

That was how she really knew all was not well. She had always been very discriminating in selecting a duty. On any minimally normal day of the past, Inez Castillo wouldn't have had a prayer. One was still objective enough to see that.

This particular duty had been over-complicated very quickly by a scathing article in the red-feminist press. Some zealot had chosen her, out of all possible choices, to hold up as an example, drawing an absurd connection between what was, after all, the use of a naked prop (yes, a further lucidity had re-established *that*, at least), from "the Underclasses," if the invective had to be quoted, and the old military tradition whereby wealthy young men had sent substitutes to wars. Absurd! There'd been no coercion in soliciting these particular naked parts, and in fact, naked parts had been available in abundance. It had been the Spanish waif's lucky day. Still, it was not a pleasant association, and one that had set here brooding at the time. But mercifully, before any social sentiments could get a hold on her, the director had died and the whole thing was *clearly* a favor to Inez Castillo. Yes, a favor and Inez's only credential for some time.

Not that the journalist had ever had a point. It would be a relief when these political types lost their moment in the limelight, truly, she had reason to think every day of the week. As if one hadn't enough to worry about, now there were threats to many of the old very necessary practices. The maniacs now at the rudder could whimsically impede the free movement of one's own money, and had done it, could appropriate one's resources for public use, put strictures on the most personal business. Who would have thought such things could happen in France? What next? Heads on pikes, all along the Rivoli?

The naked girl had also managed to hook some unpleasant old memories of her own long-ago beginnings in film, which she had thought entirely repressed. And then, soon, these battled for attention with some questions, worrisome as bees in the garden: Perhaps for those not in-the-know the body would mistaken for her own and deemed a trifle voluptuous for someone of her reputation—who could tell? And why hadn't she been invited, at least, to expose her own parts? She was 99% sure she would have declined, but in the interest of authenticity she might have been persuaded. And wasn't it customary, in any case, to discuss such arrangements with the major presence in the film? Sometimes she was not at all sorry, not sorry at all, that the misguided German director had died the early death that so often comes to the self-absorbed, even if it had brought him a cachet he hadn't earned.

Well, never mind. Once she had settled on this "duty" to shape the private and professional life of Inez Castillo from the fathomless wisdom of her own experience, she'd felt much better. In fact, this mission could sometimes distract her from everything else in the matter.

But she had her work cut out for her, the actress never failed to think each afternoon as she took up her pen to instruct her charge. Sitting at the hideous desk in the cramped and thoroughly unsatisfying chamber in this wreck of a "chateau," reeling slightly from regarding too long the poorly maintained property through a window that had been cut slightly askew, throwing the world at an angle, the actress prepared herself for her task at hand by recounting the younger actress's transgressions. First and worst, the girl had allowed unscrupulous persons to lure her from the sage advice of her new benefactor at first chance. These unsavories had fashioned a pout and a swagger for her, lots of leather clothes and such, made her a "starlet" in France and America for a few weeks, a fetish of the magazines. Everywhere the actress went, the enormous eyes of Inez Castillo reproached her from billboards and television screens. This madness had passed soon, and the actress congratulated herself that she had been generous enough to extend a "second chance." She attempted to draw *Pequeña Inez* closer under her wing, advising her on clothes (The leather has to go), general image (De-spoke the hair: this is France! Tone down the eyes—you look diseased. Buy more modest foundations: why exaggerate the all-too-unfortunately-obvious? We're not after Hollywood!), love life (None right now), film ventures (work with Alain only), finance (let me take care of it).

From the beginning there had been set-backs, stallings, lapses from the strict regimen the mentor had ordered in the hope of saving the ignorant no-talent peasant from her selfish little self.

First, though not necessarily worst, the girl was in serious debt, or so one had to let her think, and it was certainly true enough that debt was close at hand—yes, no financial sense at all. Second, by a thousand hooks and crooks had diets and wardrobe prescriptions been violated, photographs and cameos contracted for without one's approval, secret bank accounts attempted, and who-knew-what else that was a caution to one's good nature? And there had been that thoroughly inappropriate business with one's own driver, handsome Raoul (the little slut!), and a shameless-toady manner with Alain, one's own mentor, in a transparent attempt to displace favor, and lies and lapses and deceptions, enough to put one off charitable projects in future, guaranteed.

74

Well, at least Raoul could not be two places at once, the actress comforted herself each afternoon as she planned out the day's lessons and watched the well-formed buttocks of her driver as he bent over the upraised hood of her automobile, framed by the crooked window, or heard his devastating whistle as he moved here and there out of her view. But this reassurance was only good for a minute against so much undercutting in other areas, and the actress would resume her instructions with a savagery that surprised her, a sternness that she felt sure was not characteristic of her nature at all, but which she nevertheless enjoyed hugely after all the expectations on her (all her life!) to be discreet, charming, tactful, civilized, indirect, etc.

Last, and just probably worst, things had worked out (at Alain's demand—what next?) so that Inez was now leasing one's own expensive apartment in Paris for peanuts, with who-knew-what kind of lazy, lax, licentious attitudes—? And there were other problems too. Yes, several other problems.

And yet there was something in the situation that could restore her natural good humor sometimes, and, well, that was truly a blessing not to take lightly, given all her troubles. She relished these afternoons!

"Ma chère Inez," the actress had begun shortly after she had managed to disentangle her hand from the sticky paws of her groveling host that first afternoon at Auxillac. "I should have written you earlier, my dear little friend. Though we conversed only last evening, the situation was not leisurely and there was much that I wished to call to your attention, much that you should hold in mind in my absence. First, you should think of where your mentor is bound: Cannes. Yes, Cannes, and while occasionally some tart of a Roman candle will light the sky over

Cannes for an instant before fading from view in her swift downward career (Do not forget: whatever has been made of it, 'career' means the downward fate of things: consult the *Petit Larousse* that I gave you), such an imprudent fly-by-night speaks only to some random stroke of something. Actresses honored at Cannes are discriminating women of real accomplishment and maturity. They choose their work carefully, and when in doubt, they trust themselves to the good judgment of one more experienced, with their welfare in mind. I myself am going to Cannes because early in my still-rising trajectory I trusted those who were older and wiser, never assumed that any fuss of celebrity meant anything at all (and counted my blessings there was little of it!) and chose only to work on the finest films, those that were destined to become classics and would provide a steady dividend over the decades. I find myself at Cannes, 'up' for recognition again this year because I did not succumb to a cheap popular vehicle (and don't think for a minute such opportunities don't come my way every day of the week), didn't display inordinate amounts of bosom or buttock, nor engage in tasteless simulations of pigsty behavior, nor utter language on or off-screen that was unbecoming to a major presence. Instead this year I chose Alain's superb *La malheur blanc,* and that only. I didn't fritter and fiddle and strew myself about like birdseed, a bit of this, a bit of that, anything to call attention. No, I invested myself, and while I—as always—took risks with myself, for my Art, I chose a worthy enterprise. You could learn something from that, *Pequeña Inez.*

Never mind for now, though! This sermonette has gone on long enough, and besides I have much to tell you. I am dawdling on my way to be honored at Cannes, not because I'm becoming jaded after so many honors (it is just this kind of lassitude and hubris that I'm warning you

76

against, Inez), but to tell the truth, grateful as I am to Alain for all he's done for you (and you too must sharpen your gratitude faculty—never, never forget what I have convinced Alain to do for you!), the truth is I do not always look forward to the rendezvous with him on the Riviera, and you may relay that to him, as I know you will. All our telecommunications confirm that he is a maelstrom of anxiety about my fate at the hands of the critics in Cannes, a misplaced worry, since I have made a point of never having anything but the most generous and charming relations with the powerful critics, and there's a lesson in this for you too, little girl. And of course he is perhaps a bit worried about the fate of his other film, *Tu es prêt? Tout à l'heure.* As he should be. If you ask me, he spreads himself a bit thin, too trendy, two films in one year, not *my* style at all, and once you are back on your feet and have even a modicum of choice, you too should determine the one sterling opportunity and not bite off more than you can digest. You might have noticed that in recent times, I myself have chosen to do only one film every two or three years, and now that I think about it, *Malheur* is really my first film in four years, that's how discriminating my reputation allows me to be, and it is something for you to set your sights on for the future, though of course, at the moment, you truly need every bit of exposure you can wheedle, lest you seem to fall off too irrevocably from that humiliating excessive self-display of last year, evidence of the weakest discretionary faculty I've yet to encounter.

But *never mind* that now! Alain will probably smoke himself into a sanitarium before it's all done, but what can I do but endure it in respectful silence: that is my way. Besides, he knows just what to do with a sanitarium—remember me in his *L'ennui à Baden-Baden?* A case for your earnest study, *Pequeña.* In any case, in

77

Cannes I will provide him the requisite comfort, which he
has earned, a diplomacy you should master too, and desist
from your confusion between paying up and a whorish
squandering, between discreet ministrations and the vulgar modes of the Hollywood ingénue. We will talk more
of this, and soon. Did you get rid of that secret pair of
leather pants you retained, in spite of my good advice?
Really!

But why I am writing, truly, is to wish you luck when
your *Les Cowgirls du Montparnasse* premieres this week,
and to tell you how much I look forward to seeing your
little performance if I ever see it playing anywhere. Alain
was very kind to do me the favor of getting Roger to give
you that bit, and though you had to perform naked
(again!) as a baby pig, take it in stride. Roger is not without taste, and he's been having his own problems, as I'm
sure he's told you on those long, cold nights in his lair.
Yes, of course I knew about that! Did you really think you
could hide it? It's a fine repayment of your debts, isn't it?
Not prudent, not prudent. Roger has a ravenous appetite
for the firm young flesh of fryers and broilers. Against the
day very soon when he'll be a tough old capon, if you ask
me. Oh, I know him!

Well, never mind that. I wish you luck and will hope
and pray that when the critics give him his long overdue
due, they will spare you, my *manzanita.* But don't count
on it.

Well, another afternoon, another paragraph, and then
into the mail with this. My reasons for writing you today
are sentimental, sentimental. This requires explanation,
because as you well know, I am not by nature a sentimental sort, but a vigilant realist who values good sense and
reason above all in live. But sometimes I indulge myself,
like everyone else, in old-fashioned pleasures. I have been

78

tarrying this week in the rustic Lot, and my host—more about him momentarily—has two old Spanish peasants to give color to his property. When I saw them, I couldn't help but think of you, and your humble beginnings in Sepulveda. When you were not yet Inez Castillo, but Inez Huta. Oh, my *amigita*, don't take offense! No need to be ashamed of your origins, and anyone would understand why you felt like you must change 'Huta,' sounding as it does, so much like *'puta.'* I know you must have enjoyed your own wit in fashioning 'Castillo' out of that modest linguistic that housed you before your quick rise-and-fall, but to tell you the truth, I've always thought that you might have given a bit more thought to 'Castillo,' politics having become what they have become.

But *never mind*, my *paloma*. When I looked into the deeply creased and sagging faces of these peasants, I some-how produced you on my eye: a barefoot urchin, absorb-ing quaint lore at the knees of some approximation of these two old treasures; and at the same time, I had a vision of a future you as well. My host, of course, does not value them in the least. He is in many ways a naif, but for myself, I've never noticed such refinements of service here before, though I suppose these old retainers have al-ways been here. Well, it comes to nothing really, attempts at the special this, and the special that, nothing substan-tially delivered, but the old woman is especially cheerful and alert to one's comfort, or perhaps it is only your sin-gular indifference to me that makes me notice. Re-member how you refused to unpack my luggage that time in the wilds of Nembia, remember how

My dear, I broke off some time ago, to be honest, the actress now wrote. But let me try to pick up where I was when summoned away by an irresistible quality of the late afternoon light.

79

As said, I am lingering in the Lot, at a droll old country 'estate' (more of rock-pile, really) that could well be Roumanian, making much of the gothic. It belongs to a queer little man, a nobody really, but I think a friend of Gustavson's wife, so I string him along. Poor pigeon—he's barely hanging on, the place going to ruin around him, and yet he paints and decorates and cuts corners, and has even taken in renters (more about these later perhaps), all in some sentimental project to save his 'ancestral Big House' (!), not to mention his 'ancestral Caveau,' a former chicken house, I think, with several casks of acid he tries to pass off as wine. Oh, if people could only see themselves as others do (a caution for you to keep in mind, too, Inez: others see). It would be funny if not so pathetic.

Well, I should be fair: the property probably does have some Carpathian charm, and the raggedy little host (I think he is in love with me: he broods, is jealous of my conversations with his renters, can you imagine? one of whom, the female, is painting my portrait—perhaps I shall give it to you, *Aubergine*, I really am fond of you, in spite of your habit of disappointing me at every turn and taking advantage of my good will and influence. Do you really think this won't have its consequences as time goes by? Well, think again). Well, the scruffy elf means well, giving me what I know he thinks of as his 'best room' (terrible! moldy, a mélange of decorations, a veritable *history* of bad taste, the mattress like bedrock, spiders and wasps in the eaves), and he himself, round as a pomegranate, clothes full of wrinkles and tatters of the sort one rarely sees outside the poorest regions of your native country, my *gallinita*. Still, he is my host, and will be for a few days more (Yes, I have my reasons, and maybe I'll tell them to you. And then again, maybe I won't—you'll just have to wait, won't you? While waiting, you might meditate on the many times you've kept me waiting—at restaurants, at the homes of influential friends where I'd hoped to make a dent in your solid failure, what about that time in Biarritz? Yes, you'll just have to cool your round little heels, as the Americans say, won't you?).

I try to spend at least an occasional evening meal with the man—he is a terrible cook! Several times I have had to send Raoul out on the sly for provisions (Yes, I'm aware the mention of Raoul is not a comfortable one for you, do you think I'm as sunk in myself as you are? Well: Raoul, Raoul, Raoul, take that. He was, after all, my employee long before he was your lover, and if it's of any interest to you, the mention of your name to Raoul does not appear to be uncomfortable for him in the least), but we go through the motions, and if I guide his hand a bit, he can come up with an almost edible ratatouille, though he serves decomposing cheese and rancid ham and butter. Oh, well—once he drinks himself into a stupor (he apparently finds nothing wanting in the rot from his 'caveau'), then I come alive. . . . Now, now, now! You'll have to bide your time—Don't skip ahead! No patience at all! This is important, so pay attention.

I need a favor of you. As you understand, I won't be returning to Paris for six months and all I own and treasure is in your care. While Alain and I are in Brazil (rumor has it that *Brasil Cru* is going to be a masterpiece, lush and sere at once; so sorry there's nothing for you, I being the only character, but then you do have my apartment, don't you—treat it with the care you'd give your dear dead mother's grave, Inez, or I'll ruin you). Anyway, the favor: the cleaning service is still on, and unless you want to pay for it yourself, kindly cancel, but I trust that if you cancel, you will do the necessary housework yourself, I'm not kidding. And one other thing: You were probably surprised to find that two of my larger rooms are locked up, and I did have every intention of letting you know that

81

would be the case when we signed our agreement, but it slipped my mind. I just want you to know that no distrust of you, *pajarita,* led me to seal away some special items (my best chinoiserie and some rare upholsteries and rugs—I wouldn't think of burdening another person with the pussyfooting these things require; and of course my private papers and some of my more expensive clothes— why present temptations?), no, I'm sure you will be a most trustworthy tenant. Never having had private property yourself, your raw envy will tell you much about how to comport yourself with another's. No, I was not concerned about you at all, my fig, knowing I could trust you not to besmirch my satin chaise-longue or misuse my best linens. But the truth is, and your conduct in the past will bear me out, women of your wild and rowdy generation often entertain disreputable friends, and while I like to think that you grow more prudent in your selection (and might I suggest M. Pigalle of *Le Monde?* I have it on good authority that you've piqued his interest, at least), still: anyone will tell you, check it out, that it doesn't do for just any hoodlum to drop a buttock in one's genuine Louis XVI chair, and so, I've tucked some things out of sight, simpler in the long run, since it will save you the trouble of keeping your somnolent Spanish eye on them, my cherub.

As for the rent, in case you didn't understand, though I tried my best, send it directly to M. Jean-Francois Dupont at the Banque Sauf Avis Contraire on the first of each month, *punto.*

Wishing you all the best for a pleasant vacation in my humble quarters, and with all professional interest, and maternal affection,

Yours."

Putting away the stationery on this particular afternoon, the letter in the box in case she thought of more

82

she wanted to add, the actress felt depressed. Her head was swirling, her teeth sore from repeated clenchings, perhaps a danger to her dentist's patient restorations. She wished she'd never laid eyes on the little bitch. And yet a duty, if anything was, was something to see through to the end, however it turned out. But these slathering fits. . . .

She pulled her chair up close to the crooked window. Below Raoul was putting away his equipment, pausing to scratch the fearsome muzzle of the DuBonns' dog. Then he was leaving her purview, the dog getting up too and trotting behind like a courtier. She shifted her eyes and looked out on the rocky contours of Auxillac.

Suddenly one of her visions was on her: the jutting rocks forming a large Necropolis that stretched out to the horizon, dead upon dead upon dead. And just as suddenly it was gone—more a glimpse than a vision, but Terminally Lucid in the extreme. She was shaken anew. How long would she hold up, she wondered, as she forced herself to sit back from the edge of her chair and take weak possession of her self. How long could she hold up, between her strange fits of duty and these epiphanies?

Rubbing a thumb across a sensitive cuspid, she looking again onto the rough terrain and the rougher habitations of Auxillac, but now she felt a sharp remorse. How unfair to make her poor host the butt of jokes, teasing him mercilessly about his tenants. The whole general torment was unconscionable. Didn't he just want what everyone else wanted: his property in order, the general admiration of large numbers of discerning people, before he died? How else to account for his odd behavior with his renters, his doomed "repairs"? His perpetually open house and all the miscalculations of hospitality?

But someone should tell him about his lack of discretion in guests—really: on her last visit the place had been over-run with members of that pathetic crowd who had

put on such a display at the Trocadero two years ago on July 14th. Her poor boorish innkeeper thought them brilliant. It was hard to think of such things: excruciating. Compounding in some way her own general anxiety about her apartment, suddenly not in her control. And if she thought about it, what could she count on as "in her control," now that the political situation was what it was? Could one know, from day to day, that one's beach property hadn't been "nationalized" in one's absence from it? What about one's tiny farm near Fontainebleau? One's little hideaway in Morocco, even? Even Alain had been officially cautioned about taking his hard-earned capital to Brazil. No, one couldn't be sure of much at all anymore.

While brooding, she hadn't noticed that Raoul, her driver, had sneaked up under her window and now was standing with his muscular legs widespread, his shirt a bit open, the sleeves rolled, eyeing her in an amused, proprietary way. When she turned and saw him, she felt a tremendous start, particularly taken aback by the monstrous dog that had planted itself firmly near the driver's knee, its huge jaws open, a ludicrous drape of tongue tented on either side by the lower canines, sharp as daggers. She emitted a shriek before her special eyes construed the dog in its context and she realized it was just the DuBonns' pet; she could hear the footsteps of her solicitous host start up the stairs. Oh, well, why not a brief stroll with "Monsieur Edouard" before her rendezvous with the Du-Bonns? That might make her feel a little better about things, she thought, already growing steadier with the thought of her host's arm beneath her hand: He, if little else, was predictable.

She turned back to the window where Raoul still stood, and gathering her loose hair to tuck into its discreet bun, she paused for a moment, both hands behind her head.

The posture was one that had been favored by the droll "bombshells" of another film era, and sure that "knowing Raoul" would appreciate the wit, she slowly allowed one eyelid to drift down into a languid wink, obscuring the dog entirely.

8. The Case Against the DuBonns

Saturday night the actress, who had announced her plans to leave for Cannes the next afternoon, following a picnic with the DuBonns at an "adorable spot" in Edouard's woods, was putting in a perfunctory final evening with her host. Edouard was watching her as she curled in a chair in his library and sipped a brandy. She had gone to the village that afternoon and returned with a bottle (a bottle only!) of ordinary armagnac to repay her "marvelous host" for his hospitality. Edouard repressed a sneer as he took in her indiscreet posture, the ether-brandy, and especially the way her eyes lazed across the finished portrait of herself, resting against the wall.

It was a large canvas glittering with specks of bright acrylic paint, "After the style of Monsieur Vincent Van Gogh," the actress was saying. Edouard regarded the portrait sourly. It looked very little like the actress, he thought, though there was some fidelity to the color of her hair and eyes and clothes. Otherwise, the figure in the portrait was large and square, whereas the actress was slim and angular; the flesh was blotched and ruddy, while the actress was smooth and bisque-like. The smiling face of the painting seemed to have been scrawled on at the last moment with a crayon—"After the style of Monsieur Paul Klee," the actress explained with barely reined excitement. Didn't Monsieur Edouard think it was very clever of Jenny to use the acrylic medium *and* these old styles? Showing that she *knew* the New, but refused the mode? Wasn't the painting really a comment on Art itself. . . ?

As she ruminated on the cleverness of the DuBonns, Edouard fiddled with a strip of paper. Finally, as the conversation wandered to the fact of the DuBonns' being his tenants, he seized the opportunity to stride across the room and pulled up a chair to the actress's side. Then, he shoved the strip of paper into her hand.

On the paper, he had carefully listed—item by item— his "Case Against the DuBonns."

As the actress read the list with a puzzled squint, Edouard raced ahead and outlined what he himself, once the evidence was listed in front of him, believed to be a very sinister operation indeed. Did his guest not find it *bizarre* that the DuBonns lived so far in the country, so far away from their *own* society, without even a car? And might he add that their imposition regarding his own little Renault, while not exactly sinister, was provocative? Couldn't one almost say that impositions were always provocative? And though he hated to suggest that there was something unattractive about people that she, his guest, obviously found intriguing and congenial—and of course he had no intent to *malign* the judgment of his discreet guest (here he raised an eyebrow to suggest that such judgment might well be maligned), but didn't Mme. DuBonn seem just a wee bit *too* quiet, M. DuBonn just the tiniest bit *too* congenial? No? Well.

That was very easy for her to say, he supposed, since the last week seemed to have produced a *transformation* in the DuBonns—though that might be entirely attributable to the copious charms of the actress herself. . . . Oh, think nothing of it! But—and again, he hated to dampen any enthusiasms, but wasn't there a *concurrent* possibility—namely, that the actress had something the Du-

Bonns wanted, perhaps needed? Oh, who knew what! She, his guest, would be a much better judge of that than would he himself, for she had been most often in their company. As for his own part, before her arrival he had found the DuBonns unwilling to exchange more than a "good day" or a "May-we-take-your-automobile-thank-you-very-much," except on the few occasions when the male DuBonn had seen some advantage (who knew what?) in chitchatting about nothing at length, namely when borrowing a bottle of wine from the caveau—never replaced, might one add—or when insinuating a complaint about firewood. Well.

Didn't she think it odd that *suddenly* the two had become the *soul* of affability and charm—though he must add that for his own part he did not find them in the least possessed of charm—no, no, he himself did not buy their little clevernesses, no—now this was not to impute the actress's own excellent judgment—no, no, to each his own—but for his part, he did not care for Mme. DuBonn's little costumes—if the truth must be told, he found them—well—well, if the truth must be told, if he had to give them a name, it would have to be—well, "trite," he guessed, would have to be that name—yes, yes, sorry, but "trite."

And while he was on the subject—and, please believe that he had no desire to detract from his guest's pleasure in her new portrait, but frankly, he himself wondered if it were not a trick of the charlatan? Oh, please! He begged his guest to remain calm—no, no, he had not realized that Mme. DuBonn's work came very dear—really? Well, yes, he supposed that one had to expect as much when the artist had been such a success in *Bordeaux*. . . .

But, well: enough debate on Mme. DuBonn's little talents. Such was merely gossip, was it not? Besides, he

87

knew very little about the woman—merely what his guest had told him herself. . . .

But the problem that had instigated his "Case Against the DuBonns," which she now held in her hand, was much more severe than whether Mme. DuBonn was more than a clever imitator—whether a chic innovator of fashion or merely a cunning magician whose designs were more obscure than at first seemed probable—yes. Though, as just said, he had no desire to belabor the amusements of Mme. DuBonn.

The male DuBonn was the one whom he himself knew more about. Now, granted, he did not know the illustrious *history* of M. DuBonn, only what he had heard from his guest, who, of course had had it from the horse's mouth. . . .

Well. Didn't she find it strange that he lived so far from civilization, with all his fine history and fine intellect and fine . . . well, whatnot? That the tenants had been so reserved with their landlord, whom they had been living close by for some time, yet immediately *preyed*—well, no, that was not a polite word—might he then say "seized"? *Seized* on the actress the very first day and made her part of their oddball society? Touring about in her Mercedes—Well, that was nothing, really. After all, they used the little Renault as though it were their own, though he supposed that a Mercedes. . . .

Nevertheless, one might include these items on a list of suspicious behavior in the interest of getting the broader picture, no?

And wasn't it odd that the dog, that monster of an animal, had never been mentioned prior to the tenants' takeover of the little house? It could be a very dangerous beast, one had to think—large, bred from who-knew-what stock, as these ungainly dogs were? Rather like certain odd personages . . . about whom one knew nothing . . .

And of course she knew the dog's name? No? How interesting. Yes, the dog's name was *Sangrito* . . . The choice of such a name might tell one much, didn't she think? After all, it was an odd name to give a dog, and though such a large dog could hardly be called "Fifi" or "Frou-frou," wasn't it strange that this large dog was called the diminutive "Sangr*ito*"? Something a little misleading, to say the least, and something a little sinister in the obvious: "*Sangrito*" . . . Not to mention their fascination with things Spanish, like one's own peasants. The Spaniards being a strange race.

Edouard, despite the energy with which he pursued his "Case," was having a hard time judging the actress's attitude. While she had seemed to waver a hair during his charges about the probable trickery of Mme. DuBonn's art, now she merely twirled her glass in her elegant fingers and stared into the lights twinkling from her brandy. But sure that he could seal his suit with the most dramatic points of the business, which he had ingeniously reserved for last, he forged ahead, pulling his chair still closer to that of his famous guest.

Would his guest like to hear a pair of tales that might do some small bit to convince her that he was not merely whistling in the dark? Very well.

On the absolute *premiere* night as his *tenant*, M. DuBonn had come—well, really *sneaked*—up on the kitchen doorstep as he himself had sat at his kitchen table well after dark, and if it had not been for an accidental scraping of the man's boot on the pavement, one might never have noticed him, and who knew how long he had been standing there at the door watching in secret. . . ? And when one had motioned the tenant to enter—well, it had been almost as if the man had not seen one's gesture, as though his eyes had been *glazed*, if she followed—well, she was after all in the entertainment business and knew much

89

better than he how these things worked, yes. Finally the fellow had entered and offered some pallid excuse about wanting to borrow wine—and while he himself, ever mindful of his duties as host, even when the guest might more properly be called an intruder, would certainly never begrudge a bottle from his caveau—might he say his ancestral caveau? Oh, but yes, the stock had been chosen by the knowing palate of his father, the celebrated restaurateur, 5 stars. But listen to this: When he had gone out to the ancestral caveau to select a wine for this tenant and had come back into his kitchen, what did she suppose that he had found? M. DuBonn *bent over* one's *mail* and one's *ledgers!* Of course, one had nothing to hide, but nevertheless. . . .

Oh, he was a sly one, this tenant: all of a sudden coming on with his relentless chitchat about this and that and nothing, taking the wine as though it had indeed been his object in invading one's kitchen—all full of smiles and backslapping, returning, finally, to one's little house, taking something more than the wine with him—oh, no, of course one had no idea *what*, but something, you could be sure. And he hated to repeat a trivial detail already alluded to, but: the truth was that his guest's aristocratic friend, for all his history, had never shown the civility of replacing the wine—not that it could be replaced, of course, being of the ancient stock of one's ancestral caveau, but one would have thought at least. . . .

Impossible to tell how the actress was receiving this tale! The woman was *infuriating*, having swung her body around in the chair and scooted the chair itself away from his own. And now she was staring at the portrait resting against the wall. Her face seemed impassive above the jut of angular jaw, virtually all she revealed to him now.

But since he had saved the *coup de grâce*, as a *coup de grâce* might and should be saved, for the end, he had little doubt that in a few moments her desultory sympathies would be entirely on his side, and so he pushed on.

Did his friend wish to know what mysterious thing had transpired only an hour or so later on that very night—might he add on that very *strange* night? He had mentioned, had he not, that there was a full moon? No? Well, there had been. He had noted on the way to his caveau that it was very full indeed, the very kind of moon often observed to promote queer behaviors in those that were basically up to no good to begin with. Yes, it had been a clear night with a full moon, a cold night, he could assure her of that, for he had had to make a little fire in his bedroom. Well, not to over-embellish a tale that was suggestive enough in its *bones:* he had gone to his room an hour or so after M. DuBonn had borrowed the wine and had made himself a fire. And since the room had retained a few wisps of smoke—she knew, of course, how the flues were in these old places; one was likely to get a few wisps of smoke, as perhaps she herself had noticed on the several nights he had made them a little fire in the fireplace in front of her. Well, to hurry things up: he had cut off all the lights in the Big House and was slowly making his way up the cold slate steps of the front hall—yes, yes, of course he knew that she knew the way, but he must tell things as he told them. So, slowly, slowly making his way up the cold, cold slate steps, everything still as a tomb, still as death. The moon cast an eerie light—yes, *eerie*, no other word for it—across the steps as he climbed and it seemed as if his steps were the only noises in a vast *sea* of silence—could she imagine what he meant? It was as if he were the only *human* presence for miles around under that great blue-veined moon—pallid as a corpse, it was, didn't she know? Of course one might remember that Old Pablo and Miranda, his degenerate retainers, were nearby, but had she ever noticed just how far was the trip from the Big House to the hut of these old persons? Yes, yes, it was quite far, quite far indeed. And if one thought about it, these two were hardly more alive than corpses themselves—why this very moment (and indeed on the night under discussion) it was anybody's guess as to whether they had not passed on in their sleep. So. Well, slowly and alone he climbed through that pale light, through that fearful silence, until he came to his room and went about the task of making himself a small fire. As was sometimes the case, the room retained a few wisps of smoke once the blaze was going and so he had gone to his window, which happened to overlook the little house and its side yard—the very yard where, he believed, she took her late bite with his tenants, no? Yes, that very yard. In any case, he had opened his window for a moment to let the wisps of smoke drift out at the night and what did she think he had seen? No, of course she would never be able to guess, so he would tell her. He had been leaning out of his window, just the slightest bit, and had noticed that the windows of the little house were very, very—almost preternaturally, yes—dark. Well, he had been ready to close the shutters and head for his bed when, suddenly, he had seen a movement in the yard of his little house. The motion had occurred behind his tree, unfortunately, and he couldn't be sure what had made it, so naturally he had leaned out further into this eerie night, under that corpse-like moon, and peered toward the strange activity going on upon his property.

Well: he could see nothing, that was the fact of it. But there had been no trick on his senses, because the unidentified motion had gone on for quite some time. Very mysterious, was it not, since there was no movement whatsoever within the little house? Since such a thing had never happened before, and happened to happen on the very night of the tenants' invasion of his estate? And

92

then, very mysteriously, very eerily, an insidious cloud conspired to move across the moon like a hand in a black glove, if she could imagine, cutting out all light and leaving the sinister business below to advance on toward who-knew-what mischief without being discovered.

Was that not an interesting story? Did his guest also wish to know that several days later he came upon the male tenant from the rear and almost startled him out of his excuse for clothing? Yes, and found him composting, of all things, tulips—*just* at the spot where the mysterious motion had taken place on that peculiar night. Of course, she had since seen those very tulips, had she not? The color of blood, more or less, were they not? Well, what else? He could assure her that, before the galvanizing ministrations of Dr. DuBonn, those tulips had been dead as dead.

At last he had made his impression! The actress some time before had twirled around in her chair and watched every nuance of his face as he had unfurled his tales—riveted to her seat, was she! This had allowed him to relax in his own chair and watch as his guest's eyes swung like pendula between his face and the "Case Against the DuBonns" resting in her lap, her crisp little fingers clutching the empty brandy glass for courage.

Well, what did she think? Was this not some very incriminating evidence against her precious DuBonns? He did not want to belabor the facts and cause her any embarrassment about her initial judgment, certainly—after all, first impressions did not always bear out—no, that was very true, indeed. One had come to know that very, very well. He paused, lifting a telling brow. But he felt sure that she could see herself that there was something questionable, to say the least, about these tenants, did she not?

For a long time, the actress was silent, her eyes fixed on

93

Edouard's face. Finally, her lips parted and, her eyes never wavering, she said, "Monsieur has . . . I think . . . a gothic imagination. . . ."

With that, she set her brandy glass on the table near her chair, rose, and marched out of the room and up the staircase, allowing the "Case Against the DuBonns" to drift from her lap and flutter along the floor to settle in front of her host's presumptuous chair.

9. The Following Morning, the Actress Took Her Leave

The following morning, the actress took her leave early, coolly thanking her host for his hospitality with a dry swipe of her fingers against his hand, and requesting that he inform his tenants that she would be unable to take part in their little picnic after all. Entering the seat behind the driver, she turned her head and gave Edouard a strange wide-eyed look, punctuated by two or three sudden squints. Then she quickly looked away, becoming absorbed in a periodical that she had been clutching in her hand. Edouard watched her ride away, a rigid smudge against the back window of her Mercedes.

Well, good riddance, he thought. All night long she had disturbed his sleep, even roused him up once, with mysterious noises and movements. Enough.

Wandering through the Big House after her departure, he discovered the woman's portrait, a florid cartoon staring at him from its place against his library wall. Oh, but he believed he could say that he saw a resemblance in the crayoned *artifice* of its face!

For a while, the master of Auxillac traversed his rooms and regarded their dank elegance and the sunlit grounds outside their windows. Would all this ruin him with the

Circles? Would Mme. Gustavson, the film director's wife, come to partake of his hospitality in the summer as planned, or would she soon decide to take her children to a Finnish island or some such, dismissing him with a note of false regret? Would M. Roland Lassalle, the writer, laze in one's courtyard, his mind gathering incriminating details on his host and Auxillac that might one day be seen in print? Would he himself ever know now whether any of the attention shed by the Circles was genuine, or merely laid out to dupe him, to have a private joke at his expense?

Finally he climbed to his bedroom, almost in a seizure of anxiety, and extracted his moldy ledger from its hiding place beneath his mattress, and then went back down to his kitchen to spread it out on the table, reconsider everything. He would pore over the figures again. Perhaps things were not as bad as he had reckoned. Perhaps he could evict these DuBonns. As it was, he was risking everything just for new slate over his head. It was madness! It would be better to let the roof go and seal off the rooms, one by one, as they succumbed to the elements. They wouldn't all go at once. He had many rooms, in *that* he could still take pride! Chances were good he could live out the rest of his days before the Big House dwindled to no rooms. He could move his good furniture into the best ones to begin with, let the others go. Why not? He would tell guests that Auxillac was undergoing major restoration, that parts of the chateau would be sealed off for years. He could complain of the sloth of workers, suppliers, the temperaments of decorators and artisans. By such devices might one seem extravagant, even, one's penury masked beyond detection. If the worst came, if the interior decayed beyond use altogether, well, he would sell off mouldings, marble, plumbing fixtures, furniture, lighting and heating implements—put everything into the

95

facade and lock it all up, move into the little house, or even the hut down the hill, assuming it would be back in his clear dominion by such a time. He would claim to prefer the simple life, which he knew held considerable charm as an idea for people who didn't have to live it. He'd live in the stable if he had to—feign the modes of delightful eccentricity like the old avant-gardist, his salvation and his bane. He wouldn't starve. He *would* be Master of his Destiny and his Fate!

All morning he calculated, re-figured his numbers, adding and re-adding, scrutinizing every decimal point, his head in a fever. Finally he heard someone, Pablo or Miranda, depositing the mail at the front door. He rose and dragged himself down the long corridor to the drafty foyer, cold even now. The chinks between his ancient stones reproached him, though covered with wallhangings depicting noblemen, fiefdoms, court life scenes and more, all exotically patterned with a sage-colored mold, reproaching him on two further counts. There was no hope of routing the tenants and still maintaining the property even at its present level of decay, that was the lesson of his ledgers. It would have to be his wild-haired second plan or none: dislodge the DuBonns and live as he might, waiting for everything to turn to dust around him.

At the door, two envelopes lay ominously on his cracked marble floor. The long official one was the news he had been dreading. Well, there it was: the bureau of revenues assessing his property upward, upward, insult to injury. Was there no end to the conspiracies to separate him from a life of charm and remove from the ordinary, the unwashed masses of restaurateurs and accountants, the diabolical forces that had had it in for him from his conception?

He retraced his dragging footsteps to the kitchen, open-

96

ing the smaller envelope bearing only his name, no more. Curious. Inside the kitchen, he felt a monstrous hilarity building up as he pulled out and read a long page written in a graceful cursive. A brief note, then two columns of "facts" and figures descending the page and collecting in a ludicrous sum at the bottom, the same graceful penmanship affixing the signature of Miranda, followed by a handsome calligraphy spelling out her husband's name, and the signatures of two "Witnesses," the actress and her driver! Following still was the notation that a copy of the document would be forwarded to the office of an attorney in Cahors. Amazed and reeling near hysteria, Edouard lifted his eyes and let them be pulled down again by the column of "items" on the "Bill for Services Rendered," each one more absurd than the next:

telephone messenger service—5 years
refuse collection—   " "
personal laundry—   " "
mail delivery—   " "
general cleaning—   " "

Then, "occasional shopping," "breakfasts for guests," "pruning of shrubbery," "general care of vineyard," "maintenance of small residential building," "financial advice" . . .

Edouard collapsed at his kitchen table, his body shaking with mirthless laughter, the demonic sounds seeming to come from somewhere outside himself, he himself unable to tell when the laughter changed to sobs. He himself unmindful of when these gave way to a pathetic mewing and then a comatose sleep, sudden, deep, and dreamless.

Some time later, exhausted, Edouard collected his ledger, tried to steady his pained head, its neck wobbling from the contorted nap at the table, and dragged himself to his stairs and started up. Damn it, he murmured.

97

Damn it, he didn't try to live in the world! Why was the world always coming to him? Why was Nature, too, always pounding at him, wearing away the stones of housing that he had come by honestly? Why couldn't things return to their old order, the Master of the Property in control, exacting rents and tolls from everyone who tarried or traversed—rich in authority and in the fruits of his own land, deferred to by his less-favored neighbors, eagerly sought out by his equals, given the benefit of the doubt by his betters—

At the head of the stairs he aimed himself toward his bedroom, his legs heavy as stone. By chance he glanced down the corridor toward the actress's vacated quarters. The door was ajar and he could see the tousled bedclothes within, though if one judged the light correctly, the sun had long since shifted to the downward curve. So: "Linen service," was it? "General cleaning," was it? He would have to get photographs of these things, begin to build a case in his defense.

He turned down the corridor and came to the bedroom door. The room still gave off the floral reek of his departed guest, and as Edouard stepped inside he felt a momentary panic. Oh, what the woman could do against him! A torment raged in his brain, and in other organs: she had betrayed him already.

Well, one would have to speak to Miranda, and speak to her in the tones persons of her sort well understood. It was shameful to come across such intimate disorder so late in the day. For what did one release the fruits of one's vineyard if not for a little order of the kind one couldn't manage for oneself? A "Bill for Services," indeed. No, he wasn't worried about any attorneys in Cahors. But: the age of the faithful retainer had passed, no doubt of it. Just one more hideous sign of the times. Well, he would summon the old body by telephone, have the room tidied and aired of this ungrateful personage before the goblins of night were on him.

Just as he was turning to leave the room, he spied a rubble on the vanity, left behind by his guest in her cool flight. So. That was what he was worth to her now? If he'd had doubts about how he stood in her eyes, here was the proof. Hair clasps, used tissues, a used razor blade, no less. Oh, he was less than nothing to her, less than nothing! So casual an entity was he, to her, that he might view the residue of her toilette—? But what was this?

What w-a-s t-h-i-s???

A thick letter—sealed, stamped, and addressed—rested against the mirror of the vanity, a tiny trellis of leaves etched along the flap. Obviously left behind in the actress's haste to be rid of her host, yesss . . . Edouard held it in his hand, sniffed in its forbidden scent.

Did he dare?

"*Ma chère Inez,*" the letter began. Edouard put his depressing ledger on the vanity and sank into a chair near the window. It was indeed toward the end of the afternoon, and the walls of the room reflected a claustrophobic apricot light from outside that was not pleasant, that was for sure. But—well, he would see what he would see. What was one more letter on such an active day for poison pens?

The light was the sort that prefaced violent storms by the time Edouard had read several pages, and by the time he had finished several pages more, the sun had taken on a blood-like cast.

What else? he was thinking, the evidence of the actress's nature and her devastating critiques of the accommodations at Auxillac, and of himself, all resounding in

99

his head, as if rendered in her trilling little voice, dipping
and cresting. What else can be done to me? What else. . . .

". . . In any case, once I met these tenants, I decided
that Fate was instructing me. How often, Inez, does such
a situation present itself: a chance for love, laughter, a
few days of respite from the pressures of a pressureful life,
the kind you are never likely to know, exactly. Yes: your
star has risen and it has sunk, and whose fault is that?
You will have all the leisure you need to think on your
folly, *mosquita*, and it may be true that I will sometimes
envy you that, busy as my life is and will continue to be,
but frankly I wouldn't be in your shoes for all the turtles
in Australia. In any case, as for Raoul, perhaps you might
comfort him when this is over, though I never approved of
that liaison of yours and his for a minute. There's nothing
in it for you, Inez, nothing of consequence. On the other
hand, I certainly understand (now!) your impulse, and
maybe there wouldn't be anything wrong with your indulging it briefly again when I have to toss him over ever-
so-gently before reaching Cannes, where gossip and Alain
will be dangers. I will, in fact, send him directly to you, so
be ready and don't complain. As for the gentle 'tossing
over,' I'm leaning toward some blow to the (absurd) Spanish pride which you must have had a sense of one time
yourself, but then pride of any sort is not your suit these
days, is it? The rumors I hear—! Well, this blow to Raoul
will be something choice, something to insure that he
says irreparable things before he's thought the situation
out vis-à-vis his cinematic hopes, then he will be properly
remorseful, puling about, not inclined to reveal particulars of any dalliances or indiscretions or anything else
that might displease anyone of influence. Oh, so greedy
for a 'break' of any sort—why does everyone, everyone
long for this lonely life, Inez? It beats me. Anyway, I'm
surprised you can see anything at all in this man, his

100

'pride' being so flimsy that he'll put up with up anything. Well, I'll work it out. If you'll pardon my saying so, my tiny apple, it will be a stratagem much like the one that gave me my tender hold on you. . . . Oh, *don't* be angry now! Can't one tease?

In any case, having let your charming Raoul tickle my interest on the drive down, I clearly saw the opportunity for amusement here, the camouflage of these pseudo-intellectual tenants, so sure to put off my little host and thus free me from the *burden* (I can't tell you!) of his sycophantish sucking-up, no self-respect at all, you know what I mean? Beware these types, Inez, they're not harmless.

Already Raoul and I have trysted in the stables, in his little room near the kitchen (as said: by mid-evening my host has drunk himself oblivious), and in other outbuildings on the property, including the 'ancestral caveau,' think of it. And we have even made good use of the drollest *sepulchre* of a room which I believe the little rooster said had been the nesting place of his parents (he is a sentimental fool, keeping the room like a shrine—as our American colleagues are prone to scream: Too Much!). And handy Raoul is everywhere when needed: behind a bush, a door, a wall, at the ready whenever my host drifts off for a minute—oh, bliss!

I hope it's not painful for you to hear any of this, *Estrellita*. As I told you, it isn't painful for Raoul when I tell him all about you.

Anyway, the tenants are somewhat amusing, but a little too self-possessed for people of no known recognition. They are Leftists of some kind, I think, but harmless, and the little wife quite talented in her way. They much approve of my egalitarian relations with my driver, who as we both know is a bonafide *lumpenprol*. The wife, as said, is painting my portrait, very amusingly, and the husband is an obvious Jew but very congenial, if sometimes tedious. They know of my early film with Zifakis, so I have a meager credential with them, and all in all, the week in their company is by far the most tolerable time I've ever spent at this place. The female has plans for another portrait which she will sketch in at our farewell picnic, a sort of *Déjeuner sur l'herbe* tableau of me, Raoul, and her husband, which I finally convinced her to try. I've been thinking that it might make a whimsical frontispiece for my projected *Memoires*, you know how I'm always on the outlook for something original and exotic. If, of course, she can bring it off with taste. She does have a diverting way of working her stilted oils in the other-century modes. They are truly innocents, and I tease them sometimes about being remnants of the Baader-Meinhof gang, or old colleagues of Danny the Red, and they are very amused with my ribbing, though if you passed them on the street in Paris, you might think twice before letting them follow you into an alley. Oh, but here they are the perfect camouflage, my Gang of Two, and absolutely out-to-lunch. When we four drive, they sit in the rear, I (very enlightened: sitting up front with the driver) lean over and engage them in my inimitable pitter-patter while my devious hand wanders. Raoul's face, which must be perfectly reflected in the rear-view mirror, betrays nothing that I can tell. He is a marvel! You must miss him dreadfully, my dear little Huta. Well, if you ever approach even the lowest pinnacle of success before you die, why not take these rough lovers from the doomed but aspirant classes of men? Very exciting, but then I forget myself: you aren't likely to leave someone like Raoul very far behind now, are you, and it is an instruction to see that after all this time and all the care that everyone has taken, trying to help you out, you still aren't much better off than

102

Raoul himself, not far at all from that fetid alley in Madrid where Messerschmidt and I found you and you couldn't wait to strip yourself down for 100 francs a day! So forget it, I was only musing."

At this point Edouard noticed a shift. The parsimonious script of the actress suddenly lurched and sprawled on the paper, as if written in haste, with mental distress.

"P.S. Oh so I haven't sent this yet, that's the last thing I'm worried about. Listen Inez and listen carefully, or I'll make a rug out of your hide. I've had an awful time of it and I don't know who to trust right now, but you owe me.

I spent last evening with that stupid little man, who filled my ear with what I thought were ridiculous tales but have proven to be merely *criminally* negligent in their indirection (I might sue). Then I came upstairs, and what a night! But I am older and wiser this morning, make no mistake, and whatever it was you had up your sleeve in taking over my apartment has just dropped out on the floor, never mind that it's still an inscrutable blob, I'll figure it out. I'm leaving when the sun is up, but *no* picnic with your tenants-in-arms, *Ratoncita!* It didn't take me long to sniff out their plot to lure me to a desolate place and do whatever. To think I thought it was all my idea, when they had led me to it like a horse to the butcher, I wish I knew for sure how much you were in on it. Oh yes once my host had planted a most useful seed and I began to put two and two together, I saw everything, more or less, the original picnic idea coming from Karl DuBonn (mark that name well, Inez, he is the male tenant, unless of course you already know that name like your mother's) whose abuse of my car and driver my host (more perceptive than he looks) led me to see very well. And once I saw one thing, I saw a dozen: How they feigned reluctance and amusement when I put forth the picnic, in-

103

creasing my excitement about a project that would never have occurred to me on the last day of my life, a frontispiece by a neo-nobody, think of it! Yes what I said earlier in fun seems more and more the truth of it: they are of some radical group, if not the Baader-Meinhof (they *said* they originated in Germany) then any one of a hundred, there's no shortage, that's France now. You remember that car bomb near the apartment of my masseuse on the Avenue Rapp last year going off only minutes after I passed it, blowing out windows in Mme. Marie-Laurens' office and spilling her precious oils all over? Where were you when that happened, by the way? If I remember it was you who recommended Marie-Laurens to me shortly after your skyrocket began to dip back down to earth, even though you must have known that I would hate that terrible music she plays loud enough to wake the dead, and she didn't do anything about those pouches at my waist anyway, so she can't have been a professional, it was a simple job. I should sue you for that, what a waste of time and money. If I'd just had a decent masseuse five years ago, that idiot Messerschmidt could have worked with the materials at hand and never taken you on, robbing me of every minute of peace-of-mind I'd earned for myself. If there's a good masseuse in all of France, I don't know it, I've tried them all. I'd give anything to know what you and Marie-Laurens hoped to gain by having me blown up. Kidnap and torture I could see, but blown up I couldn't even give you the key to my box at the bank, you idiots.

Anyway I went upstairs and lay in my bed thinking of the tenants and then suddenly everything that my overly discreet host had been hinting at all week fell into place. Why, just then, after driving me around for all these months, would Raoul suddenly begin to flatter and flirt? Why would this happen just as my host had let out his little house to two unknown persons of such disreputable looks and secrecy, owners of a dog the size of an elephant and trained to kill, if its looks don't deceive, he'd never let out his little house before? Why did the female Du-Bonn who has no sense of art at all talk me into having my portrait done if not to detain me here, knowing (how should I know how? You're the one who knew and could have told Raoul) that I have a fortune of jewelry in my suitcase and a box of cheques for Brazil in my bag? And again making it all seem like it had been *my* idea, demurring, stalling. I have read stories.

As I lay in my bed putting all this together (and isn't it just a little strange that *just now* you should be taking over my apartment in Paris with everything I own inside behind the flimsiest doors? And isn't it strange that this suggestion should have come from Alain? He's never suggested such a thing before, I want to know what's going on, I mean it you little tramp), something else kept preying on me, an aspect of my host's ghost-story that I'd dismissed at first, but as I thought, it got its hold on me. Something had been buried some weeks before and well it just *preyed* on me. I tossed and turned and worried, not a wink or nodding off, until I finally put on my robe and very quietly tiptoed down. Oh, Inez, my only comfort in life: this cavernous house, it is frigid as the grave must be, *Infanita!* The moon was out full, veined and swollen like a piece of cadaver, casting an eerie light over the ghastly marble of the stairs, do you follow me? The floors cracked and groaning, the shadow thick and fearsome. Picture me: I move bravely, silent as a martyred virgin, clutching my robe with wide eyes and slightly tremulous underlip, do you see me? Down the stairs with the moonlight glinting on my hair, I shimmer, sylph-like. Oh, it is dangerous! Someone surely is lurking: could it be our Raoul, my darling little *Pequeñita* Inez, that traitorous rogue? Perhaps

105

as you are watching me shimmer on the stair, he is slipping around a doorway below with a knife raised high, giving new meaning to a term like *liaison dangereuse* . . . no? Of course at the bottom of the stairs, I strike off in the opposite direction (close-up of his dumbfounded face in a moonbeam), and then tippy-tippy outside (large tree branching out over devil-moon) and carefully make my way to the fatal spot (a quick breeze loosening the robe, a *glimpse* of perfect thigh), a tulip bed, a looming tree. . . .

Enough! I fell to my knees, began to scoop at the earth, which came up easily—someone *had* been digging! I began to shake, but no choice: no choice but to persist: something was in the balance. I dug on, dug on, scooping up earth and putting it to the side like a ghoul myself— and Inez: I swear that the tulips, which that afternoon had been past their prime and fading (the saddest of images and I had noted it very well, no mistake) were suddenly glowing red as a Russian flag in the dark. I'm not inventing, though you know the prodigious effects of my unique visionary gift, to which you owe so much, upsurping chicken, these electric tulips were real. I was shaking, I tell you, but digging, digging on. I discovered the large bulbs of the tulips, abnormally large and sullen, like cabbages or certain tumors gestating impatiently but with cunning stealth in the body until the stupid unvigilant host is more them than herself, then they take it all to the bank, dust to dust, it makes me burn! Next to these were larger tumors still, dark and lumpy, telepathing and conspiring, call them "cadres" if you get my drift and I know you do—none of my special effects were working here: these monsters signified! Not letting them slow me down, I dug past as one must dig past roots of evil to the primal compost and its subtler facts, taking the opportunity as I dug to rake my nails across several of these ganglia, enjoying their quick shrieks and taking an extra dig at the one I silently labelled "Jenny DuBonn," she charged me a fortune for that gimmick! In the glow of the tulips I saw a thread of her phony blueblood circle my fingernail, felt its cool rivulent on my hand, whiffed its iron and was *delirious* with pleasure, but it was hallucination, all my senses agitating in high gear as I neared my quarry.

Well, what can I say: I dug another complete foot, squaring off my little grave as I went, imagining the powerful figures that would ring the mounds of waiting coverlet on that cold day, exchanging this personage for that until I had arranged a stunning ensemble, you were not among them, who needs that kind of display? Digging deeper even, the earth putting off its stale after-dinner breath as I gave my little spot an extra pocket or two just in case there were a few things a true friend might wish to tuck in with me as was the prudent custom of the ancients, who can tell anything about it all, best be prepared. This whole line of thought was strangely soothing, and I just stopped where I was: nothing was buried in that man's yard! Then suddenly—as always, so sudden—my uncanny sight overtook me and I peered down into the hole I had made, past the huddled backs of that gang, and I saw nothing. I'm telling you, I saw *nothing!*

But here's the worst: Just as I had stood up, just as I was taking possession of my living, breathing self again, beginning to think that maybe that crazy little man had made a fool out of me, knock on wood, just as I was bending over to wipe the dirt off my robe, the moon normal again, illuminating no flowers that I could see, only my hands and my white, white feet, just as I began to turn with my head still bowed—Oh, *Cariña!* Just then I looked up, just then I collided with the blue corpse of Karl DuBonn!

It was walking upright, its arms slightly to the front of it, as if feeling its way, its cold fingers brushing my

107

throat—Are you still with me, little one, still with your mentor? This is not for the faint-hearted. Oh, its beard beamed silver in the moonlight, the skin was Gorgonzola, and the eyes, oh Inez, they were wide open and staring into mine, I almost died on the spot! Wildly, almost by instinct, because I had no sense of my direction now, that's for sure, I ran for the door, letting out a scream as I went. Well, the DuBonns have a large bloody dog, as I told you, and it set up a terrific howl, and by the time I had secured myself in my room (back to the door, head turned slightly to the side, chest heaving, a discreet triangle of cleavage, she listens) I could hear my host fumbling with his door, making his tentative, cowardly way to the stairs. Even he didn't go further, and he thrives on such details. Soon I heard his fat little steps retreat and all was silence.

Of course all this means is that the male tenant was slipping up on me as I was digging, and when he realized I would catch him in the act, he slipped his weapon in his pocket, put out his arms and pretended to be sleepwalk-ing, no more or less mysterious than that, but who knows where precious Raoul was when I needed him? Lurking in the bushes with a hatchet? Quailing under his bed? In fla-grante delicto with Jenny DuBonn? That's the mystery and when I remember that it was your succumbing that called my attention to him to begin with, setting me up, and when I feel it in my bones that you are waiting for the scoundrel now in my apartment, waiting for him to take his hatchet to my two locked doors, if I don't miss my guess, when I think of you there waiting, languishing even now on my prize Empire sofa, in my own peignoir, perhaps tipping your claws with my specially mixed (House of Dior!) polish

Well, it's too bad, Huta, you could have had a real friend and benefactor in me but you blew it. And don't think you can count on the DuBonns or Raoul. Yes I've

cancelled the picnic and as for my trusty 'driver,' I'll give
him a momentary benefit of the doubt, let him start off
driving me to Cannes, but at the same time having
stashed away in my handbag a tiny pistol I *always* carry
(you didn't know that did you? I could have blown out
Marie-Lauren's ounce of brains if she'd had the nerve to
try anything herself), and I don't expect either Raoul or
tenants, should there be a rendezvous, to be similarly
armed, they think I'm a fool. I'll hold them off, or maybe
I'll just blow their stupid faces away, you'll just have to
wait, won't you? Then I'll drive myself to Cannes, I'm no
shuttlecock waiting to be picked off or divested of my
money or property, no matter how thick the plot is, I can
penetrate it with reason and my uncanny sixth-sense.
People have always said to me, 'You know what it is
about you: you *notice* everything,' and it's true: I notice, I
see, and then I reason things out, and what can't be seen
because it's lurking in the pulpy selfish organs of grasping individuals whose mental resources are no match for
their unbounded greed, I construe it the best I can, and I
act on it!

On that note: I have to trust you to do what needs to be
done if I've miscalculated and worse comes to worst.
Should the worst transpire, *Ingrata mia*, instruct my attorney, M. Lasseau, Raspail, if he's not in league with
them/you too, to relinquish *nothing!*

I can't wait to get to Brazil where the government is
less lenient with everyone of shadowy origins, that's the
truth"

10. *Some Kind of 'Return of the Repressed'*

Edouard refolded the letter and rubbed his eyes. They
were aching with the strain of reading the actress's erratic

script in the declining light. Well. What *could* one think? He did believe that his erstwhile guest was, as she had so rudely said of him, unhinged. That would take care of much, much. No one in the circles would believe a word such an hysterical woman might say against him. He was just going to have to be much more selective about whom he invited into the Big House. Poor woman—for a moment he had felt sympathy, toward the end of her letter when she had had the full terror of the tenants' implications crash onto her like a ton of granite. How she must have suffered, down in his little garden, digging away with her diminutive fingers while the terrifying presence of Karl DuBonn hovered behind her back with who-knew-what vicious scheme in mind. He had himself been half scared out of his wits by the sudden howl of that Hound of the Baskervilles in the courtyard, in the middle of the night—

But one retreated to one's room on "fat" steps, did one? One was rotund as a pomegranate? Tattered like a Spanish peasant? A naif? One's property "Roumanian" in its aspect, was it? One's mattress not of the requisite comfort for such a delicate member of the human species? Funny, but no one had ever before lodged any complaint against the accommodations at Auxillac! And though a minor actress of rather questionable sensibility and ethics, not to mention one whose very touseled bedclothes reeked (Edouard sniffed the room and sniffed it again, to be sure) of turpitude, might attempt to discredit those who celebrated at Trocadero *and* Auxillac, one suspected that such a depraved person merely grimaced on the taste of sour grapes. No doubt such a one had long since suffered the inevitable rebuff that persons of such *surface* charm and discretion might well expect from the more exclusive groups. Ah, but—poor thing! He was entirely sympathetic with her fear of these terrorists that roamed the country,

110

roamed the whole continent. How could anyone with so much as a private tent sleep nights? Oh, it had struck the poor old dear hard, indeed. It sounded as though she suffered from a psychological disorder one read much of in the papers, some kind of 'return of the repressed,' very typical of females in hysterical circumstances.

Still. She was addled, and that he could forgive (seeing the useless albatrosses in the hut on his hillside as "old treasures"—!), but never, never could he forgive the indiscreet exploitation of his property. Trysted in his sainted parents' bedroom, did she? With the chauffeur. He could hardly take it in.

To think that this woman, whom one had thought so refined, had actually rutted like a ewe in one's caveau, in one's stables, with her employee. It was without question perverse. He himself was no prude, and had had a perfectly normal youth dallying with the young girls in his parents' employ. But that was the custom, *de rigueur*, for a young man. But a woman—well, it was nothing short of radical, and one could only wonder how his deceptive guest could have felt herself so estranged from persons like the DuBonns, the Red Brigades, Basques, Moluccans and the rest. Oh, the poor, poor demented, debased woman!

Turning away from the room and its tangled sheets, Edouard gazed out the window onto his property with an easier eye. The actress would be no threat to him now. Should one get wind of any damaging remarks, one would only have to produce excerpts from this hysterical letter in defense. Oh, his property was beautiful in this pink light of dusk!

But—well. What next? There were the troublesome tenants walking about the lawn, and— Well, who knew what to make of it? One supposed it was more of the radical fancy, what else? There below: Karl DuBonn and his

111

wife: strolling along, tossing objects to their awful dog, dressed in *costume*. The male tenant wore a more or less formal suit of the style of the Nineteenth Century, it seemed, his hair and beard swirling like fine wires in the evening light. The wife had on a long dress, her hair twisted up in some old-fashioned configuration. Actually, they looked almost pleasing.

But . . . "The Gang of Two. . . ." Could it be? Oh, it did give one pause! However necessary these persons might be to one's *immediate* economy, it gave one pause! Could they belong, as the poor actress had suggested in one of the few lucid passages in her discourse, to some radical organization? Perhaps with designs on the Big House? Were they also in some sort of conspiracy with Pablo and Miranda to overthrow him? Hadn't it been Pablo, now that he thought about it, who had pronounced it fit to take on the tenants in the first place? And what of those early confabulations in the garden?

Oh, it was a terrible, terrible pass to which things had come. Why should a citizen of an ancient civilzed country have to worry about such matters? Things were out of control—gangs, terrorists, brown persons from every country on the planet *presuming* asylum in France. . . . The government itself infiltrated by Communists, Socialists, and worse. Only this last year he had heard rumors from a passing guest that some official agency planned to take it on itself to remove all the private walls that protected the beaches of the Riviera. . . . How could a life of charm be led with all that going on?

He glanced back at the tenants, persisting on his lawn in their nineteenth-century garb. If one ignored Karl Du-Bonn, would he go away? If the world were rid of his type, would order return? One's fiefdom be restored, by some miracle?

Edouard's rippling flesh sagged in his chair, and the

112

master of Auxillac brooded on the pink sunset that only a few moments before had seemed so promising. The hard red ball of the sun fixed on him like an eye. Well, soon the infernal thing would sink and the night would be on him. Perhaps he could sleep through his terror, while the eyeball lay dormant on the other side of the world for a little while, gave him a tenuous peace. Against the light he could see the solid forms of the tenants as they moved about, tossing some object—who knew what grisly thing?—to their monster dog. Behind them, down near the crevice that was the tarn, with its grim reminder, darkness gathered in a black knot, waiting for the moment to burst out, to spread and encompass everything in the known world like an ether.

Edouard looked back at the tenants. In the last wisps of sunlight, he could see their curious, removed smiles as their beast lunged for the object again and again, clods of turf spraying the earth as its great red toes penetrated the property in front of the Big House and claimed it for its own.

Manosque

*

W<small>HEN</small> the Wheats were in their early forties, they retired, and moved from their little Tudor house in an
immaculate suburb of Philadelphia to a village in the
south of France.

Mr. Wheat had never actually been employed. But he
had had an "avocation," as a scholar of the Classics. (And
why not? he often thought. Didn't his wife avocate music? Play her relentless flute night and day, though her
talent was minimal, if she had talent at all? Didn't he,
didn't he tolerate the situation in prudent silence?) In his
career he had mastered virtually all the works extant from
the Latin and Greek traditions. Mastered in a fashion, for
it was a great sadness to him that he had read them
mostly in translation. For all his desire, he had no talent
for languages. Though he had the warmest of feelings for
the idea of languages.

Mrs. Wheat had been a music teacher. While her husband puttered in his professorial study, she gave lessons
to the children of her neighbors on the flute and piano. (A
man who claimed to have nothing to profess, she'd suddenly remember, as a child tortured "The Happy Farmer"
on the keyboard. Who claimed to be beyond profession,
and yet with a professorial study after all! She sometimes
was not tolerant, not tolerant, though she had been edu-
cated to tolerance, tolerance and civilized procedure.)
While he persisted in the University library not far away,
she resolved to take up something too, a modern language

115

or a special cuisine, in earnest. Sometimes she felt an overwhelming need to *do* something in life. And even though these spells quickly passed, they left an unpleasant weakness for a while afterwards. Sometimes the flute didn't seem enough. As time passed, she began to think, too, that should she have any talent for whatever it was she might one day take up, she might earn more money. Theirs was not quite a living.

Though of course there was Mr. Wheat's annuity, she never failed to thank her lucky stars. It had been left to him by an unknown relative in his babyhood. Manna from Heaven, she and Mr. Wheat often said, gratefully. Between this and her music tutorials, they had managed. They had acquired their house at a good price *(exactly* the amount of interest that had amassed from the annuity, they often marveled) several years after their early marriage.

That event had taken place in 1963, "The year things went to Hell," Mr. Wheat always said. At the time, he'd been a student of political science, full of hope for the Camelot White House and all it might come to mean. Perhaps even raising the "cultural level of America," it was theorized in a favorite phrase among the Young Democrats at his University. He was a Young Democrat too, and so was Mrs. Wheat, who greatly admired the First Lady. At last, people of taste and culture in control of things. It had given them all such hope.

And then, everything had changed. Their Hero was gone, and soon things were getting very unpleasant, all the way around.

There was no Unrest on their own campus, where they had stayed on to attend graduate school after their marriage, but they couldn't avoid rumors of what was happening elsewhere. It seemed there had been something approaching a racial war across the country in Los An-

116

geles. Then there was that business half-way around the
world. At least Mr. Wheat would not be in danger, as long
as he stayed at the University.

And why leave? he often thought to himself. "Why
leave?" he often said to his wife, though Mrs. Wheat had
not said a word about leaving. She loved the University,
with its great green malls. "Why leave," she would an-
swer her husband.

As a graduate student, Mr. Wheat had switched to History. He could no longer believe in politics as a science,
after what had happened that monstrous day, in that
monstrous state two-thirds of the way across the Nation.
History was better. He would concentrate on the Spanish
Civil War. He had developed a particular interest in the
martyred poet, Garcia Lorca, so pathetically done in, he
never tired of relating to Mrs. Wheat, in some lonely
Gethsemane of an olive grove. He would have considered
Spanish Literature, even, just to study Garcia Lorca, if he
had had a talent for Spanish. If that area had not been
thought to be, in his University, somewhat *déclassé*. "It's
a very sad story," Mrs. Wheat always commiserated,
moved by its connection with painful recent events, and
by the useless twisting of her husband's hands as he told
her about the martyr.

Mrs. Wheat continued her practice of the flute and
piano, though she too had shifted her field of concentration. After seeing the former First Lady tour the artistic
marvels of Angkor Wat in Cambodia on television, the
ruins of an ancient city, sacked by some ancient horde,
she had switched to Art History. The ancients were fine,
but she found that her own tastes ran more to the paintings of the Impressionist period, rendering the world in a
satisfying blur. But not so satisfying as the miniatures of
Fragonard, Nattier, Boucher, and Isabey. Yes, miniatures
were the most satisfying of all, she often told her hus-

117

band, displaying reproductions that were much larger than the actual artifacts themselves, a fact she thoroughly disapproved of. "It makes *no* sense," Mr. Wheat thoroughly agreed, touched by the angularity of his wife's somewhat bony face as his study lamp cast her half in light, half in shadows.

These had been days of solace, after all they'd been through, days of agreement.

But finally even the pastoral world of their own university was becoming, more and more, disrupted. More and more, they observed, the students were beginning to dress like derelicts, or to dress not quite at all. Mrs. Wheat had seen a woman not much younger than herself walking down the main street of their little town in jeans and a skimpy leather vest, no more—the vest unfastened, flapping open with every step. Someone had offered Mr. Wheat drugs in the student lounge of the library. Often they thanked their lucky stars that they hadn't been born even two or three years later. Even two or three years, they often agreed, could have made the difference. They could have been swept up in this madness themselves, swept into harm's way.

"Who needs it?" Mr. Wheat had finally said to his bride, shortly after turning twenty-six and leaping beyond the clutches of the Selective Service. He had his annuity, after all.

"Who needs it?" Mrs. Wheat concurred. The annuity was very pleasant to have, indeed. Not enough to require apology, but very pleasant to have. She often thought that she should have been born much, much earlier. In the 19th century would have been best. All she wanted, all she had ever wanted, was a gracious life, a chance to perfect her music, her study of art, in a civilized nation run by the best and the brightest, good feelings all around. If things hadn't gone to Hell, she could have been a concert-

118

level flautist, she knew it! Her husband might have had a profession in the Law, or in service to his country in an administration dedicated to the cultural requirements of its people. She would brood on this for years to come, while everything raged around them. They might have had summers in Europe, a small collection of art works, a tiny *caveau* of distinctive wines, brilliant guests, children at good schools. Why couldn't she lodge a Protest?

It would be somewhat painful, giving up the formal study of the miniatures, Mrs. Wheat conceded to her husband when he made his suggestion. But she would have more time for her flute.

It would be a shame to forfeit the Spanish Civil War, Mr. Wheat hastened to counter, but he'd find something else. Besides, he thought more and more, Garcia Lorca had become too painful a fact to contemplate. More and more, he was finding the ancients the most satisfying of all poets.

They had given up the University with few regrets, in the end. They bought their house near Philadelphia, whose Greek name appealed to Mr. Wheat, already fashioning his avocation. And to Mrs. Wheat too, who admired more than she could say the idea that the name encoded.

Soon they settled into a life. They saw few people except each other. Their speech grew somewhat archaic, though neither could have said why. A certain personal reticence became their habit, even with each other, which they silently agreed had been a good rule of an earlier, more gracious time. Invariably, they called each other Dear. Their neighbors knew them as Mr. and Mrs. Wheat. Their given names, Harper and Linda, disappeared from their lives for all but the most practical purposes.

Sometimes they talked, wistfully, about their dead

119

Hero, the President. Neither would countenance any of the unpleasant theories that had been batted about as to his part in that business half-way around the world. It was the quality of everyday life that counted, they both agreed. Their Hero and the First Lady had been models of the gracious life, that was what counted, in the end. They remembered, with a pungent fondness, their youthful hopes, the ideals, the Young Democrats, the old belief that a nation of semi-barbarians could be transformed. They rarely mentioned what things had become, what things might become.

Within their little house, now that they had withdrawn, their needs were very few. A well-tuned piano, books, modest food and drink. They didn't require a car since Mrs. Wheat worked at home and Mr. Wheat walked to the library. They rarely went out socially, so a very spare wardrobe sufficed. For recreation, they gardened. Mr. Wheat grew a salad garden. Mrs. Wheat grew prize dahlias, her mother's hobby. These she exhibited at the annual flower show, her one significant social event, one which Mr. Wheat declined, but no matter. She did not attend his annual conference of Classics scholars, after all. Occasionally, they visited a museum. Mrs. Wheat remained fond of Impressionism and miniatures. Or they went to the opera, or to a concert. Chamber music was best, though a symphony sometimes would not be denied. Very rarely, they went to a play, a revival of some forgotten treasure of manners. Or to a movie, usually European. Mr. Wheat said "cinema," his wife "film." Both liked British comedy, and the droll *ennui* of the French, always good for a laugh.

All in all, they were not unhappy. No, not in the least unhappy with the way they had worked things out for themselves. They took pride in the neatness of their day-to-day routine, and both derived great satisfaction from thrift, their special order. Sometimes Mrs. Wheat's shrill flute irritated Mr. Wheat, as did the intrusion of her pupils, and sometimes Mrs. Wheat seethed at her husband's leisurely study, but on the whole they were happy enough in their little domain. And they intended to stay that way: they hadn't even a radio, much less a television or newspaper in the house.

If they had one unmet desire, it was to go "abroad." But there was nothing in their close economy to give them hope of it, and so they made their peace with the facts, content with the idea of abroad: embellishing it occasionally with a dinner prepared in one of the European cuisines, capped with a dessert of cheese and fruit, in the European manner, and a small toddy or port, which Mr. Wheat took in his study, which Mrs. Wheat took in her bath.

Each year they promised each other that they would learn French or one of the other modern European languages before long, just in case. They had a book entitled *A Dozen Languages in Simultaneous Translation*, which they kept by the dining table and dipped into sporadically, directed by their menus. They acquired a small store of random words. They loved the idea of being fluent in French or German or Portuguese. Besides, Mrs. Wheat still had hope of a bit of extra income.

Their only terror had to do with mysterious cataclysms in the world of finance. The regular lurches in the economy after the first years of their retreat sent their neat ledgers into disarray, rocking their tranquil routine. Every motion dwindled their resources, so that many of the small luxuries they had allowed themselves in the early years were becoming available only rarely—the cheese, the port. Even some of the necessities (the piano tuner's services, the scholarly books necessary to Mr. Wheat's re-

121

search) were moving beyond their fiscal ability. Mrs. Wheat could take no satisfaction in her students' oblivion to the maltuned piano. If a job was worth doing, it was worth doing well; this was an idea she had never once had cause to doubt. Even if she herself had been deaf, like Beethoven, poor man, the *idea* of an untuned piano would have troubled her as much as its sound, she felt sure, just as she felt sure that the same had been the case with the famous composer. As for Mr. Wheat, he was having more and more trouble going about his work, unable to buy several crucial books in his field. Rather than expose his ignorance of their contents, the proof of his falling behind, he did not attend the annual conference for the first time in years. He allowed himself the mild pleasure of self-pity as he thought of his colleagues going about their business without him, but it was short-lived. He was becoming quite depressed. Mrs. Wheat could no longer afford the best fertilizers for her dahlias, and so they grew pale and stringy. She missed her flower show and was surprised to find herself passing that day in fits of tears, as if a world where one could take the vast leisure and calmness of mind to nurture plants of no obvious utility, altering their make-up in the most subtle ways—as if that world were receding from her, or had never really been possible at all.

Both brooded on all the hope that had been thwarted that bright day in Texas, the year things went to Hell, the year of their marriage. Now that their little comforts were made smaller still by the disappearance of their few indulgences, they began to complain aloud about the impossibility of ever being able to go "abroad." Mr. Wheat complained daily about rumors he'd heard at earlier conferences, of how the Coliseum was being ruined by auto fumes and worse, how there was graffiti on the Parthenon, how the weather was ravaging the monuments of the Acropolis beyond recognition, even as they, the

Wheats, sat in their overly-cool parlor wrapped in shawls. Mr. Wheat had a new habit of borrowing his wife's less-feminine shawls: he knew that men in other regions of the world wore such garments. Why shouldn't he?

Mrs. Wheat repeated her own particular distresses often. Was she to go to her grave without ever having traversed L'Orangerie or the Jeu de Paume? The famous symphony halls and chambers where the most divine music was performed?

These topics entered their conversation at an accelerated rate as unwelcome rumors reached them—through Mrs. Wheat's students, through Mr. Wheat's contacts in the scholarly world—of crime, political scandal, of heart attacks suffered by several of Mr. Wheat's colleagues in Classical study. In a particularly bleak month, Mrs. Wheat's sister died in Seattle and Mr. Wheat's last living relative, an uncle, perished in a boat off the coast of Tampa under mysterious circumstances, mysteriously leaving no money or property behind. One night, only a block away, thugs invaded a private house and ransacked it, beating the owners severely. Nothing was stolen. No perpetrator was arrested. The idea of it curdled the Wheats' dreams for weeks. Even when the weather grew warm, they decided not to remove the storm windows from their little house.

In their unhappiness, their small irritations with each other disappeared. Why *shouldn't* one who chose not to profess have a professorial study? Why shouldn't someone whose musical talents were *minor* have an "avocation" too? They grew closer than ever, closing their "ranks" of two completely.

"I do think that things have gone all the way to Hell," Mr. Wheat told his wife as they took their plain meal with water and no dessert.

123

"All the way," his wife agreed whole-heartedly.

The only positive note in it all was that, even as their income deflated almost to the point of being no income at all, the value of the little house had trebled. In spite of the hideous crime around the corner, the neighborhood, which was so close to green parks, so stable in its comfortable population, was one of the most desirable anywhere near the City of Brotherly Love. The Wheats had been calculating this fact within their separate heads for many weeks before bursting out almost simultaneously at the dinner table one evening:

"Who needs it?"

Once the house was on the market, Mrs. Wheat broached a subject much on her mind one evening as her husband struggled to untangle a particularly unresponsive passage of Pliny the Elder in his study. She rarely disturbed him at his work (especially when he worked on Pliny, that inscrutable man who had died in harm's way, having left the safety of his home and, *voluntarily*, sought out the disaster near Vesuvius: he was Mr. Wheat's bane), but they really had to talk, make some plans. Neither doubted that after the sale of the house they would go abroad. This country wasn't fit to live in, and there was no way to get out of it from within. The news of things was always worming in. The silent language of money might as well have been a sermon. No leadership, no protection, no peace of mind, no chance to pursue an art or avocation in peace and leisure. Daily they counted their blessings that they had never been caught up in materialism, the national disease. They had little they wanted to take with them, a few books, the flute, some clothes. Mrs. Wheat cared less and less for the piano, so woefully out of tune. She'd sell it. They had no cats or dogs or birds or fish to unload, no great friends to take tearful leave of,

124

though they had, and had ever been themselves, sterling neighbors. Mr. Wheat's passion for ancient works was paling, in spite of himself. The theatrics of heroes, battles. He would sell most of his library to some novice in the field, revise his avocation once things settled down again.

"I think we should go to Greece," Mrs. Wheat said firmly, sacrificially, standing in her husband's doorway in an old gray sweater she had had at college. "Or Spain."

Her husband looked up in horror. "Oh, no—I couldn't let you—" said Mr. Wheat when he gained composure. "We'll go to Paris where you can see Art, and have music every day, a proper teacher for once in your life, I insist. Dear—"

Mrs. Wheat blanched. "Let's talk tomorrow, Dear. There's time—"

"What about the Côte d'Azur?" they both blurted in a duet as they prepared for bed, later in the evening. "Could we afford it?"

Both went to sleep, after their turmoil, dreaming of seawalls on the Mediterranean, bougainvillaea spilling over whitewashed stucco, quaint fishing boats; dreamed themselves: Mr. Wheat in a striped blouse and flat straw "boater," Mrs. Wheat in a disarray of white linen under a parasol, all in some slippery physics of light, circa 1874.

After the house was sold they took the cheapest flight to Europe, to Luxembourg, and then took the train to Nice, all their possessions in several suitcases. As it turned out, they couldn't, by any economy, afford even the worst the Côte d'Azur had to offer. Which was just as well: it didn't look much like what they'd imagined after all. The light all wrong or something. Would it have looked any different in the 19th century? Mrs. Wheat, for one, couldn't help thinking that it would have indeed.

Finally they brought out a map and scanned the to-

125

pography of Europe, the names of things. With relief, Mrs. Wheat saw that it was not really far to Greece at all. It should be only a matter of sailing around Italy to . . . well . . . Sparta . . . Arcadia . . . . She could see her husband walking with some Pericles of a shepherd, trailing a well-mannered flock, conversing philosophically while she, at a distant window, accompanied his activity on a primitive set of panpipes. Then, there was Spain. . . .

Following Mrs. Wheat's forefinger with a damp terror, Mr. Wheat finally whisked the map from the table and folded it so that Greece and Spain were beyond their purview. He left only France exposed. After all, they had already purchased a large amount of francs. Look how close they were to Paris—couldn't they negotiate the troublesome peaks of the Basses-Alpes by auto or simply take the train? He could see them in Paris, himself cloistered in a bistro with cigarette smoke thick as fog, men in heavy black-rimmed glasses carrying on the wry, removed debate so typical of French intellectuals, or at least his idea of them, which he had from somewhere. Across the city, he could see his wife playing her flute by the window of a room with a high ceiling, a famous impresario watching from the shadows, contemplating a move, a touch to the soft material of her skirt or maybe something more distracting. But she—wonderful woman—kept her eyes closed, persisting in her transported rendition of something from Debussy, tempted by nothing else.

Horrified by her husband's posture as he leaned over the little portion of the map left to them, scrutinizing Paris as if he were lost to her, Mrs. Wheat quickly placed a book over that whole portion of France. Even she had not been able to avoid the news of Paris, a city with a knife at its throat, terrorists, bombings—

"Let's be sensible," she said. "Let's travel only so far. We must, after all, think of our means."

126

"Yes," Mr. Wheat agreed reluctantly as Mrs. Wheat's book blocked out the scene in the impresario's lair. "Let's be sensible."

Both returned their eyes to Nice and started over.

Suddenly, in one motion, as if their hands belonged to the same body, their forefingers converged on the word "Manosque" some centimeters northwest of Nice. Both were relieved that they concurred, and so their enthusiasm was much increased.

"It could be . . . Arabic," Mr. Wheat said. He had no intention of ever looking at the real Classics again, but the idea of Classics was burning brighter than ever in the unsubtle light of the Mediterranean. He would fashion a new career . . . "Manosque."

"It could be anything," Mrs. Wheat said hopefully.

In Manosque, the Wheats bought a little stuccoed house in an olive grove on a hill above the village, a little house with a terra cotta terrace, "Spanish" tiles as its roof, arcade windows, beams in the ceiling. It was a charming little house, and very serviceable for their needs. Those needs would be more simple than ever. The climate was not right for dahlias, hence there would be no need for fertilizers, though Mrs. Wheat could readily see that if fertilizers were required, the economic waste of barnyard animals would be abundant and reasonably bought. But they would not be required—no, she had moved beyond dahlias, she felt sure. Mr. Wheat no longer grew a salad garden. All the vegetables and fruits, and flowers too, for that matter, were available in the village market, very reasonably priced. Mr. Wheat took as his special project the supervision of his tiny olive grove. He would cure that produce, press the oil, perhaps sell some eventually in the market below, commission a vendor, etc. It was a splendid olive grove, full of healthy trees, burgeoning with

127

fruit. Quite as good as any olive grove in Greece, he felt sure, and not nearaly as problematic. Mrs. Wheat decided not to take in any music pupils. One's art should never be one's vocation, she had read somewhere, she felt sure, long ago. Instead, she took in several local children for English lessons, though she knew nothing of French. The children managed very well in her tutorials without her knowing French, just as she managed well at the market and so forth, managed very well indeed, as did her husband. No, it was a little late in the day for learning French. But both she and her husband liked the idea of French, and the idea of France, very, very much.

On market days, Mrs. Wheat took her straw basket and walked down the path of their hill, a path the color of a peach, to the small paved road to the village. These were her favorite times. She could observe from a distance the town about its business, at a distance even close up—herself existing in the single word *"Madame,"* knowing others only in *"Madame"* and *"Monsieur"* and *"Ma Petite"* and *"Mon Petit."* The simple economy of it all yielded a profound pleasure and peace. Here was community, cooperation, civility. If culture was lacking, well, one didn't miss it in one's middle age nearly so much as one would have thought. The men and women in the square, with their red cheeks, their laughing, their little seriousnesses, were like dolls, gesturing, taking care of things, their language drained of all content, music to her ears. She could almost imagine all the quaint and harmless points of debate, all settled amicably over a glass of something at one of the tables outside the little establishments near the square, the square itself shaded by lush trees, cool and comfortable, entirely. For a while she had believed none of them could die, even, so animated and doll-like were they, going about the silent movie of market day, their words like musical notes from some sprightly piano be-

128

hind the screen. Even their tiny hearses, like the small vans used for delivering bread, but black, with tiny black drapes, seemed almost comic, not real at all. Even the tears of the little widow walking behind one, which she had seen by accident, coming upon things with no one to warn her, had seemed to express a diminutive kind of grief, a doll's distress. The graveyard in Manosque, she discovered on one of her walks, identified anyone of any recent life with a photograph sealed in plastic and fastened onto the headstone. Photographs of persons looking much like the persons who still gestured and laughed in the square, and so there was the effect of no death at all, no death and discord anywhere in Manosque, which had now—she felt sure she could safely say—subsumed the world.

On the way home from the market, her basket bulging with fruit and cheeses and salad greens, a picturesque loaf of bread protruding, Mrs. Wheat practiced a further economy, gathering a great bouquet of wildflowers in all the colors of the spectrum for the table, for the meal she would make for her husband, nourishment for his honorable and indispensible work in the olive grove.

In a chair on their little terrace, outside their little house, Mr. Wheat reposed in the sun and waited for his wife to return from the village. His olive trees, which he regarded from slitted eyes, gave the impression of silver left too long in moisture, growing a green patina, some mossy residue, but not the least unpleasant, in spite of what he might have thought at first. No, he couldn't have been happier with how things had worked out. Here he had, if not the life he had wanted at first, the life he had come to want. Here, anonymous completely, he could wear a shawl on a cool evening, or a pair of swim trunks, as he did now, or dress for dinner like a gaucho or peasant.

Study or not study, as the spirit moved him, collect his annuity in shameless gratitude.

He could not see anything of Manosque, except the geometry of its red-tiled roofs among the trees of the town square. That was perfect somehow. At first he had thought he would learn something of the village, the region. He had ordered a history of Provence, several books of Provençal literature in translation. But they were, after the Classics, depressing: one invasion after another, Visigoths, Franks, Saracens. . . . No, leave well enough alone. In his spare time from his orchard, he had begun to read FitzGerald's translation of the *Rubáiyát*. That was more like it, a Classic that would perhaps be the only book he would need to study, a philosophy of simplicity *and* utility: live life to the fullest, while you can.

It was all, all so sumptuous and fortunate. Should he flatter himself? Hadn't they—hadn't he—wrested opportunity from the most awful historical circumstances, taken the bull by the horns, engineered their sunny fate, got them out of harm's way? Why couldn't you take credit for anything in this world with an easy conscience?

Well, conscience be damned. They had their life.

Below, on the russet path that led up to the house, he could see his wife come into view, her red kerchief, the rest of her still a blur. He knew she would have her basket full of all they required, her hand stained green from the stems of her flowers. She rarely played her flute these days, but she had taken to humming very pleasant little tunes as she went about the work necessary to their domestic comfort. They would have a leisurely lunch, complete with an economical wine of the region, and he would take his customary nap before going out to check again, as he did every afternoon now, every morning too, the health of his trees and olives. Sometimes, as he drifted off to sleep, something rose, out of *A Dozen Languages in Simultaneous Translation,* no doubt—

Man—Os—Que
Man—Bone—Why
Ma—Nos—Que
Manos—Que

He would wake, heavy as lead, heavy as marble, into the prickly sun of the afternoon, into the strange sounds, from the other side of the house: his native language on the tongue of a local child, his wife's pupil:

"Good afternoon, Sir. What do you do?"

Sometimes he knew he imagined it. Once, he had heard his patient wife murmur to the child, correcting him, saving the day.

"No, no, *mon petit.* The question is too abrupt, almost rude. It is '*How* do you do?' Of course I can't see your book, but I feel sure that it is, must be, '*How* do you do?' Let's try it again."

Leavened by this kindness, by the persistent memory of it from afternoon to afternoon, he could count his blessings, thank his lucky stars, draw himself up from his vicious bed and get ready to go out into a world he was convinced to be of his own making. There he could wander like some Greek without philosophy: in an olive grove, even, where he knew—felt he could be sure that— no violence, no betrayal waited.

131

A Summer Afternoon

*

*Summer afternoon—summer afternoon; to me those have always been the
two most beautiful words in the English language.*

Henry James to Edith Wharton

I<small>T IS</small> approximately two o'clock in the afternoon of July 4,
1912, and the plush summer estate of J. Clement Coole,
Esq., on Long Island is wrapped in a gauze of sun and
humidity. Swarms of insects and pollens diffuse the
light around the bright green lawn of the great house,
spanking white with yellow awnings, but silent now and
shuttered against a brutal temperature and the time of day
that most of its residents, for various reasons, find troublesome.

In a dark parlor near the rear, the mistress of the house
repines on a too-short couch, her feet in an uncomfortable
arrangement with the floor, a cool cloth draped across her
eyes. It is the time of day she once enjoyed with her husband, now estranged from her in the city. Beneath the
damp line of the cloth, two smudges of pink flush her
normally pale cheeks. She has just had a very surprising
visit.

Down the hall from Althea Coole's parlor is the library,
where J. Clement Coole is a most present absence. Its
doors are closed, but inside, the snooker balls are pressed
into a gleaming geometric on their green-felted table,
waiting. His favorite port is waiting too in a crystal de-
canter, and a glass has been freshly polished, as it is every
morning, though Mr. Coole has sent no word to expect

133

him. In a glass case, his collection of rare books always waits, unread but highly prized. A photograph of The Late Queen Victoria, much enlarged, glowers from the wall.

Across the courtyard from the library, in a dim room over the carriage house, Karl the chauffeur has skewered Frieda, the young pastry cook, to his bed and is whispering erratic endearments against the hot blush of her cheek. He cannot wait for the afternoon to be over so that he can take Mr. Coole's spit-polished new Ford out for its daily run. Frieda is filling the lull between meals with a mental inventory of her baking ingredients, holding in reserve a recipe for a Lady Baltimore cake she plans for the boy Coole's birthday dinner this evening, and behind this tallying, never far off, are several entertaining versions of her own cake shop, in one of several resort villages close by.

In the servants' quarters on the third floor of the main house, in a room perpendicular to the chauffeur's lair but higher up, Caitlin, the aging laundress, has lain down in her shift to pass the afternoon and is suffering the excesses of her own demonic hand, her eyes wild and ranging the room's partitions. Occasionally, as they snag on the crucifix that hangs on the opposite wall, she emits a groan of mortification and doom.

Reposing in his own room, his lipless mouth clamped on a thin cigar which he saws back and forth through the air with a flourish, is the new tutor of the Cooles' young son, reading a detective magazine that is part of a large cache of similar periodicals that he stores beneath his bed.

Such is the activity within the Coole compound.

But back outside, back beyond the formal gardens of the house:

The meadow is undulant in the haze, sage-colored, and flocked with daisies and buttercups, milkweed and

134

sneezewort. Two chestnut mares, their noses sunk into grass from which butterflies flutter in drunken gyres, swish their tails against large green flies, keeping them more or less at bay, and down the meadow, at a distance that leaves the big white manor house looking like a very elegant doll's house, a great oak spreads in its prime. It is ninety feet tall, and just as wide, its limbs stretching in every direction, shading a throw of thick dark grass and patches of flesh-tinted mushrooms: *Agaricus elongatus* and *velutinus.*

Here, a passerby, had there been one, might have walked out of the heat for relief. The oak was all the shade the meadow offered. And once under its protective leaves, this gentleman would no doubt have delved into the breast pocket of his white linen suit, extracting a white linen handkerchief, and wiped his brow, blotting the evidence of his reckless excess—going for a hike on such an afternoon!

But once such evidence was obscured, even from himself, he might have smiled in some contentment. After all, Nature was thriving all around. And the respectable prosperity of the white house in the distance was proof that things were going well in the human world also.

Hitching the pleats of his trousers with thumbs and forefingers, he lowers himself into a comfortable squat. Why not pass a moment or two? Resting on the heels of his white calf shoes, he watches the butterflies and the horses and the twin flappings of Old Glory and the Union Jack, caught just this instance in a rare gust, from a flag-pole atop a small hill that bears the manor house. The Union Jack is very large, the observer notes. It billows and furls gracefully, if in somewhat faded hues, from the top position on the halyard. A much smaller, but very bright, stars-and-stripes batters the air beneath.

Transfixed for the moment, the observer does not no-

135

tice the beginnings of action to his left. His eyes, their
whites streaked with red, their blue irises blanched pale
from the glare, are rested by the scene in front of him and
gradually glaze over.

But suddenly something sparks in the corner of his vision, as if a wearisome gnat were seeking a drink. Suddenly there is action much too vigorous to be ignored. A
mass of pink and black and white is thrashing about only
a few dozen feet from where he squats, and he can see the
wild basil and bloodroot and pieces of sod being tossed
into the air like shuttlecocks.

Oh, dear. He will have to make a choice.

Depending, as his generation is wont to depend, on his
Sensibility, and a lingering notion of the True Nature of
One's Heart, he will have to shout and break up the
shocking scene or race away, clutching his elegant hat in
a trembling hand.

Or he will slip quietly behind the massive trunk of the
oak and settle down to watch.

On this afternoon, because it was his birthday, Mlle.
Ghislaine had brought young Standard Coole out to the
tree for his French lesson. Normally she avoided such
nonsense. After all, didn't the Master provide a perfectly
well-appointed—perhaps overly lush—room for the boy's
lessons? But there had been something in the child's eyes
as he gazed out the window of his "school room" after
taking lunch with the servants in the kitchen; it was a
look of longing, and of deprivation, despite the luxury of
the room around him, Mlle. felt sure. That had moved
her, and so she had suggested that perhaps, just this once,
they might take their French lesson under the meadow's
great oak.

The boy had leapt up delighted and tucked his book under the sleeve of his middy blouse and hurried outside.
See how little it took to please him, Ghislaine remarked

to herself, as she propelled her bulk after him, across the
meadow, releasing her breath in labored puffs.

Ghislaine had been with the family for six years. She
had arrived at their summer farm when the boy was only
six years old and received him into her care from the
weak little hands of Althea Coole. But she was not really
his governess. For such an important position, the Cooles
had always been careful to employ an Englishwoman.
There had been many of these during Mlle.'s tenure:
young, blond, blue-eyed, transparent of skin at temple and
jaw, the veins delicately webbed beneath. They had given
Ghislaine, who was dark-haired, hefty, and somewhat
thick-skinned, cause for many moments of self-recrimina-
tion. But all the governesses had left in time. In fact, all
had left in very short time, and very suddenly, never to be
heard from again.

The latest, Miss Emma Cotting-Jones of Southampton,
who had been a special caution to Ghislaine, had left only
several weeks before. And she had left a clue: a letter to
Althea Coole, written on Althea's own stationery, that
had been delivered to the breakfast table on the morning
after the governess's flight, and then dropped—along with
a coffee cup and a saucer on the rich Turkistan carpet, as
Althea sank into a bloodless daze in her chair. J. Clement
Coole watched his wife's fit over the top of his morning
newspaper with a mild interest, until a servant happened
to enter the room, and then he rose calmly, extended his
cup to the flustered girl for a refill and, on his way to his
library, pointed to the telephone and then to his distressed mate at his back, as he passed the butler in the
hallway.

All this Ghislaine had from the maid.

The doctor, on examining Althea Coole in the sanctum
of her bedroom as she languished on a very elaborate
fainting couch of wicker, decorated in intricate Ara-

besques, made the following prescription: rest, cold com-
presses, absolutely no contact with her spouse.

On leaving the house, the doctor glared down Coole
with a look more appropriate for a blasphemer or snake-
oil salesman than for an officer in the petroleum industry.
This Ghislaine had of the butler.

J. Clement Coole left for the city immediately on hear-
ing this presumptious "prescription." He was an important man with Standard Oil, for whom he had named his
only son; an important man all the way around, no time
for domestic squabbles. The governesses were more trouble than they were worth, as his little family had turned
out to be also, though a man had to have a little family.
Well, he would take care of it all neatly and forget it.

Thus did Toby Tobias, recent Dartmouth graduate,
come to take over Standard Coole's studies in grammar,
mathematics, ancient languages, and the sciences. As for
the French lessons, they were for some time in limbo
while Mrs. Coole tried to make up her mind if Mlle.
Ghislaine was any threat to her household. Finally, in
council with her physician, it was decided that the
Frenchwoman—overweight, hirsute—was no threat at
all. Besides, she took very good care of the boy, never
bothering Althea. The French would remain.

In the boy's care, her regular duty, Ghislaine was and
had always been very thorough. She woke him in the
morning, dressed him, took all meals with him and, at
night, bathed him and put him to bed. Though it might
seem that by the time the boy had reached the age of
eight or ten, he might have preferred to bathe himself and
put himself to bed, such was not the case. Even on the eve
of his twelfth birthday, the night before the outdoor
French lesson, it had still been a matter of mutual, though
silent, agreement that he and Mlle. would share that re-

138

sponsibility. It was their custom, and as a child who participated in few human interchanges that could be tagged with the warmth of "custom," Standard Coole would have been lost without the ritual of his bath, a ritual which had become such a natural part of his life that to be without it would have been very strange indeed.

Each night after supper and after Standard had put in the two hours of study his father had long ago and arbitrarily required, he would undress in his room and go to the adjoining bath where Ghislaine had prepared a tub of very hot water. When he was younger, there had been toys to float in it. But now that he was growing up, they had been abandoned and the ritual more or less confined to the business of washing itself. But, oh! What a business! He would get into the water—slowly, slowly, getting used to its heat—and then he would lie back, relax, almost bobbing finally, indulging in some daydream or other while he waited for what he knew, from custom, to expect. Ghislaine would come with the towels and then . . . Oh, but he was getting ahead of himself. First he must wait. Often, while waiting, he would balance himself on his elbows and try to make parts of his body actually float. Parts of it—the knees, his "acorn" as Ghislaine called his member sometimes, pronouncing it solemnly ("hay-corn, hay-corn") from deep in her throat—would exit the water and shrivel in the cool air of the room while the rest of him remained warm in the tub. It was an exquisite contrast. Soon Ghislaine would come with the towels, lay them on a table, and get down on her knees by the tub to attend his washing. First she would have him stand and she would soap him all over and rub briskly with a cloth. Then he would sit and rinse away the suds; then stand and have it all repeated. Then he would sit silent and passive while Ghislaine took care of the most intimate parts of his toilette, cleaning his ears, between his toes, between his legs. This last was a very pleasurable step in the ritual and it always went the same. He would raise up on his elbows and float his parts out of the water. Mlle. Ghislaine would soap her plump pink hands and massage him—first the inner thighs, then the *mons*, she chanting the word in a whisper as she worked: *mons, mons, mons.* Then catching his little "zee-zee," as she called the "acorn" too, in her fingers and rolling it, pulling it, stretching it, cleaning its every side. Then she would add more soap and rub his scrotum, lightly pinching it and rolling it between her fingers. Then she would dunk the lower part of his body beneath the water to rinse the suds away and have him stand and submit himself to the process again. And then his favorite event: the great pink hand tugging on his "zee-zee," rolling the nutty business beneath—and then moving back and running up between his buttocks. He felt a light shiver when the edge of the hand crossed what he thought of as his Secret Button, and he couldn't help himself: his "zee-zee" would shoot out straight and taut as a pointed finger! And in spite of his friend's stern face, he would giggle, always. Then he would sit down and allow the woman to rinse him, and then step out into the soft white towel.

Ghislaine would dry him, running the towel over his belly, back, arms, and legs, and for many years this would be the grand finale of the ritual. But in the last year, she had begun to do the most amazing thing. Just as he would be all dry, she would bend her head and slip his "zee-zee" into her mouth. Baffled, he would stare down onto the fine terrier's moustache that capped her upper lip and ponder her action. It made no sense, making as it did the part wet again which had already been dried—but what fun! And even when the stern Mlle. would give one of her rare smiles as he stepped into his nightshirt, he could barely respond, so caught up was he in this baffling and intriguing turn on what had been customary.

Afterward, he would go to his bed, his breast pounding.

140

Then Mlle. would cut out the light, close the door, and go to her own room on the third floor.

On the afternoon of the outdoor French lesson, Ghislaine had first settled under the tree with Standard. The long walk across the meadow had left her winded. She felt hot and fluent, her clothes sticky and unnaturally constraining, and so she did what she could never have done closer to the house. She undid her garters, sure that the boy would not mind, if he even noticed, and she rolled down her stockings and gathered their tops into neat quoits at her ankles. As she'd suspected, the gesture made no impression on her pupil, who was chattering away in French about the variety of butterflies. She could see that he was up to nonsense, but she let him get away with it, using the moment to recover her strength.

Actually the butterflies were a ruse. Standard hoped that he could distract Mlle. from his real activity, which was the surreptitious reading of a very thick book entitled *The Royal Path of Life,* which he had found much-thumbed in his father's library, its cover and early pages, and hence the author, missing, the rest of it generally battered, as if someone had once tried to destroy it. Standard hoped that it was now sufficiently camouflaged in its bed of opened French books on the grass so that it wouldn't rouse the interest of his Mlle. No good would come of her reading it, that he knew.

After a few minutes of alternating chitchat with reading snatches from this precarious text which threatened to fall apart at any moment, Standard felt himself slipping away from the hazy meadow and entering a metaphysical realm. The remaining early pages let the reader know that this was a book that offered the secret prescriptions of "Success and Happiness," and buried in this major matter, he had found some striking particulars. He had managed to locate, undetected by Mlle., a passage that he'd

141

already found riveting, a section called "To Young Women." Now he read:

"Beauty is a dangerous gift. It is even so. Like wealth it has ruined its thousands. Thousands of the most beautiful women are destitute of common sense and common humanity. No gift from heaven is so general and so widely abused by woman as the gift of beauty. In about nine cases in ten it makes her silly, senseless, thoughtless, giddy, vain, proud, frivolous, selfish, low and mean. I think I have seen more girls spoiled by beauty than by any other one thing. 'She is beautiful and she knows it,' is as much to say she is spoiled. A beautiful girl is very likely to believe she was made to be looked at; and so she sets herself up for a show at every window, in every door, on every corner of the street, in every company at which opportunity offers for an exhibition of herself. And believing and acting thus, she soon becomes good for nothing else, and when she comes to be a middle-aged woman she is that weakest, most sickening of all human things—a faded beauty! These facts have long since taught sensible men to beware of beautiful women—to sound them carefully before they give them their confidence. Beauty is shallow—only skin deep; fleeting—only for a few years' reign; dangerous—tempting to vanity and lightness of mind; deceitful—dazzling often to bewilder; weak—reigning only to ruin; gross—leading often to sensual pleasure."

These were fascinating ruminations for Standard Coole. Beauty—why, he'd always assumed it was a good thing, especially in women. True, his tastes in women weren't quite formed yet, but he felt sure that he had known many beautiful ones, if his feelings on such things could be trusted, and that he was no worse for it. After all, his governesses had given him the best of feelings, as had his treasured Mlle., and surely these had to do with Beauty.

Even the traitor Cotting-Jones (he felt a stab of loss) had given him the best of feelings.

Maybe there was something to it after all, he thought. Emma Cotting-Jones had looked like an angel from his illustrated books. Perhaps she was the proof of Beauty's affliction. "Beauty is . . . fleeting," said *The Royal Path*, and she was gone. Of course these books illustrated with angels had already been belittled by Tobias, his knowing new tutor, something else that would now need to be pursued in secret.

If Beauty meant gratifying to look at, no one rivalled his Mlle. Ghislaine. Beauty of Beauties. But that all was not as it seemed: That was a shock. "Beauty is shallow . . . dangerous . . . deceitful . . . gross." He would have to consult his dictionary on "gross," but he knew these others to be the worst of characteristics. And was it so: these— the underbelly of Beauty?

Something in Standard's chest flipflopped. If things were so different from how they looked, how could a person know what was what? And if things were opposite from what they first seemed, did that mean that his own mother, whom he *felt* was not beautiful in the least, would be brimming with comely invisible qualities after all? How could that be so? The subject of Beauty was a deep one. He would have to ponder it, make inquiries.

Meanwhile, Ghislaine had leaned against the tree trunk. She stretched out her thick legs in front of her and fanned herself with a clever cardboard apparatus that she had invented to help the boy with his verbs. She was beginning to cool off some. The haze of light that had almost blinded her as she'd struggled across the meadow was beginning to clear, and she could feel herself winding down from her physical distress. But a mental replacement was starting up, as she regarded her legs, the color of skimmed milk, bearing a fine covering of long dark hairs. How different from the slick, shapely legs of Emma Cotting-Jones. Several weeks earlier she had spied on Emma as she took her bath. Emma's legs were firm and thin, and lit by the sunset coming in the window, they had seemed the color of ripe apricots. Though Emma by ordinary light was extraordinary pale, there were enough blushings and bloomings and flarings to brighten her up, nothing like the lifeless white that Ghislaine saw in herself.

Watching Emma standing on the rough wood floor, one foot in a basin, Ghislaine had felt indescribable misery. She'd watched the younger woman bend and gather water from the basin and let it run over her knees and calves and shins. Ghislaine's chest was pained with the memory. Against this misery she now measured her distress with her skin, her bowed and stout legs; why she was putting these together with the bath, she didn't know. It was more than knowing that Emma had been a favorite of J. Clement Coole, who, twice during the past six years, had climbed in and out of her own tiny bed in great stealth and greater swiftness, though they had never exchanged a personal word. No, she was used to the Emmas of the world being the favorites of powerful men, and of weak men too. She didn't resent Emma. Her misery was tied up in some way with notions of grace, pains in eye-head-chest, and some mystique of the bath that had never failed to move her, and that was now suddenly out of hand.

She shook off these mysteries. She must put her young man to his task, birthday or not.

They did some preliminary work with the verb apparatus, though the boy was distracted, she could tell. Then she assigned him some phrases to copy and some further work with the verbs—after all, with these he was strangely inept or unmindful, she didn't know which. Then she watched as he leaned against the tree, raising his knees to prop up his notebook and setting about his work dutifully, though his mind was clearly elsewhere. Oh, well, why not? Wasn't he twelve, a little man, today?

He was a thin child, and that was part of the charm he held for her. His large gray eyes scanned everything so seriously, and he was very well behaved, the mustard-colored hair the only unruly thing about him. She was very, very fond of this child. There was an innocence in his pink lower lip moving slightly as he wrote, and a pathos in his earnest grasp of the pen that had a profound and sympathetic effect on her.

[Six years later, Standard himself would have a similar feeling. Sitting in a muddy trench in France, watching a British soldier weeping and flexing his finger on the trigger of a Vickers .303.

The delicate strings in the top of the hand formed a fan, so delicate it might well be used as an ornament, placed at a woman's bosom or in her hair. Hands, Standard would think. The agents of our defense—futile, futile, futile. Fragile claws, moving after success, always. The sinister masons of our infamy!

. . . parts of the body too accessible, showing veins, bones, and tendons—]

Was it an innocence she would destroy? She—clawing after things so far from her grasp? She—propelled by something that did not feel awful, and yet she knew it was awful, cracked.

If she were to look him up half a dozen years down the line, would she find that she had cracked him in some way?

She didn't think she could help things. Her life was breaking her with its monotony of meals, lessons—even at times, its toilettes. But sometimes the sweet pain of it all was a comfort: the memories of nights, nights when He, the Master, had turned the knob on her door, and moved quickly to her: raising her sheet, raising her shift.

Oh, but then the days: Of passing Him in the hallways, He looking neither right nor left. The odor of Him, His tobacco, as He passed.

Then, once the apple was bitten: the exquisite pleasure of bathing His Son. At bath-time, she would half-convince herself that he was not the Son at all, but J. Clement Coole Himself, half-grown. The smooth childish skin . . . the hard little groin . . . Oh—was she, was she wicked? (But she *was* fond of him, did her duty by him—)

And her memories of the Father: fondled at night in a sweet pain, her only recent memories of romance. Embellished, she knew, so far beyond the facts as to be utterly transformed, fictions.

But sometimes she found herself thinking too that there was something very, very wrong with an idea like "sweet pain." Where did it come from, and what was it doing to her and causing her to do? And yet she seemed to feel it, feel it at every turn. Oh, how she missed the hitherto proximity of her colleague, Emma, into whose beautiful form she had several times dreamed herself metamorphosed, bathing as He pressed His eye against the keyhole and watched her spill handfuls of tears down onto her legs in the apricot sunset, He Himself beginning to weep with the sweet pain of her beauty. Why couldn't she live in such a dream? Earlier in life she had dreamed that the world would change everything around and all the features of herself, so arbitrarily and cruelly disregarded as not beautiful, would suddenly be valued. It would be like the miraculous shift whereby flimsy paper money had taken on all the solid strength of gold—who would have believed it?

But such miracles were unlikely for her. For a woman's organs and parts to function well, to serve, was not enough. Sometimes this basic logic seemed to be out of the picture, as with her non-functioning, often-ill mistress. Oh, but now: she would settle for always living in the dream of her self as Emma, object on the god-like eye of Him: Sweet Pain!

But even as she reflected on this under the tree, fanning herself and squinting against the light, suddenly like a dozen suns, Ghislaine knew that there was something very, very wrong with such an idea. And in some place very deep she knew also that, in important ways, her life was over.

What had happened to her? She had come to America to work and earn a dowry, nothing more sinister than that. She had planned to return home and marry a not-too-powerful man who would be satisfied with her as she was, nothing more ambitious than that. She had saved and forfeited her youth in that pursuit, and nothing had come of it, not even a decent bank account, for her employers were stingy. There was no other word for it. They cut corners at her expense, and at the expense of the others. But how could she ever have left, after He had come? Coole the employer and Coole the Lover were not the same.

Any night, even now, He might return from the city. The door to her room might open, her sheet might be raised.

But things were off, cracked.

Lately she'd begun to save all the evidence of passing time: Envelopes of her nail clippings, strands of fallen hair, even several crude cloth bandages encrusted with her menstrual blood.

Where would it all end?

While Standard transcribed his verbs and ruminated on the strange information he had gained from *The Royal Path of Life,* transforming the promising heat of the present into the stony past with a skillful suffix, frowning over the mutability of mutability . . .

. . . Mlle. looked at her skimmed-milk thighs and felt the flutter of mortality, tasted the stuffy years ahead. She felt cold, cold, as if outside in the snows of the Basses-

Alpes, under the tombstones of Sisteron. She must have the sun, she must have the sun—

Abandoning her charge to his ominous verbs, she moved twenty feet or so away and rearranged herself in the hot grass. The smell! The odors of wild basil and burning earth. How they carried her back. She could barely hear the boy's voice now and the sun was already thawing her calves. She couldn't help it: she must have more.

She unlaced the old black oxfords and tore them off, along with the widow's stockings that her Mistress insisted that all the women in the household wear, summer and winter. She undid the cuffs of the prim blouse, another item to Althea's vigilant taste, and she rolled its sleeves to her elbows. She ripped the buttons from her collar and bodice, let the sun shine on her. And she couldn't help it: Oblivious to the boy and his droning conjugation, she quickly removed her bloomers and raised her heavy skirts, as He had raised Her shift.

Warm at last and transported, she let her fingers drift within her blouse, touched the moleskin of her breast, felt the nipple harden like a dried pea. No longer quite sure where she was, Ghislaine fell back into the grass and opened her heavy thighs wide, wide, wide . . . to the sun (to the Son!), her eyes roaming half-blind across the hundreds of tiny acorns that the great oak had spilt on the ground over the years of its life.

Standard had finished the "ir" verbs, and was in need of further instruction. He could see Mlle. fallen in the weeds, but she didn't look particularly approachable. Still, she clearly wasn't asleep: he would chance it.

He moved forward quietly, whispering her name very softly. She looked wonderful lying there like that, her blouse undone, her legs bare. Oh, *truly* his Mlle. was a Beauty! But did that have to mean that she was all *The Royal Path of Life* despaired of? He stopped and marvelled at her nipple, discrete as a berry, rising from the gauze of her clothes. The breast beneath was a large blue-webbed globe, animated. He yearned to put his hand out and give it a squeeze.

Deep, deep in his brain certain disturbing echoes were barely audible: deceitful . . . dangerous . . . gross.

Oh, but no. Those words could not have to do with his treasure.

He could feel a certain compelling turbulence drift out from his friend and swirl around him, urging him forward, and it seemed natural to obey.

Suddenly, Mlle.'s bare forearm shot out and her great hand grabbed his wrist. In a motion too swift to measure, he felt himself tumbling into a storm of gauze and grass and earth and flesh, spinning and spinning into some bright explosion, a fusion with the sun.

That evening as dusky clouds floated above Long Island Sound, the sun a weary red eye, Althea, who had rapidly begun to revive from her illness, summoned her son to the porch where she had just finished her supper of cold fish and asparagus. Now off her fainting couch, she reclined on a chaise-longue covered in a rose-patterned chintz, her delicate whitestockinged feet barely peeking from beneath an eyelet shawl. She wore a white organdy dress with a high collar, and her dark gold hair had been swept up from her neck and caught in a deep wave and pinned with a rose that matched the flush in her cheeks. Her hands lay long and pale, the color of certain shells, on the arms of the chaise and there was something in her pink and alabaster looks that reminded Standard of a birthday cake. For a moment he fought a foreign urge to step up to the chair and take a deep bite out of her frail little hand.

Interdit, something said.

The unsuspecting Althea smiled and beckoned him forward. He shook his head almost imperceptibly, even to

149

himself, and then approached his mother. After all, it was not her fault that she didn't have Beauty, he supposed. He would need to be more tolerant, especially now that it seemed possible that Beauty might be a curse.

"And how did your day go?" she asked vaguely.

"Very well," Standard answered formally, allowing her to adjust his perfectly straight shirt-front and pick imaginary lint from his shorts.

"How did you lesson go? Did you have it outside? I thought I saw you going into the field—"

Standard felt his ears go red. He fixed his eyes on a pitcher of iced water sweating on a fussy little wicker table and mumbled "Very well" again.

"Good," Althea said. "But get dressed. Put on your nice white suit and pin a flower in the lapel. I want you to look like a little gentleman tonight—you haven't forgotten? The fireworks—"

"But you said—"

"I know, I know, my *darling* boy! But I'm feeling . . . better." She pursed her little rosebud of a mouth into a flirtatious coil. To Standard it looked like the Secret Button on his father's pet terrier. He turned his head and stared out onto the yard.

"Do get ready," his mother demanded in her deadly sweet tone. "I don't want you to miss anything. Besides, Mr. Tobias has agreed to accompany us. We mustn't keep him waiting."

Standard noticed the color in his mother's cheeks deepen a degree. "Hurry now," she repeated, turning him around with her weak little hands. "Hurry."

Later that evening, on the walkway that ran close to the Sound, Standard, Mrs. Coole, and Mr. Toby Tobias strolled abreast. Standard had dressed himself in a suit of his own fashioning—the jacket his regular jacket, but the pants a pair of long pants, cut from a pair of his father's that he had found in a pile of refuse to be burned several weeks earlier. In secret he had cut off their legs to fit his own and stitched a clumsy hem. The waist he had gathered in with a cord and covered with his buttoned jacket. He was glad that it was almost dark so that the less-impressive aspects of his suit would not be noticed. His mother had not said a word, as he had expected, and so he strolled about with some small puffs of pride, his thin legs, brown from his afternoon in the sun, hidden in the loose fabric of his father's cast-offs.

Mrs. Coole was as glowing as her son. Discreetly she clasped her lace purse to her waist and nodded at acquaintances, but her mind was sloshing about in a tempest of indecision. Beside her, her son's tutor hooked his hands in the small pockets of his vest as he had observed his employer do, and as he walked silently by the stunning older women who paraded along the walkway, he watched with a covert interest, his face carefully angled to shield it from his companion's hungry little gaze. Like a drunken firefly, the tip of his busy cigar left a golden zigzagging trail in the dusk.

A few hundred feet away Caitlin, the Cooles' laundress, exhausted from the ravages of her afternoon, had settled heavily onto a bench, and thumbing her rosary, she waited in sorrowing penitence for the fireworks to begin, her sad eyes roving over the Sound. She was oblivious to the damp gentleman in the wrinkled white suit slumped on the bench next to her as if exhausted from a long swim. The man's straw hat floated on his fingertips, and the great dark hollows in which his eyes were lost were turned on the Sound also, as if he too were penitent, waiting to be absorbed into the darkness and distracted from himself for a blessed moment by star-spangled heavens.

A half-mile away, the laundress's fellow workers, Karl the chauffeur and Frieda the pastry cook, lay hot and disheveled in the cramped seat of the Ford, which they had slipped out of its berth only seconds after the tutor had

151

loaded the mistress of the house and her son into the old brougham and mounted the driver's seat himself, the chauffeur's bribe stuffed in his pocket. Karl reveled in the leather upholstery, the pungent undersmell of motor grease. This was the ticket! Frieda was hot with worry. The boy hadn't touched the cake—well, yes; he had touched it, tasted a crumb and rejected it. Had she over-estimated herself? No, the cake was delicious. She had tasted it herself. She waxed hopeful, then felt despair again, as her dream of escape from the Cooles' kitchen, as always, faded in and faded out.

On the Sound, Mrs. Coole and her two escorts watched the fireflies and waited for the first bursts of red, white, and blue fireworks. Standard had always taken these as a personal celebration of his own birthday, so often ignored by his parents, though he had never understood why, the holiday itself seeming a pointed reminder. Tonight he waited with special anticipation. He had been born into something today, all right.

The threesome had settled on a bench and Mrs. Coole now demurely gazed into her lap as Tobias, deprived of the other women around him now that it was dark, turned his attention back toward her, wrapping her eyelet shawl solicitiously about her shoulders, the name "Althea" surfacing from his toady murmurings and giving Standard a quick thrill of shock. So!

Then the first rocket began its long sputtering climb into the sky, hesitated, and burst into a hundred stars that fanned out, faded, and sank into the Sound. "Just think," murmured Althea Coole. "America is one hundred and thirty-six years old *today*."

Standard's heart hung still in his chest. Would she remember after all? Already he could feel himself forgiving her everything, everything. . . .

"Standard," his mother cooed, opening the clasp on her little purse. Standard felt his heart beating hard. Oh, he

152

had been too hard on her! "Darling, take this . . . take this, and get Mr. Tobias and myself two cups of lemonade, if you please, Darling?"

Standard felt the warmth rush away from his skin. He hesitated a moment and then took the dollar bill and disappeared into the crowd.

At this moment back at the otherwise empty house, Mlle. Ghislaine rushed erratically here and there. In the foyer, a small tapestry valise held her possessions and a few mementoes of her sojourn in America: Mr. Coole's (signed) edition of *Les Misérables*, a small *nature morte* by a minor Impressionist that Mrs. Coole had bought on her last shopping trip to France and then, having lost interest in it, had given to her son. Both objects had seemed to be begging to return to France with Ghislaine, and she had buried them in the middle of the valise for protection, along with a pair of J. Clement Coole's unlaundered socks, found deep in his closet.

With the valise stuffed and waiting, Mlle. made a last tour of the house, stopping now and then to finger the private possessions of all the residents. In Mrs. Coole's bedroom, she stopped before a vanity and regarded herself, imagining for a moment that she was the wife of such a man as He. In the funereal light of her mistress's Tiffany shade, she could almost imagine it so, as she brushed her thick hair with Althea's silver brush and touched the stopper of a perfume bottle to each ear lobe.

Nearby, in Standard's bathtub, she had left the weird contents of her hope chest for the little bastard: the nail clippings, the knots of hair, the stiff and crusted repositories of her womanhood, lost forever to her now, herself less than nothing to a *succession* of powerful men, a dirty thing never to be cleansed and a mason of infamy too, a grasping pair of hands, and faceless. Just as well, having no beauty—

She took a deep breath, her mad eyes swirling, and

153

rushed for the door, dropping Mrs. Coole's elegant brush in the hallway, its bristles tangled with her coarse dark hair.

By now Standard found himself at the end of a walkway, regarding the wares of a sleepy vendor by the man's pale lantern. In a few hours he would know that *The Royal Path of Life* had been right. Beauty was "deceitful" . . . "thoughtless" . . . "selfish, low and mean," "leading often to sensual pleasure," a thing for sensible men to beware. But now he selected a pair of delicate lace gloves and passed the buck to the vendor. He slipped the gloves into the breast of his new man's suit. He would tell his mother he had lost the dollar.

Turning back to the dark Sound, all the rockets and flares having fizzled in the brine, he imagined the flush of pleasure that would illuminate Mlle. Ghislaine's face when he gave her the gloves. They weren't quite worthy of her, but he knew that she would know what he meant. Yes, *The Royal Path of Life* was all wrong about Beauty, all right. His Mlle. would never deceive him, never, never.

154

What I Did For Aunt Berthe

*

MY AUNT BERTHE never married, but I believe that everyone thought she was very beautiful, and I observed myself that she had many admirers, so not getting married had to be a matter of choice. I heard many rumors of old romance in the village when I spent summers with her, in her farmhouse on her wild Bretonian coast, a white stone house with low ceilings, which had belonged to the parents of my Aunt, and my mother. (Other rumors too— rumors and wispy gossip, and full-blown gothic mysteries about my Aunt, who had admirers and detractors alike.)

This was right after the War. I heard little, romantic, gothic or otherwise, from my mother and father, nothing about Aunt Berthe. Nothing much, all the way around. They were busy with business. Getting their little shop going again in Cherbourg, after "that terrible business," which was how my mother spoke of the near past.

"Anton," she'd say to me, whenever we found a few minutes to talk. "Anton, we have nothing to be ashamed of, don't you forget. We have to put that terrible business behind us and get on with things."

She'd look off into the distance and suddenly her pupils would zoom into dots, like the sharp-focus on a fine camera. Like the eyes of a falcon when it's getting ready to plunge onto the soft body of a hare.

My father said even less. This had been, after all, his second great adjustment, the first being Minsk, 1917. The second time History had plucked him up in its massive

155

talons and lifted him, flailing, above the rocks by the tenuous cloth of his collar. Oh, yes. Father counted his blessings and said little.

At my Aunt's during these summers, I found my calling. It took some time to call, but it was my calling, coming at my invention. If others drifted into businesses and
professions whose every rule was set already, I didn't. I
called myself. But more about that later.

At first, I thought I'd go into Natural History. In the
fields near the village, with their wild grasses and flowers
and shells and fossils, I began to make my collections, a
natural pursuit for a young man suddenly at loose ends,
rusticated to the nether regions of the modern world.
Moths and insects in the conventional jars, and then on
the conventional pins. Occasional fish that I kept in
crocks of seawater. The insects did very nicely when
alive, though some consumed others, all in the nature of
things. But the fish died quickly on their own, and having
no notion of taxidermy (you could hardly pin a fish to a
paper and put it under glass!), I waited somewhat impatiently for their decay, and then for their skeletons, which
I carefully saved in a box under my bed, evidence of the
logic that underlies the most grisly things.

Oh, but how soon the illogic of the human world, and
of Histories unnatural, intruded. As I went about the
fields and beaches, nosed around the little village, and occasionally made a pilgrimage to the nearest large town, St.
Malo, catching a ride with an itinerant of some sort or a
villager driving there on business, though few in the village had private cars, I was always coming across something of primitive, emotional, erratic or naively hopeful
gesture. The stone Calvaries erected against the Black
Death, three centuries earlier. Crude monoliths from the
rituals of old Druids. A human chain dressed in the tall

156

lacy headresses of the region, blessing the birds, the boats, the fish, in a colorful, if useless, supplication.

Yes, I'd thought of Natural History, but of course much had already been done in that field. Perhaps all of it already done, and I discovered in the end that I had many interests in the human world, though much had already been done there as well. Lamenting the loss of the scientific tools of my first false calling, but vowing myself to make the most of the slippery matters and methods of the other (legends and accountings + the unreliable sensors of oneself and everyone involved in the formal and casual amassings of material), I investigated: Nature, and History, and my Aunt, and the men who came to the house in deferential postures: the grovel, the Quasimodo hunch. Deliveries of mail, milk, bread. Offers from "painters," odd-jobbers. Any excuse to come around would do.

My Aunt paid no attention. That's *immensely* to her credit. I can still see them, skulking around like thieves. Pretending to prune an already perfectly pruned shrub, rooting around in the bulb-garden, wheeling earth here and there, for no earthly reason, except for their own devious, earthy afflictions. These were primitive tactics that my Aunt didn't note. Or if she did, she didn't remark on them.

Of course there was much that she didn't note, things she ought to have noted, and remarked upon. Take myself—I, fourteen, fifteen, sixteen—her *"petit"* Anton!

But life around her seemed to fall on blind eyes, deaf ears. Even Henri, the large, muscular brute with the sweeping moustache, who rode out from the village on a bicycle twice a week to bring provisions (when once a week would have sufficed: after all, separate village-idiots brought the breakfast rolls, the daily loaf, the milk and cream and eggs and butter; a neighbor—a little man with

157

tufts of white hair sticking out from the sides of his blue wool cap—adding his petitions: a bottle of wine here, a confit in apple brandy there, sweeping off his hat in an elaborate winglike motion, stuffing it into his pocket, bowing toward her, his cheeks red as poppies, his teeth two or three nubs in the vast space of a wet mouth).

Even Henri, though he managed to bend the local virgins this way and that, made no headway with my Aunt, I noted with reassurance that first summer. The atrocities of Henri and his flawless animal's instinct and cunning in matters of romance and more, much more, were much remarked on in the bistros of the village. Old men would recount, laughing and bobbing their domes up and down over glasses of cider, telling tales, whole histories of the conquests of Henri, *"le grand peu,"* how he seduced the daughters of the pharmacist, the baker, the clothier, beguiled the young laundresses, twins, had them both, leaving one a bastard with a crooked foot—*"la signe du diable!"* they'd shout all together, their rasps echoing loudly around the room. Even Henri escaped the noting of my Aunt, I noted that first summer.

She, after all, was not a young virgin. No, the rumors in the village had made their point: she was not young. Not young at all, the women were always insisting when I went to shop or to pick up the mail during one of those weeks when the postmaster's wife forbad him to pedal out to deliver some trivial missive from my mother, who didn't seem to trust my Aunt. The point was made: when I went to the confectioner's or to the laundry for the sheets. Sometimes the point was made by the woman with the club-footed infant. She would hand me the pile of linen with the gaze of a peregrine, the child rolling on the floor nearby with a toy. The mother's twin would be folding sheets in the background, her cheeks blooming like flowers. Her breasts forcing out her apron into a pouf of white cotton that even I could see, blind as I was with the subtler charms of my Aunt, did indeed merit the enormous confidence of her tone when she addressed the large middleaged woman of frontal planes and no beauty who ironed in a further background yet. Addressed her in the bright scent and steamy glare of the freshly cleaned linen, on the matter of my Aunt, in my presence: not young, and not a virgin.

Everyone knew my Aunt had lost her Lover. Some said that it had been in the bombing of Rouen. Others said that my Aunt and the Lover had worked in the Resistance together, and that when what had happened, happened, my Aunt had escaped (saved herself, smote him with her own hand, and made a deal, abandoned him to die in the rubble of a destroyed city, left him bleeding in a field while she hurried through the dark to one who would "make arrangements," sold him out before the fact, had been a spy all along, an opportunist, a whore passed among the underground, the Vichy, the Germans themselves, etc.—no end, no end to the variations on this theme). Some few, among the less-timid men who admired her, advanced a case for her, as an innocent bystander to unsavory events outside her jurisdiction, as one who had suffered enough (time to let old sins rest in peace), as someone not quite in control of things, a self-exile in a house built on sand. But these were the few, the very few. Even Henri had something to add, and there were other rumors too, more rumors and more rumors, and rude remarks, and someone always making the point that she had been old enough, with enough experience, to have known better.

Such a woman was bound to inspire stories, stories and theories, legends and the crudest gossip. I learned to take

159

it. My Aunt herself heard rumors of rumors, but I don't think she noted them.

My Aunt had disengaged.

2

She was a woman that *looked* remote. Tall and pale, with her hair held back by combs. She smoked in the pensive way I associated with film stars, her hands large and square and ruddy. She wore gabardine slacks cut full and my grandmother's gold-rimmed eyeglasses.

"There's nothing wrong with Berthe's eyes," Mother complained to Father as they were settling me in under the eaves that first summer, in a small room that had been used by a housemaid many years before, guardian of my Aunt and mother's childhood, disgraced by some local debaucher and rusticated beyond rustication many years before, but remaining a subject of fascination for my mother, who alluded often to the tale, and to the small voyeuses, herself and my Aunt. They had spied on "poor Anne and that brute," through the cracks in a springhouse wall, "Where poor Anne rolled in a *flurry* of clothes on the mossy floor, near the cream and butter crocks," my mother never tired or relating with a giggle half suppressed. My father, her audience, never responded to this prattle, never looked up from his rolls and jam, never took his eyes off the road if my mother sprang these pathetic details on him as we took a quick drive in the country on a Sunday afternoon. I, too, listened with reserve, though there was never any indication that the tale was meant for my ears.

"Nothing at all wrong with her eyes," my mother said. "But if she wears those things—! Who knows? Mama was almost blind."

I found the glasses fascinating, especially the way my

160

Aunt sometimes wore them, down on her nose, like a grandmother in a cartoon. This revealed her real eyes (by turns sharp and dreamy—sad, *I* thought), and the two circles of glass alluding to eyes, which could be transcribed as vacant or as a tabula rasa of some sort. Or as they caught lights and impressions of things, they could be read as reflectors or palimpsests or whatever a person could come up with. When she didn't want to be bothered (almost always the case) she would push the glasses up on her nose and the lenses would magnify her *distant* eyes as she wandered elsewhere, giving the painter, the mailman, my parents, but never myself, surreal evidence of just how far they were falling from their marks. Oh, it was satisfying!

Eccentricity that is truly eccentric, unconnected to a central design, to nature or history, etc., is little more than a vulgar peep-show, wouldn't you agree?

Oh, but the odd that is centric, or can be so construed: it is powerful, long-lived. As it turned out, discovering these centricities became my calling. If something is lost in such endeavor, well, something is gained.

To the surprise of everyone who noticed it (me, my mother, everyone in the village), my Aunt took up the traditional Breton lace, a kind of net on which a heavier thread is embroidered. She made gloves, working for hours in the evening under a bright lamp, the glasses near the tip of her nose, reflecting the light and her hands at work, but looking to me like the things you can make of clouds on a lazy afternoon. The large fingers that looked so unsuitable to the task managed a cunning delicacy and some intricate designs after all, I thought, though I'm no connoisseur of lace even now. I never knew of anyone to come and collect this work for sale in town or for export

161

or for the tourist trade in the favored cities. But she must have had some such arrangements—why else would she have done it? I asked myself at the time. The work was exacting, hard on the eyes, time-consuming. Sometimes she would stretch the finished item over her red hands (nails clipped to the quick) and leave it on as she smoked a cigarette.

As for our own relations, remote as she was, I have to think that she favored me:

1. She never chastised, even when I pelted the bread-man (I'm sure she saw it) with his own stale rolls from my window under the eaves, pretending that I was poor Annie and he the irresponsible churl responsible for who knew what misery.
2. She endured the rumors I brought from the village with admirable tolerance. I never told her the worst, only extended a tiny piece of bait, something to set her nibbling near my hook, something calculated to draw her out or to make her angry enough to leap into the fray, wrestle Rumor to the ground and claim the tale of herself.
3. She must have known I occasionally spied on her bath, but no confrontation.
4. My delicate questions about the cheap tittle-tattle from the village were not met with anger.
5. She allowed me to loll on the arm of her chair as she worked on her lace in the evenings, eventually to reach out and pluck lint from the gabardine of her slacks.

"Anton," she would croon, often enough to give me courage. "Can't you, can't you part with one more of your treasures, *mon petit?* One more only?"

How could I resist? I would go for my collection. Together we selected. Sometimes a fishbone, more

162

often a moth the color of her thread. We would stop its
fluttering with her needle, then attach the form to the
net, begin the operation.

The gloves are popular with tourists, even now—I
mean the Breton gloves in general. If you don't believe
me, if you have never been and never intend to go to the
region, check out the vendors near the Chartres Cathedral
in your travels. My Aunt preferred the white ones, though
she tried all of them out. They come in white, black, and
ecru. Go see for yourself. Buy a pair.

3

"I think she should see a doctor," Mother said to Father
as they were helping me unpack in poor Anne's little
room the fourth summer after the War. Their business in
Cherbourg was back on its feet, close to thriving. Now
they could note things.

My mother was noting everything.

"Maybe she should see a doctor," she said to Father.
"Or get a job. Or marry, or emigrate."

The summer passed as it usually did. My Aunt made
her gloves, I made my collections and generally tried to
guard our quarters from the relentless men who swarmed
on its outskirts, never mind that my Aunt could never be
confused now with a young woman receptive to such attentions, though she remained very beautiful—her hair
beginning to gray, the skin at her throat like a petal on a
delicate flower crushed in the cruel fingers of an unthink-
ing child—oh, *painfully* beautiful now: the rumors were
flying!

In August, having stayed close to home, ever zeroing in
on my quarry (my collection was enormous, filling the
walls of Anne's little room, stacked in boxes under my
hard bed, under the table and chair), I forced myself to

make time for the usual pilgrimage to St. Malo, arranging to travel part way with a purveyor of the region's special cider, the rest of the way by foot if need be. We took off early one morning from the village square in his tiny vehicle, crates of cider in the rear, waved off by a dozen people on their way to work, including the twin laundresses who were growing stout and benevolent, the sturdy child balanced between them by each hand, the crooked foot apparently no hindrance at all to its steady persistence through the murk of childhood.

I had made it: seventeen now. Even she no longer called me *"petit."*

After a tedious ride that consisted of much babbling and rasping, queries and innuendo, rumors of this, of that, and of nothing that could possibly be known, titters and whispers, a near fit of rage and a bona fide hysteria and weeping that lasted a good thirty seconds, the garrulous fellow dropped me off quite a few miles from my destination. It wasn't a spot I'd visited before, only one I'd heard rumored to exist, though I'd never seen a word about it in print nor ever heard anyone claim to have been there. After I watched the man and his truck disappear down the road, I turned to look at some squat nubs poking up over an unusual swell in the earth, the reputed remains of a site of ancient rites and rituals, some say of the Druid, some argue for the sacrificial altars of a barbarian horde now dispersed into the population at large. Curious, and increasingly fascinated by the memories of certain wisps of history acquired at school, thinking maybe the ruins might offer some chips and fragments, teeth or bones for my collection, or an amusing story to tell my Aunt, I left the highway and struck out on an upwinding footpath toward the hill, over which a white disk of midmorning sun hovered like a headlamp.

Maybe it would interest you to know something of the

164

history of Bretagne, a.k.a. Armorica, Gaul, Lugdunensis, Brittany, Breiz, etc.

1. Conquered by the Romans in the Gallic Wars. But since they couldn't be everywhere at once, soon enough Celts (pried off Britain by fierce Angles and Saxons) swarmed onto this *terra incognita* like sea drones. And why not? One has to live. Before the Celt, much is buried, as they say, in History, never to be disinterred. After the Celt (about whom little is known, but much is speculated), there was one struggle after another. Against the Franks, the Dukes of Normandy, the Counts of Anjou, the Kings of England and France, etc. One barbarian after another. All these left their marks, leading to a troublesome question: What is Bretagne? From whom does it wish to Separate "itself"? . . . Really? (How quaint!)

2. One source, written elsewhere, claims: "It was not until the 17th century that paganism was even momentarily abolished in some parts of the Region, and there is probably no district in Europe where the popular Christianity has assimilated more from earlier creeds. . . . Witchcraft and the influence of faeries are still often believed in."

3. In the great French Revolution for *Liberté, Fraternité,* etc., the region was Anti-Revolutionist. Another source reports that by then the inhabitants were staunch Catholics, preferring the corpulent French Court to the lean and godless mobs ranging city and countryside. Lopping heads from dukes, statues, cats—no matter: as if even such dull and stony heads as these could fathom the logical problem underlying this bloody lurch for the Enlightenment.

4. But now we come to it. *Easily* the most historically luminous woman to come into or out of this region was

165

Anne de Bretagne (1477-1514). Picture this beauty, slumbering on a lacy pillow in her twelfth year, the sun just creeping into the room and laying a golden tint across the round forehead, the soft cheeks and bud of a mouth. A tiny puff of pale gold hair lingers loosely in a top-knot but with a small filigree escaping onto the brow and neck (forgive me, but this is the only way; otherwise History, as they say, is "dead"), one long curl reposing on a smooth breast not yet poufing out in the expected configuration, but still very promising. The sweep of lash is wavering, and suddenly the eyes open into yours and the little beauty's pink tongue flicks her lower lip as she sits up into the sunlight and croons: "Could I trouble you for my dressing gown, just this once? It is right there on the chair, near your hand. . . ." What can you do? Your hand is on the soft material before you know it, your feet taking those fatal steps toward the silky disarray.

But there is a sudden clamor at the gate, stopping you in time. A mob of babbling, slavering entrepreneurs. Anne's father, the old Duke, has died in the night and this little one is up for grabs. You hurry to her with the dressing gown and quickly wrap it around the pink shoulders, sash it (hurry, hurry) at throat and wrist, covering the treasure. But even so, she is slipping away from your fumbling hands, moving toward the door without a word. You can't see her face, only the loosening robe, the hair coming undone and trailing down the back, the naked feet making their white steady streak against the floor as the figure leaves the sunlight and passes into darker regions.

Before he died, the Duke had promised (at sword-tip) that Anne would never marry without the consent of the French Court. But what had she to do with France? You don't know much for certain, but speculate that she's

166

made of stronger stuff than the tender scene in the bedroom just now hinted. It was a *stalwart* back moving toward the door, and Rumor has it she resisted, resisted. But who could say why? A regional loyalty, mysterious enough in itself? "A mind of her own" (what could that mean?) or a Lover? Who knows? Besides, as always, others had other opinions.

Either way, neighbors rushed to aid her:

* Henry VII of England, stray vine of an old root, himself once a fugitive in Brittany. (That's right: History repeats itself.) Maybe sentiment tempered his greed in the end. (But did his chancred lips brush that cheek?)
* The Archduke Maximillian of Austria, chief engineer of the perpetual Hapsburg and of the "Diet of Worms." No slouch, but the records say he never saw her.
* Ferdinand II ("Ferdinand the Catholic"), King of Sicily, Sardinia, Aragon, Castile, Leon, Naples, a testament to his nickname, and surely in the Case of Anne, a neighbor only, being husbanded already to invincible Isabella, patron of Cristo Colombo, pirate *extraordinaire*. King of This, King of That already, busy cleaning his own house (installing the Inquisition, banishing the Jews from Iberia, etc.), but still he came to Anne's aid. Give him partial credit, even if on other occasions History has him condoning some of the most notorious *autos-da-fé* of that dark area.

These were the champions of Anne de Bretagne.

They failed. They failed her one and all, all around, though Maximillian made a great gesture, marrying her by proxy sight unseen. Romance then was never what it has become, never mind the favor it's enjoyed as a literary

167

genre and species of entertainment. By all accounts the author of the "Diet of Worms" never laid one rheumy eye on her, and that's fine with me. But she: flowering now in her season. The bosom poufing out at last, swelling up over the elaborate lace of her bodice. She is sloe-eyed, mysterious. Her top lip puffs a little over the secretive one beneath it, as she bends in the garden to break a pale rose the exact color of her blushing throat:

"Oh," she says, startled. The finger is already beading with blood. Instinctively she puts it into her mouth, but it's too late. The blood is running down her finger, covering the palm of her white, white hand, dripping off the arm onto her dress, running in a rivulet between the random rosebushes, this not being the century of the formal garden.

Married her, did Maximil, positioning his daughter Margaret between Anne and the sure contender for the Region: the French dauphin. (Did Anne have any choice in it? Could she, should she have refused? In this case, it didn't seem to matter.)

Sure as a dog follows a bitch in season, the dauphin assumed the throne of France, jilted poor Margaret, cuckolded Maxi, declaring the "marriage-by-proxy" a fake, and became himself Charles VIII. He sent a pack of soldiers on horses (how else?), spurred by a relentless pack of hounds, barking, sniffing, snarking, all of them breaking into the old Duke's compound, trampling the roses and the remnants of the rivulet, pounding, pounding—

I know she's above, in that childish room where I first saw her, but I'm hiding way below, behind a makeshift arras, and I can't tell you if she's dressed and ready to go

168

or if she hides under the bed or in an armoire behind her clothes, holding her breath.

Well, yes, it's possible: maybe she preens in front of a glass, crushing petals between her breasts, scenting herself up for this bigamy with no regrets or second thoughts. I only speculate, and only that for a minute, because a soldier is nosing his horse into the area, a cur sniffs near my shoe and begins to moan. I can't hang around to find out any more, though certain knowledge is a wonderful thing and hard to come by. Still, when a choice must be made (as it must now: I turn away from the whole scene, run out the gate and head for the forest), one saves oneself.

And is that something that requires apology? Well, that's a large question, not one I'm about to take on myself.

So, Annie was no longer the Archduchess. Married to Charles VIII, she was now: Queen of France.

And how could one be Anne de Bretagne and Queen of France? She was a moth caught in a web, unless of course she was an opportunist or frivolous butterly.

Max was livid. But always an enterprising fellow, he recovered, made arrangements for Margaret with a son of Ferdinand's, leading in turn to the marriage of his son Philip ("Philip the Handsome") to Ferdie and Bella's daughter Joanna ("Joanna the Insane"), who had already been spurned as defective goods by Henry VII of England, Annie's first champion. Insane or no, Joanna conceived, and the rest is History of a very military sort (see the Invincible Armada), but with some touches of Romance—see the

169

tragic story of Don Carlos, rumored to have dismantled with love for his stepmother, Elizabeth of Valois, wife of Philip II after the death of Don Carlos' mother, Maria of Portugal, in childbirth. Any vulgar Freudian could render this classic "Case"—not *my* calling, I'm relieved to say. (See also the ridiculous promotion of Don Carlos as a champion of *Liberté, Fraternité*, etc., by the German Romantic, Schiller.) But most accounts agree that Don Carlos was a homocidal maniac, perhaps an unfortunate legacy from Joanna the Insane, whose own symptoms have no clear origin, and so who knows if anyone can be held responsible for anything? Genetic collisions cannot be resisted, and something breathed into the natural air of Vienna by these old Hapsburgs, hacking and coughing on return from a wedding feast in Aragon, might have incubated—growing, growing, in a dark nook or niche of the city, until one day hundreds of years on, a breeze "wafted" idly in, gusted suddenly (who could say why?) and lifted the thing aloft, sustained it as it invisibly crossed the chimneys and spires to where a surly youth perched on a ladder poised his paintbrush on an eave and dreamed himself for a moment free of his stupid job. Dreamed himself, actually, King of the World, a personage luxuriating in the fresh mountain air near a Bavarian lake. Breathing deeply in this momentary diversion, he sucks the thing up whole, right into the brain pan.

Don Carlos was finally locked up by his father, whether because of an adolescent lust for a female relative or something else, we haven't a clue. It is even rumored that this poor unhappy unfortunate confused diabolical fiendish brute was finally murdered by his father. In my own calling, it is tempting to read it all as an allegory: a general condemnation of the unholy union of Spain and Portugal, of which this aberration was the telling issue.

170

So does History accumulate under the spinnerets of the meandering spider; besides, Max didn't live to see any of it. Maybe it would have been best to focus on Anne's two legitimate husbands and their exploits, suborninating Max the illegitimate, though he took special interest in the exploits, as anybody's web of History will bear out. But enough, anyway, in this elaborated mode. In the interest of time, I'll stick to the dead facts, fascinating for me but tedious I know for you, dear and gentle. Please be patient.

When Anne's first husband (who was Charles VIII, the former dauphin, you remember—but note: he was the son of Charles VII, "Charles the Well-Served," who lolled idly by and let one little servant, the Maid of Orléans, streak the night like a Roman candle), when this first husband died, his throne and Anne-de-Bretagne-Queen-of-France passed to a cousin, Louis XII, along with the other chattel. Louis (also of Orléans) of course had to dump his own wife, Joan of France, which he did for all the understood reasons, and it seems that neither Anne nor Joan had any choice in these marital arrangements, though I suppose either one could have cut her own throat, or his.

Immediately the goat mounted Anne (no longer so young, but still a beauty), and sired little Claude, an only child, then flung himself on the narrow flank of Italy with undiminished gusto. But there he languished in searing frustration. His daughter grew and his wife acquired a pensive ripeness, a studious remove, that was very appealing as I see her now: the throat almost imperceptibly etched, its delicacy enhanced something like fine gloves by her travails.

171

Over and over, Louis failed to penetrate Naples, still in Ferdie's domain, and Max cleaved to F. like a tick. Louis finally grasped the double-threat, offered up little Claude, forty years younger than old Max, but give him credit: he had the good sense or something to decline. (No record of whether Claude or Anne got wind of any of it.)

Finally Louie pulled out and returned to his family and by all accounts ruled France for the rest of his life in benevolent moderation. By the end he was known as "The Father of the People," though literally only the father of Claude, whether in benevolence or moderation, we don't know.

Down the line another Louis (XVI) did marry some progeny of Maximillian—the indiscreet Anne of Austria, granddaughter of Philip the Handsome and mad Joanna, but no good came of it.

It's time for discipline, Restraint of the severest order. This is how History does you and why I relinquished it as a possible calling: always leading you down a garden path, into some Gethsemane more often than an Eden, that's the truth. Addling you with its lacy intricacies and intrigues when you'd been after something else. Doubling back, linking up and drawing asunder, repeating, digressing. . . . It's maddening. My own theory is that it's best construed by the objects and images it throws up, its telling phrases, by the (can I say it?) psychological content of the un-psyched. All the messy details just rendered are useless in the face of the rose harboring a bloodied thorn, a woman flaming at the stake, or a diet of worms, etc. These are the bare bones. The rest is gossip.

172

Nevertheless, all the complications, ambiguities, and whatnot must have weakened the resolve of Anne de Bretagne—but by what stretch of credulity can we even lend her the name now? There were treaties or capitulations, depending on your point of view, and there were mysteries and confusions, and surely moments of vainglory and self-doubt, as that little possessive "de" twirled endlessly among meanings and implications, duties and indolences, greed and the finer sentiments. But rumors have come down that she was a fascination for the people of the Region, if enormously unpopular.

After her death, Claude (then fourteen) married Frances of Angoulême, later Francis I, and Brittany became officially part of France.

Did she resist, our Annie, to the proper degree? Heroine to Blois in the Orléanaise, far from her native province, where even today there is a small inn commemorating her? Blois—ancestral seat of the horde of barbarians who became feudal lords, the Counts of Blois. A line begun in the 10th century by Thibaut the Cheat and ended when the last old Count, childless and besotted with debt, sold his fief to Louis, Duke of Orléans, grandfather of Louis XII, Father of the People, husband of Anne.

But it seems like it was all stacked against her.

But my adolescent self nears the crest of the queer little hill. Enough of these episodes. A last brief note on History less remote.

5. Rumor has it that the Bretons resisted that recent terrible business, resisted with the best of them.

173

At the top of the hill the sun burned into my eyes torturously, relentlessly. I could barely look about the site, and in fact, saw nothing particularly remarkable, old stones stacked or falling or crumbling. Well, maybe something significant, but more likely something eccentric and of no real matter. In the midst of this physical discomfort to my eyes and the silence cramming itself into my ears, producing great pain, and then the discomfort of the brain and all that lay behind everything, I felt a quick jolt of anxiety ("Anxiety: a *sourceless* dread" as our century has conveniently defined it, and who am I to argue?), I couldn't tell you why. It was as if I knew that everything was about to shift, all the way outside my jurisdiction and logic.

I stayed only a night in St. Malo, ancestral home of Cartier and Chateaubriand, half in rubble still from a bombing during that terrible business. By the next afternoon, I was walking out from our village where a stranger had dropped me in the square. I was heading for the white house of my Aunt Berthe with a dislocated feeling that, even now, I cannot describe or truly remember.

I passed through the gate with a foreigner's stealth, cryptic to me then as now, and walked straight to the window of her bedroom, why I couldn't say, and leaning down, peeked through a crack in the shutter where the white sheets of my Aunt's bed gleamed like snow, on which she rolled under the brutal ministrations of Henri, her wide red hands on his shoulders, her eyeglasses all the way up on the bridge of her nose, the eyes in their sharp mode, staring at me in something like bas-relief.

Shortly thereafter, over my protest (which included a determined fast that pushed me to the precipice of true illness—visions, nocturnal sweats, etc.), my parents sent

174

me to Switzerland, to what they have always called a "Special School." Perhaps. I certainly studied there, invented my calling, and designed my training in it. There were many famous doctors, not all of them encouraging, but I persisted, refining, refining. "Historical Psychology," I finally pronounced it, a specialization that you might say I invented single-mindedly.

Some time later, my Aunt went suddenly blind.

It was some time later still that I visited her, with the perverse encouragement of my "colleagues," and over the objections of my mother. "Look the other way," Mother admonished me, in a fury. "People don't have to make more trouble for themselves. They don't have to get caught up in something they can't do anything about, what's wrong with you?" All this in her chic retirement "chalet," my father doddering around with a small herd of goats outside the window, his white hairs lifting in the wind like the strands of a worn-out cocoon.

Of course I went. I was still a young man, more or less.

In her house my Aunt stroked my face, stubbled with a beard now, "looked" past me with perfectly normal-looking eyes, and murmured in a mother's voice, pure and simple, ". . . petit Anton, petit Anton." She stroked my face with her small white hands, while a monster from the village, a barrel-shaped woman with enormous eyes and ears, took it all in from the doorway, my Aunt being her charge.

Later, I walked by the ocean, that blissful resource of my childish summers, pondering these changes in my Aunt. I sniffed the brine, its tolerable odor of dead things, sifted sea-matter through my fingers, and I saw a spectacle. Great winged insects were copulating in mid-air, their dangerous propellors whirring, their shit exploding into shit-clouds when it hit the ground. There were large mournful fish, leaping from the water and delving back—

upon spying me—with such force that waves shot into the sky and hovered there, threatening to break on me, threatening to break on my Aunt, who seemed suddenly to be there.

I watched with my usual professional distance. Such hallucinations are my stock in trade.

I'm sure that in some way, all this is centric. You might want to say it spewed out of a feverish brain unrecovered from a belated Primal Scene. Tsk. For professional purposes, I have described it and much more as a "demanded imposition of Psychology onto History and this in turn onto Nature." What do you think?

And of course I have made much of this description in my work, the well-received "Case of the Nature of B. in Her Historical Moment," later revised by me under a new title, "The Case For B. in Her Historical Moment," well-received also, but in a different quarter. Both, if I might say so, are models for further study, not "classic" at all.

But to tell the truth, I'm something of a phony, not entirely sure I've done justice to "B." or anything else, not entirely sure about anything much, but I stand by my calling and its method of revelation, and not being entirely sure, I've given my Aunt, all the Anne's, and the people of France the benefit of the doubt.

As for my Aunt Berthe, she died some time ago, and I was very sad about it, whatever the truth. I've always planned to visit our home one last time, and take it from me: I will, when I can.

I'm willing to scan it from top to bottom, I think. I'm sure that she sold them, the black ones with the white ones, that they were dispersed a long time ago to their targets in America, all over Europe, any place where hands might well be covered with a flattering lace. Even to Switzerland, this mercifully ecru place, such a boon historically to nature, psychology, business and history alike. Even here there might be one or two who might well want to cover their fat pink hands. Though I have to say that I've never seen a pair here, even in Zurich, where I live. That's not to say that there aren't thousands of pairs for sale in the shops and department stores. I'm not one to go out much on the streets anymore, and haven't gone out of the country in the last several years, but I feel sure I didn't steer you wrong about the vendors at Chartres, should you need them. No, not one for the streets, or the parks, or even the country anymore.

If by the smallest chance, I am wrong—if they are packed in a trunk in her attic, along with the powerful glasses, or in a dusty box under her bed, and if there are no moth corpses in their webby fabric, and if I look up Henri and find him playing innocently with his perfectly normal grandchildren, while his smiling, much-adored old wife faithfully darns his socks in the background, no hint of a village brute anywhere

Well, then, everything will have to be reinvestigated, won't it? Reconstrued. . . .

When Things Get Back To Normal

*

HE HAS a strange tooth. It has been filed, or maybe it just grew that way: like a guillotine. It is long, vertically and horizontally, metal-gray. It has a very sharp edge. I can see it as he speaks, lurking deep inside his mouth, among the molars of the upper right.

"Mami," I say to my mother, yanking the soft wool of her best dress. "Do you see his tooth? It looks like a cleaver."

"Rude child," my mother says. "Pay attention."

We are standing very close, very close to the dais from which he speaks. He is in his uniform, wearing his hat with the visor. We have to bend our necks backward so that we can see his face. That is how I can see the tooth: I am looking right up into the cave of his mouth. Later I will know that if we had been standing further back, where he had the photographers stand, I would only have seen the oncoming vigor of him, sharp as his visor, only the firm gesticulations of his head and hands, and that it might have made a difference. But no—my father has arranged *this* vantage, especially for me, and for my mother. I am grateful. Many years later I will know that such a view as that of the tooth could have come to only a few. Like Eva Braun, lying in the rumple of her peignoir, staring up into the perilous tunnel that leads to her lover's heart.

"*Heil!*" my mother emits, heartily, with the rest of the

179

crowd, jerking my arm up with hers. *"Heil— . . ."* again. And then a whisper: *". . . —ig."*

The tooth has retreated behind a hard rim of lip, which in turn has withdrawn under the famous moustache. My mother's face is bright pink. The fat lobes of her ears are bright pink below the pale blonde hair that sweeps back into a crescent-shaped roll, like some exquisite seashell on display. She is looking at my father, who stands in a row within several rows of stiff officers at the Führer's back. He doesn't look at us, but he knows—of course— that we are looking at him, from somewhere in the vast ocean of clear blue German eyes staring through the Führer at him, Colonel Erich von Rundstadt.

"I don't care if it was what you call 'a very special honor,'" my grandmother grumbles to my mother later in the afternoon as they lay out things for our snack in my grandmother's dining room. The room has thick puce-colored drapes trimmed with lace and they smell of buttery cakes that have gone stale. "If you want to make a spectacle of yourself, banging your fist in the air for that insect, I don't think you should drag the child along. *Sieg heil*, indeed."

"He's a powerful man, Mami," my mother says, unwrapping the *Bundkuchen* and *Blutwurst* we had bought on our way to my grandmother's apartment. My mother is always very deferential to my grandmother, just as she is to my father. She is a very beautiful woman, and most people are charmed by her quiet, fawning ways. But if they could see her, back in our apartment, now that my father is away with his soldiers, they would see a different side of her. With me, she is harsh, always barking commands about my posture, my lessons, anything that catches her attention. When we are alone, she doesn't fix herself up or smooth her hair back into its roll. Instead,

180

she will wear her oldest bathrobe all day long and let her hair hang inside its collar. She puts off the odor of musty bedclothes.

I don't know how my grandmother looks when alone. With us, she always wears a nice suit of wool or linen and one of her soft printed blouses, very chic, in spite of her short somewhat chunky body. Her gray hair is always in its roll. She wears opaque stockings and very square shoes, black. Her skin hangs in freckled rolls at her neck, in front of her ears, beside the downward crescent of her lips, like a delicate fabric.

"He's a vagrant," my grandmother pronounces on the Führer. "Whoever heard of him before everything went to hell." The fabric billows slightly. "Your sister Else was very smart to get out. If I weren't so old, I'd give up everything and follow her."

My grandmother pauses in arranging her cups and saucers and makes a feeble sweep of her arm around her little apartment. She has seen better times. Before the Führer, she lived in a large house and had several girls to tend her.

"You're not always democratic, Mami," my mother says in her deferential way.

"She's a *snob* about the Führer," my mother explodes when we're alone. "I wish we could see her if his name was *von* anything!" My mother goes through this every time her mother has held forth on her favorite subject: how mother and I should take as much as we can and join Aunt Else and her children in Lausanne. How she herself will stay here, just in case the insect brings things off and things get back to normal. How when all is said and done she will go to him and *plead* ("I might have pride, but it's not *foolish* pride!") for the return of her great house, which is now headquarters for some official business of

181

the Reich. Plead on the strength of "von Rundstadt," her trump card.

"After all," she always says, "If he manages things and things get back to how they were, what use would his officers have for my house?"

It is as if she had never sold the house.

My father says on one of his brief visits that the Führer is a snob too. My father is also a snob about Hitler, but he believes that he is necessary to our own interests. We three sit together in our sitting room, drinking coffee and eating sausages and some little cakes that father sent me out for, from a bakery some distance from our apartment. I knew it was a ruse to be alone with my mother, and so I took my time. Now my mother's face is bright pink, such a bright pink that I fear she is ill. My father is his usual alabaster self. Both seem to have their clothes back in place, though my mother has not put back on her shoes and stockings. Rather she is wearing a pair of ivory satin house-shoes, with little satin roses on the toes.

"He's really quite crude," my father sniffs. "Careful, Maria," he says to me. "This is a private conversation. I'll be more surprised than anyone if he can bring things off and get things back to normal."

"He's a very powerful man, Erich," my mother says softly, lowering her eyes and sipping, barely, from her cup.

My father snorts. "Where would he be without me and the others—von Brauchitsch, and von Mantueffel, and von Choltitz—? Standing behind him, propping him up?" He takes a large bite of his cake and crumbs fall heavily on his trousers.

I have been reading a little in recent years about Eva Braun. But it's hard to get much information that would seem to the point. I have, of course, seen her photograph, many times. She appeared to be an ordinary woman: curly hair down to her collar. Light brown, or dark blonde. She wasn't glamorous in the way you'd expect the mistress of a world-class dictator to be. She was nowhere nearly as striking as, say, Eva Perón, or even Isabelita Perón, and she was never in a glamorous profession as those two women were, though she obviously had her aspirations. Some of the photographs are of Eva dressed in costume, dancing around the apple trees in Tyrolean clothes. Others show her picking flowers in a meadow, wearing the peasant's apron. Others show her in a bathing suit, doing gymnastics. Actually, these photographs are stills from Eva's own home movies. Others include the Führer with sundry dogs and children, of which much has already been made. Much might also be made of Eva's habit of making movies of herself. In any case, my encyclopedia says only that she was a photographer's assistant. It says nothing at all about the home movies.

We know that she and the Führer married in the last days of the War and then committed suicide. This is of course very romantic, and it—like the Führer's devotion to children and dogs—has been very much held against him, as if there were not enough already. Much is made of the Führer's love of his faithful dog Blondie. Much (negative) is made of the romantic and sentimental impulses of others, who are not the Führer. This is very crude reasoning. I have sometimes found myself implicated, not at all because of the geographic, national, and racial facts—but because of certain abstemious practices I have taken up in recent years. They breed hostility, even in friends. Someone is always saying: "*Hitler* loved dogs." Implying more connection than logic might bear. It is more than the love of dogs that keeps me, like the Führer was, a vegetarian.

It is more to the point that the Führer commandeered

183

cattle cars, to my way of thinking. But perhaps this is all beside the point of things.

Still, things will speak themselves sometimes. Information will rise out of things. Rise and connect, as if there is an invisible counterlogic, powerful as Natural Law—conveniently repressed by the invention of Coincidence—

(Is it more than coincidence that dictators seek out and make mistresses of women named "Eva?")

(Anything to it that it goes all the way back to the Garden of Eden?)

In any case, my encyclopedia says of Eva Braun: "She had no influence on the government."

In the fall, my father goes to France to help administer the Vichy. At first his letters come often: "Things are shaping up nicely here," he writes. "If things could just fall into place everywhere as well as everything has here. . . ."

In the winter, my mother is suddenly changed. Something has happened, and after several days of pacing around in her bathrobe, smoking and snapping at me if I so much as spill salt at the table, she emerges from her bedroom late one morning, dressed in an expensive suit and wrapping her shoulders in a cape of red fox pelts that she has had remade from an old coat of my father's aunt, the Countess Elisabet. I have always found the cape obscene. And it does nothing for my mother's pale beauty that I can see.

She says she has an appointment for lunch and leaves, trailing the scent of tuberose, which is her favorite and which I remember having read is one of the main ingredients in embalming preparations. While she is out, I go to her bedroom, where the lavish perfume masks a stale undersmell, and begin to open her drawers and chest, her jewelry boxes. Finally, in a large stationer's box I find a

184

letter from her friend Hilde, who is with the occupation in Paris, and a photograph of a group of officers, apparently in some sort of nightclub, one of them clearly my father, his arm around a young blonde woman with a theatrical look—the overshadowed eyes, the arched brows and dramatically painted lips. She is not even looking at my father, but has turned her head slightly away from him and is resting a long cigarette in a holder in two languidly extended fingers.

So.

In April, my father writes, after some silence, that he is in the South, "taking care of things" at a large railway station. Apparently there have been problems with the Italian soldiers who won't let the trains pass through as they need to. "Slowing things down," my father writes. "I thought we were in this thing together."

He says it is raining every day, that the weather is cold, the situation inefficient and boring, that he is lonely and misses my mother. My mother reads the letters and leaves them on the coffee table and the mantle, as if they were cast-off wrapping paper. I read them before folding them back into their envelopes and putting them in her desk. They are uncharacteristically sentimental. "My dearest little Eva," he writes. "I have your photograph close to my heart. . . . I have always been grateful that things between us have gone so well. . . ."

In the summer, a telegram comes. My father's car, in a freakish accident, left a bridge and plunged into a river. His body is not recovered. Soon, letters of condolence arrive from friends and those high up in the Reich, even a note from the Führer himself, which my mother carefully hides from me. Even though I riffle her things at every opportunity, I am never able to find out anything about it,

185

never see it. Lawyers come and explain important papers. It is hard to say what my mother is feeling. She has put on a stoic's face, clammed up, but she is careful to be absolutely meticulous in her grooming. Even when we are alone in the apartment, she is dressed in her best summer dresses, her silks and linens. Her hair is like a fresh-baked roll at the back of her head. She wears her pearls and small ruby studs in her pink earlobes. Always her shoes and stockings.

My grandmother comes and says, "Don't you *dare* think of marrying anyone else. At least not until we see how things are going to turn out. A name like 'von Rundstadt' doesn't come along every day of the week."

My mother demurs sweetly. "We'll see how things go, Mami."

After several weeks pass, my mother resumes her luncheon appointments, her evenings out "with friends." Notes come regularly, but who knows from whom? She never leaves them lying around, does not tuck them in with her underwear or stationery.

One night, very late, close to midnight, I hear her rustling around and smell her tuberose. The door to the apartment closes with a tiny click and I pull back my curtain and watch the street. A shiny black car with the official insignia waits at the curb, reflecting the streetlights. Soon my mother emerges from our building, a man gets out of the driver's seat, holds the door to the back seat open for her. She gets inside.

Pulling away from the curb, the car seems the size of a railroad car, immense—blacker than black. The streetlights light up the inside intermittently, and it seems for a moment that I can see the visor of an officer's hat, sharp as a weapon, but I can't be sure. Everything is very blurry, suddenly. Then the car is gone.

She returns the following afternoon, wearing a black

186

evening dress that falls low on her shoulders. Her skin is the color of a geranium. She has never, never looked so distant, so demure.

In the middle of all this, our town is bombed. The planes come at night and make a terrible racket. There are sirens, so loud I think they are right there in our apartment, until I realize that part of the noise is my mother's loud, relentless wailing, behind the door of her bedroom.

The next day half the city is in rubble. My grandmother comes weeping to our door, her gray hair flying around her head like a spider web. "They've bombed my house, Maria," she cries over and over. "Eva, they've bombed my house."

"Were you able to save anything, Mami," my mother—all calm now—inquires. "Your paintings, the silver—?"

"Fool!" my grandmother yells. "I mean our house, not that wretched closet I live in! Oh, Maria—" she sobs, turning to me, kneading her purse. "Things—things are in an awful way. . . ."

My mother confers—"with friends"—all afternoon by telephone. Miraculously, the lines are still in operation in many areas, though we have no connection to my grandmother's apartment, where she has returned to mourn the loss of her house. As the afternoon wears on, my mother begins to scrutinize lists of information she has gathered from her many conversations, her round brow pale and knotted. When my grandmother comes at dinner time, bringing a bag of canned goods and looking old and dazed, my mother announces that she and I will be packing and leaving the very next day. "We will, of course, send you things, Mami," she says, serving us all small portions of the tinned meat and crackers.

"Shouldn't I go?" my grandmother asks, her voice wan.

"Else will have room, and now that my house is gone. . . ."

"We're not going to Else's, Mami," my mother says sweetly. "I hear that things are almost over. Things are shaping up in Berlin. Maria and I will be going there tomorrow, taking a few things. I'll leave everything else here, or with you. No, you stay here. Take care of things for us, and when things get better, we'll be back. Or we'll send for you."

My mother keeps her eyes on the tinned meat, never looking up. Her skin has turned the color of a radish. Soon my grandmother's gaze settles on a wall across the room and no more is said, until she prepares to go back to her apartment. At the door she pulls me close to her. "Don't you *dare* let her change your name," she whispers.

We are in Berlin, settled into a beautiful apartment belonging to one of my mother's friends, unknown to me, when it is all over. The Führer shoots himself, perhaps testing the bullet first with his ingenious tooth, who knows? Shoots himself and falls dead, Eva too. At first my mother is in a panic, weeping, wringing her hands. For days she paces and puffs her cigarettes, snapping at me, watching "Things go to Hell" outside our window. Then one evening she throws on the old fox cape and goes out, after a telephone call from a friend. Much later she comes back and tells me to pack, that we are going to Else. At midnight or so a dark car comes for us. A man opens the door and my mother and I get into the back seat. The man in the back seat is wearing an American officer's uniform, covered with a gaberdine raincoat. My mother introduces him to me as "Colonel Brown." His driver takes us all the way to Lausanne, and the officer comes along, flashing his cards at each checkpoint. At daybreak, I can see my mother sleeping with her head on his shoulder, her face relaxed at last and blooming.

At Else's there is much excitement. My aunt pulls my mother to her and says she must hear "Everything." "Oh, what terrible things you must have endured, Eva," my aunt says, hugging my mother, her great blue eyes peering into the Colonel's face, over my mother's shoulder. "How are things with Mami? Have you heard anything of Josef?" Josef is my aunt's husband.

They turn slightly, as if in an awkward waltz.

"That insect!" my mother ejaculates, looking demurely at the Colonel, over Else's shoulder. "He ruined things for us! No, nothing of Josef."

We pass many months at my aunt's house. At meals we sit around a large table under a large, intricately carved clock. We talk about things, how things went from bad to worse, how things must be for poor grandmother, back in her little closet, how bad things must be for Josef, wherever he is, how all our personal things must be lost, except for the clothes we—all of us, Else and her children too—brought on our backs, how things can sometimes get out of hand, away from one, how things are so seldom what they seem, why things can be allowed to get in an awful fix, etc.

Every fifteen minutes an elf runs out of the clock and bangs his little hammer on a little bell: *Ding, ding, ding . . . .*

How the newspapers in foreign countries—though, thank heaven, not Switzerland!—are making things up, blowing things all out of proportion. . . .

During all this time, the Colonel is an almost-frequent visitor. He catches rides on airplanes that criss-cross

189

Lausanne this way and that, on various official business. When he is coming, my mother and my aunt dress in their best, both blooming like Alpine roses. He brings news: my grandmother is fine, happier than ever, because it is possible that her property can be restored to her when things are closer to being straightened out; Josef is in a British camp, being treated very well, things being arranged—slowly, discreetly—in his favor. Much of what was the von Rundstadt interests is being secured— quietly, pragmatically—for my mother. Things are shaping up in Japan.

On one visit he brings magazines with photographs. "The proof of things," he says slyly to my mother and aunt. They smile at him as though baffled, blush prettily, offer him more cakes and sausages. The Colonel pulls me on his lap, calls me Blondie. My mother and aunt smile and smile.

When he leaves, my mother and aunt are petulant with each other, sitting around the large table as I hold the magazine, unopened, in a corner of the room. "I'm not surprised," my aunt says. "I had already heard it at the butcher's."

"Someone is always blowing things up, Else," my mother says, pale as snow. "Out of proportion to the rest of things."

"Well, I suppose for someone with the von Rundstadt interests—"

"Maria, time for bed." I go, taking the magazine.

"Anyway," I hear my aunt say as I leave the room, "I wasn't there."

During the night, I fall ill. Mysteriously into a fever. I call out and my mother comes with water and a cloth, washes my brow and hands, then goes away. In the morning, they say later, I am in delirium. I remember almost

190

nothing. I fall into vivid fits and dream. I dream of smoke. At first, long dark streams of it, moving toward heaven. Suddenly, the smoke is pink, a thick whoosh of it shooting into the sky and then billowing out on the top like a great puffy flower.

One morning, my mother comes with a plate of sausages and cakes. "Have a sliver of *Blutwurst*, Maria," she says. "It will give you strength." I try to decline, but can't speak. She is poking the sausage at my lips. I clamp them together. "Oh, well, then," she says irritably. "Have some cake. Take something. Do you want to die?" She rams the cake against my mouth. It crumbles on my bedclothes. I am sick again, dreaming.

At some point, I remember, my Aunt Else is standing over me, peering into my face. "What things, Maria? What things are you talking about?"

Altogether, it takes two years for things to get back toward normal.

For the Colonel to arrange to get Josef away from the British and into a job with the U.S. intelligence. To get my grandmother's property back, even if it is only a lot with three walls standing. She is very happy: she will rebuild and everything will be as it was before.

For the von Rundstadt remnants to be transferred to my mother. For Colonel Brown and my mother to get married.

In the end, it is impossible to know anything much about Eva Braun. Much would depend on what she thought about, lying under the Führer, his great gray tooth gnashing right in front of her eyes. She left no record.

There is something odd, when you think about it, about Blondie, the Führer's beloved dog. As you think of the dog

191

galloping wildly about the lawn, Adolf and Eva beaming on the sidelines, it seems that there are things it ought to know, perhaps by some sensory detector. Its innocence is a puzzle. Lack of language does not seem a sufficient excuse.

"Things will be better in America," my mother tells me as we settle at a table in the little snack room of the ship, only minutes after it has left Bremerhaven, Colonel Brown on deck until the last minute, one arm around my mother's shoulder, the other around mine. We are going to the Colonel's parents' ranch, somewhere in the west of the United States, to make the best of things until the Colonel can get out of Berlin. My mother is thriving, speaking English with a new twangy accent, much like the Colonel's. Looking rosy as a rose.

The waiter brings my mother a whiskey and soda, a plain soda and a beef sandwich my mother has ordered for me, and a newspaper. My mother begins to read the paper, relaxed, smiling to herself. Soon she holds it up and shows me a photograph. "Look, Maria," she says, smiling in her deferential way, which has come to include me for reasons not quite clear. "The new Führer. Truman. *Der trau Mann.*" She giggles. "Can you imagine? Look at that face—"

I study the photograph.

"Eat your sandwich, Mary Brown," she says. "You look like a wraith."

The man is wearing a straw hat. A wide smile. One canine sinks into his lip like a rocket.

Chez les petits suisses

*

THE traveler from Cascais, slightly west of Lisbon, was sitting at a table near the wall of the little Swiss hotel's blinding white dining room with his English mistress, who bored him. But here they were: spending an interminable holiday together nevertheless. Why couldn't she at least have sat on the other side of the table, he was thinking. No, she had to sit beside him, right up against him, forcing him to recoil and hug the plaster of the wall. Unless he turned his head and looked at that wall, there was no place to look that didn't bring some part of her into his view: at the least, an ivory hand—the famous English complexion!—slithering out of the silk of her sleeve. The English hand looked weak, barely hooking the soft white roll that its mate moved to butter. The sleeve was the color of a fever. But he knew that all around the room Others who did not know her in the intimate way that he did were admiring the hand and its delicate appropriation of the roll, and marking the subtleties of the woman's attraction. Subtleties that he had exhausted a long time ago, or qualities that he had discovered not to be subtle at all.

Yes, once they were back in Portugal he would tell her it was finished, perhaps offer her a job to conciliate. He was, among other things, the owner of a prosperous boutique of women's clothing and accessories in one of the large hotels along the Gold Coast, the ribbon of beach that unfurled into the Atlantic west of Lisbon. He called

193

the boutique Elizabeth Barrett Browning. Soon he would be opening a second one with a business partner in Rio, to be called O Casabranca. Maybe he'd install her there, far from himself. Make her an emissary, in the business sense of things. As for anything personal: finished. Their relations, still more cloying than seemed reasonable, given all they knew and suspected of each other, were intolerable, and they were growing more so every day. Somehow he had managed to repress the troublesome particulars of the decline—so thoroughly that he doubted even he could dredge them up—but he couldn't help feeling that these were shaping his life still, in invisible ways he couldn't fathom.

He had complaints about this little hotel, too, he was thinking now, scrutinizing the brilliant plaster on the wall, then allowing his eyes to range the few nooks and niches not dominated by major imagery from the woman by his side. With some irritation his brain followed his eye across the room where he could see (underscored by the blurred suggestion of his mistress's hand) the American film student attacking his rolls, tiny crumbs gathering in his beard. The Portuguese quickly raised a napkin to his own lush moustache and then, with effort, shifted his eyes to the ceiling and began to run them along the line that bordered a denticulated molding painted white.

Yes, he had complaints. The little hotel was clean enough, that was true: austere and polished in the manner of Swiss hotels. But it was far too expensive, especially considering how plain everything was. Take the meal he was preparing to eat now: that was sure to be plain. And why did a person travel if not to indulge in lavish and sumptuous fare, luxurious trappings, splendid vistas? To have come all the way to Switzerland and find oneself pinned to a wall like a moth, one's range of vision severely curtailed, a pathetic and parsimonious table— This last especially goaded him. This would be his fourth supper in the hotel's dining room, and it was misery, all the way around. The food excited almost as much distress as the English.

The previous evening there had been potato soup, and then a pallid clump of lake-fish, sliced veal in cream gravy, a mountain of overcooked noodles, several spears of white asparagus. It was all followed by a blancmange in the shape of a ragged heart. And, in a comedy of errors, large cups of hot milk intended for some other guests had been delivered to his table instead of the coffee and port that was one the few pleasures he and his mistress could still enjoy in common, and there had been enormous difficulty in convincing the dunce of a waiter of just who had authority in the situation, and further difficulty in meeting his mistress's sly disdain once they were back in their bedroom.

Now the beginnings of the new meal were before him. Spongy rolls, pale butter, a cream soup that gave off a thin reek—turnip, at best. He drew in another whiff of it, appraised, and exhaled, reaching for his wine while still keeping his eyes averted from his mistress. He felt depressed. Even the wine seemed diluted in this little hotel. But he supposed that such neutral spots were necessary to the order of things. In his old age, the business of a lifetime done, who knew what he would prefer, or need?

From across the room the film student caught the turbulent eye of the Portuguese and threw him a little salute. The Portuguese returned the gesture by reflex and quickly withdrew his black eyes under his great brows and began to examine his soup. No, mustn't encourage that one. He had spent a trying hour the previous afternoon with the brash young man, preceded by an hour of observing him discreetly through the window of the library as he himself

195

played his own daily game of solitaire. The film student had moved about erratically in the drizzle, filming the little hotel from various angles. Finally, misted over like a pet left out in the weather by mistake, he had come directly into the library from the verandah, his manner petulant and accusing, but curiously exuberant even so. In his finite dealings with Americans, the Portuguese had noted to himself that their confounding exuberance, even in their misery, seemed almost like a racial trait. The last thing he had wanted was a conversation with the film student, who had been interesting enough as a moving image, but once in the library he seemed to dominate it in his surly enthusiasm, not a seemly mode for such a young person. Still, what could one do? Being the only other guest in the room, the Portuguese had had no choice but to pass the time of day with the American, or else pretend that he didn't know the English language—impossible: he had had that language force-fed him almost with mother's milk, more the pity.

"It's been a real waste, man, absolutely," the film student had said in the nasal whine the Portuguese had noticed to be characteristic of spoiled youth everywhere. The American sat on the edge of a richly damasked chair, a curious piece in the austere little hotel, and began to pry at his camera and make adjustments with his Swiss army knife. "Yeah," the student said, concentrating his eyes on the camera, eyes which failed to release the Portuguese nevertheless. An eye set to sharpening a power-driven eye of perfect memory was an intimidating thing, the Portuguese realized.

"I made it to Baden-Baden, Marienbad, even Spa. Man, I got footage for a lifetime, no shit. And now—here." The student looked up and surveyed the library dismally, making an inclusive motion with his knife, which the

196

Portuguese thought scraped into its circle, rather too rudely, himself.

"Have you ever seen any place this ordinary?" the student asked with a direct gaze. Though the Portuguese concurred absolutely, he merely smiled with a father's indulgence and placed a triumphant jack on the queen of hearts.

"That's what I get for letting them know I'm American," the student complained, returning his attention to the camera. "I should have passed myself off as Canadian. They'll tell an American anything."

The Portuguese made a gesture toward scooping up his cards in preparation to leave, and the American fastened him under his unpleasant eyes again. "Americans get a bum rap," he said. "You want the Third World? Take a look at the hand somebody's always dealing the Americans, the minute they step off the plane. For half the world, America's the Third World." He suddenly snapped the camera case shut and grasped the machine firmly between his knees, bent his head and pressed his eye against his machine, turning this part and that, as if trying to focus on the floor.

What a strange person, the Portuguese mused, suppressing a yawn and seizing the opportunity to gather his cards and return them to their case. He was impatient for the newspaper, always two days old in the little hotel, to learn the latest on his neighbor in Cascais, Umberto, the King of Italy, just released from a clinic in London and reported to be recovering from an "undisclosed" illness in Geneva.

"*Go To Montreux . . .*," the student intoned from his awkward posture. "They'll tell an American anything. *Go To Montreux . . .*, like it was a big secret. The guy looked like Boris Karloff. He said he'd had a bit in *Marienbad—*"

197

The student scoffed and raised his head, just as the Portuguese was rising and taking his cards off the table. "You leaving?" the student asked, as the Portuguese lowered himself back into his chair.

"He wasn't in any *Marienbad*," the student resumed, setting his camera on the floor and leaning back into the damask chair, crossing his hands on his hard stomach and staring at a spot on the wall nowhere near the Portuguese. "He was just an anti-American asshole, ready to lead the first American he saw on a wild goose chase." He closed his eyes. After several minutes the Portuguese, having eased the card case into the pocket of his jacket, stealthily started up out of his chair again.

"Then there was the old man," the student said suddenly, without opening his eyes. "He was on the horn from New York, saying that since I was already over here wasting his money I might as well take care of a little business for him in Geneva, so here I am. What a washout." He opened his eyes and looked up at the Portuguese, all his surliness suddenly gone. "Did you see *Marienbad*?" he asked dreamily. "Aw, Man, you missed something. I mean Resnais is on his way out and all, it's all Germans now, but that was some flick."

Relieved by this shift in demeanor, the Portuguese smiled in a way friendly enough to convey that he had nothing against Americans *per se*, but not so friendly that the young boor would think a friendship was on the agenda on some future rainy afternoon, and then he shrugged pleasantly, tipped his head in an appropriate leave-taking and headed for the door.

"What are you, anyway?" the American said, stopping the Portuguese in his tracks. "Spanish?"

The Portuguese turned slightly, exhibiting the same measured smile briefly in profile, then resumed his aim of

198

getting beyond the insipid discourse of this insufferable person.

"Great!" he heard the American exclaim with the exuberance of his race. "It's all going to be Latin Americans soon, bet your ass. Did you see *Aguirre, the Wrath of God?*"

Now the Portuguese watched the film student work on his soup, remembering with rising fury an even worse encounter with him just several hours earlier. Suddenly the American's face, with its square thrusting beard, looked like a shovel. The Portuguese wiped out the image (and the ruffle of his mistress's sick sleeve) and willed something like the student's "footage," onto his eyes, thereby withdrawing from the depressing dining room entirely.

The little hotel faded in slowly—with, oddly, a luminous quality that the film student could never have caught on such gray afternoons, and a quality that now seemed very much beyond the facts to the Portuguese guest. Otherwise, it was realistic enough: a white stuccoed buiding with spanking white wooden verandahs on three sides, and a second-story verandah on top of the one that spanned the building's facade. It all resulted in something like the colonial effect, the Portuguese realized, although a moment's reflection revealed that he had recognized this all along. Yes, it was much more as if the little hotel, rather than being Swiss, had served some early planter family in the West Indies, or the coastal South of the United States, which he knew quite well from books. Or for that matter, he thought tardily, Brazil, Mozambique, or Angola.

The verandahs had many white wooden chairs to be used by guests on warm afternoons, if such afternoons ever occurred, and the Portuguese had begun to doubt that

199

they occurred very often—and that was another complaint he had: most of the guests were very old. Not that
he had anything against the old, nor the young either,
really, though the film student had tried his patience. But
it was all such a surprise, along with the food and appointments and the persistent chilly rain and gloom that
had kept the verandahs from doing much business and
had made his relations with his mistress so much more
difficult than they might have been otherwise.

Several years before, he had passed the hotel while on a
crucial business trip that had left him not a moment to
linger. He had caught only a glimpse of the facade from
his speeding auto, but the hotel had seemed to glow like a
rare jewel in the sunlight of that remembered afternoon.
There had been guests sitting in chairs on the front lawn,
and all along the verandahs. He had not specifically noted
the ages of the guests, and even now he was not inclined
to fault himself on that score. He had the clear impression
that, in that sunny season, there had been men of vigor
lounging in rattan chairs, strong young women strolling
about the grass in discreetly dipping sundresses, their
wide-brimmed and ribboned hats floating on the tips of
their elegant fingers.

The poor souls who now occupied the dining room and
shuffled about the common rooms of the hotel were the
result of some vast misunderstanding that had occurred—
maybe in the nature of things, he had even thought from
time to time as the gloomy days wore on and there was
nothing for him to do but eat the bland food, try to find a
quiet corner for his solitaire, persist in re-reading a massive biography of Vasco da Gama, a childhood hero with a
strange hold on him.

Yes, the old folks were a mistake, he felt sure, his eyes
coming back to the dining room just as a sparkling white
china plate containing an equally white arching fish-

200

corpse was set in front of him. The old folks were not *necessarily* the rule.

But if that were the case, why did they occupy the best tables while he sat crushed against a wall, he wondered irritably.

He had his eye now on the most desirable table of all: a large round table in the exact center of the room, right under an enormous and elaborate chandelier, the dining room's only grand gesture. Occupying this table every evening were two elderly couples whose heads were as white as the table linens. He looked toward them now, over his mistress's pale hand, its claws painted blood-red and worrying the edges of his vision despite his best craning. He could see the old people at the coveted table, two of them effervescing on who knew what—laughing, gesticulating. The other two sat lumpish as the fish before him, sunk in their chairs, their eyes elsewhere, wasting the miraculous table and its favored location.

Yes, there had been some misunderstanding, a misunderstanding or two or three or more, not unlike the inclement temperatures and gray drizzle that had marked, so far, his unhappy holiday: quite outside his jurisdiction and blame.

2

The English woman was pleased to find the soup somewhat tepid. The previous evening it had been very hot, the fish course coming so closely on it that there had been nothing to do but to eat quickly and scorch her palate. The waiter had been an impatient Turk and had hurried them along as if the wishes of the guests were nothing, as if the guests had no claim on a say in the matter. And it was true: they hadn't said anything.

But then it was her lover's place to say things, wasn't it? That he had only blackened his ever-present frown,

pressing his great eyebrows into a figure something like
the wings of a bird in flight, and then eaten faster, accommodating the Turk at a dervish-like pace: This was a side
of him she'd never seen before. It was as unpleasant,
truly, as his behaviour the previous evening, when they
had been served by one of his countrymen, a compact little Portuguese whose service was impeccable and whose
manner left nothing to be desired: respectful, discreet, un-
obtrusive. And yet her lover had been thoroughly rude
and abusive, ordering the poor man here and there, de-
manding fresh rolls, even though he was not eating rolls
himself, complaining about the wine, the consistency of
the fish, the shine on the silver, the placement of the
table—

It was endless. A very ill-bred condescension, by anyone's judgement. It didn't take a similarly abused "lover"
to see what was what.

More and more, it was clear that she and the lover were
not, by any calculation, lovers.

But there had been a time, not too long after she had
gone to live with an aunt and uncle in Portugal, the uncle
involved in port and other trades, when things had been
very different. She had been recovering from an earlier rebuff, whose particulars she could no longer quite recall,
and she had been too susceptible to this little man's limited charms. After she had languished somewhat bedrag-
gled, as if still misted with the rains of England, for
several months in her aunt's house, the intrusion of the
Portuguese had had a miraculous effect.

"Oh, Dear," her aunt had bubbled spritely. "He will *do*,
for the moment. You look like one of my camellias! We'd
begun to have our doubts. Oh, not in the long-run, of
course. But for the moment, he will do very, very nicely,
Dear. . . ."

She could still see her aunt's face pushed closer than

202

was necessary to her own. The face like polished marble, but crêped where the lips were struggling to control the pleasure of a coup, the eyes blue as two robin's eggs in spring.

Well, it was true: she had *effloresced* in that amusing courtship, forgotten her earlier loss and humiliation. Sometimes she had felt like she had known the Portuguese a long time, and she had worn his attentions as comfortably as an old robe.

Not least erotic was the fact that he had fallen helplessly under her control. He was enamoured, almost comically servile, responsive to her every desire and whim. Even a casual musing on this object or that service could bring it to her in an instant: a nice piece of jewelry, a skilled masseuse bearing oils and Turkish towels.

He had been just what she had needed: a distraction from old pains, an attentive administrator of love and passion's business, mindful of detail and blind with desire. He sought her advice on every matter and what was his, he turned over to her, gladly—the keys to his small seaside villa on the isle of Madeira and to his tasteful British car, access to his credit, the pick of merchandise in his exquisite boutique, which was only a hobby, not his true business. He gave her license to his tab at the casino, took her on frequent holidays, to dinner at the Aviz, to dance at the fashionable new *boîtes* in the darker corners of Lisbon, anything that she hinted might secure him a burrow in her serious feelings.

And then, gradually, but at an increasingly rapid pace, things had changed—a complete mystery to her, even now.

The flashy new German-made automobile, for which the lover had traded his comfortable British car against her advice, was *verboten*, that was his word. A weekend on Madeira was by invitation only, and when one was

203

invited, there was clear evidence of earlier female guests. He had detached himself from certain investments in the port trade and put more into Brazilian coffee, over the protests of her and her uncle, though port was the business he knew best from his father, just as she knew it somewhat from her own diverse father. The lover, though, knew its most subtle formalities, all the minutiae, and yet he had forsaken it for something less desirable, just as he had forsaken her for—what?

Some sort of crisis had come involving the Bank of Angola, and heedless of her warning that this was a signal to return to port, he had put more into sugar in Rio. And almost as if there were a connection, all the little touches of unquestioning devotion went the way of the villa. Suddenly, the daily calls and flowers, the toady indulgences of her aunt's eccentricities and chatter, the gifts and holidays and sumptuous dinners were absent. Or if present, they seemed the wisps of habit. Her lover's investment was clearly elsewhere.

"Perhaps it's time you returned to London, Dear," her aunt said one evening over roasted goat in her gleaming tile dining room. Her aunt and her uncle had cooled along with her lover, a puzzlement. After all, hadn't her aunt said the Portuguese would do "for the moment" only?

Her aunt's table was spread with its best Madeira lace tablecloth, set with the famous Vista Alegre china, good as Spode, and with the exquisite Atlantis crystal, rumored to rival Waterford. A large Arraiolos carpet covered the floor, pink marble from the Alentajo region, and in the corner a newly acquired capital from some church of the Manueline was displayed on a pedestal, balanced by a still-life attributed to Josefa de Obidos. On an elaborately carved sideboard which had miraculously survived the Lisbon earthquake of 1755, the best tawny port waited for Manuela to bring the native oranges and demitasse.

204

"Perhaps I should," she said, feeling suddenly weak and queasy. Her uncle seemed distracted, but she could feel the damning critique in his silence.

Of course she had not gone anywhere just yet. She hadn't felt well enough to face a return to the cold misty city where her parents lived, or even to the damp country place where they sometimes escaped the pressures of their tenuous livelihood, always more than comfortable and even somewhat lavish, but always a struggle too. There were sure to be some reminders, also, of her old defeat. Yes, since her lover's ardor had cooled, she had felt weak, not quite ill, but not quite well. Though she had never—even on best day of their relations, even by the most bizarre stretch of imagining—never loved this bantam Portuguese, there had nevertheless been something strengthening in their former relations, something that had buttressed her in an almost tangible way. "For the moment" of his passion for her, she had felt an amazing power, like something she could almost remember from an earlier, simpler time of life. Oh, it had made her feel powerful and attractive at once: to feel herself, for the moment, almost the Owner of one whose own ownerships were really quite extensive.

Well, it had gone as mysteriously as it had come, and the indulgence of her relatives with it. Well? Was this such a great loss? Hadn't she been getting just a little too dependent on such favor and largess?

She gave a sidelong glance at her lover, who listed curiously against the wall of the dining room as if pushed by her look. He seemed to be staring at nothing at all on the opposite wall. Sometimes she wondered if he were not actually ill. His black eyes often seemed feverish and his lips sometimes were over-red, not unlike her aunt's camellias. Of his failing mental health she had all the proof she needed. Why would someone in his right mind insist

205

on journeying to such a distant trysting place, and one so plain and unpromising of a rekindled passion as this little hotel, and once there, act as though he had been tethered by a rope and yanked across river and alp against his will?

Clearly he was worse off than she. Feverish of eye and lip, unsteady in his chair, too thin. Actually, he had always been too thin for her taste, though it was a marvel how he could gourmandize with the best and stay in his spectral shape. The thinness and the grayish complexion had, more times than she wished to remember, reminded her of a famous painting by El Greco: "The Burial of Count Ortego," if she recollected the title. Yes, perhaps he was ill, harboring some undetectable disease that was draining him away from himself, deep in a secret place, one that was working on his mind also and obscuring his judgement. That would explain a great deal.

Still, you'd think he could will a serviceable cordiality, just to get them through this dismal holiday in this strange little place, a fiasco of his own making, after all.

She had enjoyed herself at the little hotel much more the previous week, before he had joined her.

When his invitation had come, she had been revived momentarily by the possibility that such a retreat might reinvigorate their arrangements after all, strengthen her and restore her to her aunt and uncle's favor. That it might extend her sojourn in Portugal and postpone her return to a scene of former distress and to her family's ship of fortune, always threatening to sink.

Blooming with these hopes, but still in a wan condition, she had preceded the Portuguese to the little hotel to settle in and get things on her terms in advance. She had stopped off briefly in Zurich to take care of a small business matter for her uncle. His manner, along with her aunt's, had warmed to her in light of this surprise holiday.

Her aunt had donated a sheer peignoir and a bottle of musky perfume from a famous Paris manufacturer just as she was leaving. She had had to keep the driver waiting, undo her luggage, and make adjustments—all the time the blue egg eyes of her aunt sparkling above hands clamped over nose and mouth as if praying.

After taking care of details in Zurich, she had rented a car and driven down, arriving on a sunny day bristling with flowers and the pungent reek of lawn trimmings. The adorable old guests had tucked their snowy hairs under straw hats and had crowded onto the verandahs or were shuffling aimlessly about the pale green lawn strewn with its fragrant clippings, drying even as they were shuffled upon. The hotel sparkled like an opal. Its great red awning was rolled out, the sidewalks lined with bright geraniums.

At first, she had found the whole compound extraordinary. It had something of the piquant charms of tuberculosis asylums in the early part of the century, or as she imagined them from her readings in Somerset Maugham, Thomas Mann, and so on, and as she had seen them represented in the cinema.

Oh, the sparkling little hotel with its happy guests and the clinking and bustle from the kitchen mingling with its happy summer birds—it was irresistible! Magically, her opinion of her lover's judgment altered to accommodate this choice of place.

In the afternoon, after a filling lunch whose details she had not noted, so entranced was she by the bright dining room, whose windows were thrown open to a warm breeze and whose corners hummed with the pleasant intercourse of these pleasant guests, she had taken a spot on the verandah that offered a good vantage of everything. Dozing near sleep, she had mused at length on the special charms of the earlier sanitariums.

Just now she caught the twinkling eyes of the lively old twosome under the grand chandelier and nodded with one of her most benevolent smiles, the one she reserved for well-behaved children, well-behaved animals, and elderly persons who made the best of things. These two were truly wonders, always smiling, always chatting, never seeming to get down in the mouth like the dour and cumbersome couple who made up their quartet.

What strange bedfellows, she thought, as she had thought from the first day when she had noted the robust husband and wife ushering their friends along the geraniums, then steering them across the lawn, as if elbows were rudders, to sit in four white wooden lawn chairs as prominently arranged as their choice table under the chandelier.

Again she nodded and smiled as they nodded and flashed smiles quite as benevolent as her own to her undistinguished corner of the dining room. Not to be outdone, she raised one hand slightly above her butter dish and briefly agitated her fingers. The gesture provoked an incensed look from her companion, his head whipping away from where it had propped itself against the wall and swivelling toward her like a puppet's head on a stick. She could feel his ill-temper oppressing lower, like a heavy storm-cloud, over their table. It didn't lighten, even when the head swivelled from actually meeting her gaze, which she hastily crafted to show an incredulous pique underscored by a wry and tolerant amusement: *what could you do* when people persisted as they persisted in their inscrutable passions, she hoped to convey to the increasingly intolerable man at her side.

Showing no outward sign that he had received this critique, her lover's blustery eyes came to rest on a window pane at the end of the room in which she could see them obscurely reflected among reflections of the beaming

208

chandelier and the beaming crowns of their neighbors' white heads. Suddenly she felt a surge of pity for her lover. She could well understand his embarrassment at her seeing one of his own countrymen serving the Swiss. It must have been something like she felt when they had accidentally run into one of her father's London friends in the lobby of a hotel in the Algarve, the father of an old and especially desirable suitor who had gotten away in the end. Though the situations were not exactly the same, still something could be learned. *She* certainly had made it a special point to exhibit an elaborate and almost deferential respect for this little lover to the thoroughly jovial Englishman who was himself masking a slight reservation, but certainly undetectable to the Portuguese. That was the English way, she observed with some pride.

Well, it was a consolation that you could move about the world outside England and never see an Englishman waiting table. With the possible exception of the large American cities. Human nature was human nature, after all, and America and all it represented could lead almost anyone to unseemly arrangements, and besides, it was very hard for anyone English to get very upset about anything involving the Americans, those effusive and intemperate step-children.

Still, her companion's distressing behaviour with the waiters had been recollected since with some amusement, as she tried to pass the hours in the now-gloomy little hotel. Nevertheless, she was glad to see that neither Portuguese nor Turk would be waiting on them this evening. Instead, it was an elderly Swiss, with the expected apple cheeks. Once again, she felt a gratitude of no clear source that her own family had never exploited anyone of race. Even her aunt and uncle's Manuela had made her uncomfortable. Though all of London was over-run with Indians, West Indians, East Indians . . .

209

Not that she hadn't always enjoyed dipping into their restaurants for an exotic meal—which reminded her: wasn't this a peculiarly bad meal? Proving once again the injustice of the traditional pronouncements on the traditional British fare? Wouldn't a nice banger and a Scotch egg and a side of curried lamb with large glasses of ale make that point absolutely clear, just about now?

Yes—enjoyed their restaurants and shops and services outside the home, but it would have been disconcerting even if a dark man wrapped in a turban and speaking with an almost British tongue had suddenly appeared at this tiny Swiss table. *Very* disconcerting, she realized as the scene sprang into her imagination. Still, she would never treat such a creature in the unforgivable way her lover had treated the Portuguese waiter.

Yes, an elderly Swiss waiter was what you wanted in a little Swiss hotel. With apple cheeks, she thought cheerfully, enjoying the creamy soup after all. Even though you had never been in the dining room of such a little hotel before last week, the elderly Swiss waiter would be as familiar as your mother's cockney laundress and Irish cook, and every bit as proper.

But—wasn't the old man advancing now as if to remove the soup plates?

Covertly, she watched her lover. A chance to redeem himself. Surely he would have no trouble at all instructing this benevolent old clock-figure that they were not yet done with this delicious soup.

The Portuguese still seemed to be staring at nothing at all across the room, lost to her. She scrutinized him freshly from the perspective of the scene she imagined taking place later on that evening in their bedroom, when she would break it off and transform what was already a *fait accompli* into something more flattering to herself, perhaps even engendering a little remorse and self-

210

recrimination in this pale lover with the feverish eyes and lips.

She watched as the old Swiss waiter bore down on them, waiting to see what her *unpredictable* lover would do. (If he had to condescend, why absolve the Turk?) Without a by-your-leave, the waiter snatched up both half-finished bowls of soup, spun neatly on the heel of a brightly polished shoe and was gone. She looked at her lover with his one forefinger of protest suspended foolishly in the air. She felt depressed.

Settling her eye on the dark window pane with its bright reflections, she wiped out the present moment and her lover and the ungracious help in the dining room and escaped to her sunny speculations on what might have been, back in the days when such a setting could have produced a spa or asylum. Oh, she could well imagine the attraction of the sanitariums in an earlier day: What possibilities they must have offered, those glamorous institutions for the terminally ill. For blameless trysts, agonized embraces likely to be broken by some swift tragic stroke. . . . And wouldn't there have been the utter luxury of taking the sun in an endless succession of lazy afternoons? In a happy No-Man's Land beyond reproach? Having one's meals prepared, being ministered to in countless intimate ways, no questions asked? Wouldn't everything be enhanced further by the calm that would come from knowing that everyone, everyone *understood* that you were indisposed, perhaps moribund, unaccountable, and that it would be a grievous breach of everything civilized—unthinkable!—to make any demands on the invalid, or to assign to such a one any blame in the scheme of things?

Yes, the little hotel had been, for a few afternoons, very promising of relief.

Coming back into the room, she could see a young man

211

with a beard propping himself against the opposite wall with one shoulder. Suddenly he was scrambling upright, hurrying to replace his spoon in the soup plate as a dark-skinned waiter whisked it from under his nose.

3

At the large round table under the many-prismed chandelier, the two old couples were approaching the lake-fish, as were old couples all around the dining room. Some were Dutch, some were Spaniards, others were Danes or Belgians, or Americans or Britons or Viennese. The foursome at the privileged center of things included one pair French, one German. Or viewed another way, one pair in health (the French wife, the German husband), attacking the fish with gusto, talking all the time, gesturing enthusiastically with a knife in the air and ordering frequent replenishings of the wine; the other pair (the French husband, the German wife), not-so-well. Compared to their robust mates, they knew they had fallen into serious disrepair. They couldn't help it: they felt apathetic, with a perpetual chill, a chancy digestion, sleep problems. They felt a displacement from the present moment and were subject to a morbid obsession with the past, an almost tangible past which both felt themselves to be occupying, even as they occupied the dinner table.

The healthy mates were just the opposite. They lived in the moment, and most of the time, for the moment—though they experienced almost daily the most delightful nostalgia for a version of the past. All in all, they found this a very satisfying arrangement of time, and wished that their poor unfortunate spouses could brighten up. Everyone had occasional descents, but wasn't the point to transcend all that? Wasn't that, more than any other single feature, Human Nature?

212

Still, both healthy mates curbed this irritation with their spouses and prided themselves on holding things together, on slowing their still-vigorous steps to the infirm pace of the others, on speaking up and leaning toward a dim ear to pass along this witticism or that, on smiling good-naturedly even when the witticism was met with a look of puzzlement, or distress, or fear.

The two couples met at the little hotel every summer. It was a way of life. Nobody quite remembered the exact reasoning and desires that had brought the habit into being, but it was a habit of such long standing that to break it off now, whatever its toll on the two infirm mates, would have been unthinkable to everyone involved.

They had all first met in this same structure many, many years earlier, when the little hotel was not a hotel at all, but a tuberculosis sanitarium. They had met, talked, commiserated, consoled one another, finally paired off and loved after a fashion and, later, they had married. Basking now in the little hotel's discreet ministrations, it was difficult for the healthy two to remember how miserable those early days had sometimes been, all the ways they had had to distract themselves from their terrifying circumstances, the price of stoicism and the bizarre nightmares of repression. At the time, even the locale had seemed like a plot against them, so close to the lake and its persistent mists. The locale, on the lake and so near to Castle of Chillon, site of a famous martyrdom, had seemed a stacking of the deck, and it was true that the number of fatalities in the sanitarium was rumored to exceed the norm. As rumor compounded rumor, patients whispered together about the imprudence and bad planning of the ownership.

The owners and staff of the institution, in turn, claimed that *if* anything could be proved irregular, *if* there were abnormal tolls or veiled statistics or irresponsibility or anything going on to buttress rumor—much could be laid at the doors of the patients themselves, for they had a heedless penchant for making pilgrimages to the Castle, no one knew why. There, as if mesmerized, they would make their blind descent to the hellish dungeon where the martyrs had passed their last days in chains. And perhaps there was something, too, the owners maintained, to the fact that these irresponsible persons returned sunk into an unnatural despair, and then spent their evenings reading an endless verse narrative of the tragedy by a famous English poet. Who knew? Though of course this should have no scientific bearing on the rate of patients succumbing, *if* indeed anything were untoward about that rate, and all the evidence pointed to there not being anything untoward in the least.

The old couples in the dining room knew Lord Byron's poem by heart and they did not feel that their diseases had been any more perilous for that fact! At the time, even in its original English, it had somehow been a comfort.

But now, all this was behind them, one way or another. The healthy two certainly basked in a different vision of it all! And somehow this vision was rendered deliciously poignant in the present-day hotel's particulars, reminiscent of things they had read in books, or later seen in films. Their personal stories had assumed a luminous "tableau" quality: of lover and beloved: pale, subdued, heads inclined toward each other so that the faces were in shadow, as if in sweet conspiracy, the sunlight beaming its golden halo, the lawn radiant as a gigantic emerald in the background. Sometimes, thus transported, their voices would suddenly burst out in a strong unanimous vibrato: *"Proud* of Persecution's rage!"

214

And why not? Their circumstances had thrown them together and it had been almost necessary that certain arrangements come into being. Why not put the best face on things, remember the good, forget what couldn't by any feat of god or man be changed? They had, after all, survived to tell the tale. Didn't that alone give a license to tell it as they saw fit?

The two in poorer health basked too in what the hotel offered, felt a need for all the ghosts and goblins called forth by being at the actual site of early misfortune. Unlike their spouses, they had been unable, even after all these years, to wipe out the terror and dreams of those early days in the sanitarium. There had been dreams of lung tissue disintegrating within the body as if it were a dead fish, afloat too long in an untended or tainted aquarium. There had been a necessary resistance to finer feeling, because they knew that strength must be conserved in case one were among the lucky ones who survived, who might make it to the outside again, to live in a way that added up. And they had survived, and had made it to the outside and had lived.

But after the first jubilation of their great good fortune, after the first easy breaths of life, the possibility of romance after all, after the business of love without fear and marrying—everything had begun to go downhill. They had felt a vague discomfort. It came on them frequently, and suddenly: as if the shadow of another human had fallen across the table on a sunny morning when one had thought oneself alone in the house. The worst dreams of their illness returned and persisted. They watched their children grow up and feared what might be festering invisibly within, did not trust them actually. And sometimes, just when involved in an intense pleasure of food or love or natural scenery or festive gathering, they would be suddenly washed in a subtle guilt, of no clear source or expiation.

215

As the years went on, a specific melancholy tinted their work and days, alienating them from their spouses, even, who had grown bored with them and shied away. In extreme age, so remote that they no longer counted, they knew, they watched their long-suffering mates finally blossom out from under the gloom, a consolation of sorts. As for themselves, the small hotel had become something to be suffered almost in atonement, its fish course each evening a pungent reminder of an ancient illness, the sacrificial lamb or veal or young bird that followed a transubstantiation of sorts, repugnant but necessary. Dinner at the little hotel, more than any other activity in their almost-finished lives, relocated them absolutely in grim history. It summoned memory as clear as a newspaper photograph, and it engendered, summer after summer, the not-quite-clear but unmistakable knowledge that somehow this history had been of their own making, as if they had contrived a tableau. Sometimes, occupied in these thoughts, they would mumble simultaneously, in a doleful duet, ". . . Finished as we had begun. . . ."

In previous summers, when the weather had been agreeable, the four had spent all their afternoons in a half-circle on one of the verandahs, the unfortunates lost in some private realm of ache or pain, the fortunates chatting and gossiping and sneaking looks of longing at the lawn. Sometimes it was naked of furniture, other times two wooden chairs might be placed close together at a suggestive angle. But on just as many afternoons, some thoughtful minister of the hotel business would have placed four chairs on the lawn, and while it was not always as pleasurable for the fortunates to take them over as it was to watch the empties from the verandah, nevertheless it was sometimes very pleasant indeed, especially when the problematic spouses were in netherland. Nothing was worse, though, than the rainy days. Couped inside together, the lawn seeming to absorb the gray of the day's light beyond their windows, the healthy mates sunk into mild depressions and took on some of the qualities they despised most in their spouses, a mood and manner that could be relieved only in certain ways. Among these were dinner under the light of the chandelier (a cluster of suns!), and the hint of a break in the weather.

Just that afternoon, after so many days of fog and drizzle, there had been such a hint. The sun had suddenly burst through the clouds and mists, and though a faint rain fell across its rays, the healthy mates had bundled up their charges and hustled them out on a verandah. At first there had been a manic surge of pleasure in the one pair, a corresponding density of depression in the other. They had taken their customary spots in wet chairs and looked out onto the lawn shifting its tones under a roll of cloud moving across the sunlight. But for the optimists, disappointment soon returned. First, the chairs on the lawn were visible only intermittently and clearly beyond their enjoyment in the queer mixture of weather. Also, half-enshrouded in fog, the chairs would not give up the images of lovers or anything else that was promising. In fact, the suggestiveness of the chairs' angles, the implied conspiratorial coupling coming forth from the arrangement and unrelieved by any images of human curvature: well, there was today something insidious in the implication, each member of the happy couple noted separately. The spouses noted it too, and felt some lifting of mood in the confirmation, but not enough to alter the general atmospherics on the verandah.

Secondly, and much worse for everybody, a young bearded man had surveyed them with a movie camera. He had at first been a figure of little interest in the background, taking shots of the roof, the facade, a queer little

217

cottage off to the side of things—and then, suddenly, with
no request or inquiry, he had begun to take pictures of the
verandah and of them, and had assumed for a time a site
equidistant between them and the foggy lawn chairs and
had moved his great lens back and forth between the two,
in an almost obscene gesture. As if they had no claim on a
say in the matter, he was angling in on them, rudely,
going for the sickly mates alone, scrutinizing their faces,
so pathetic in the pinch and sag of major depression.

The alarmed healthy mates had moved quickly, herding
the other two into the relative protection of one of the
common rooms. The healthy German male, so angry he
would smite the devil if he persisted, fingered his Swiss
army knife deep in his trouser pocket. The healthy French
female felt herself near collapse as she stepped in front of
her poor husband. At the window, even though their outrage was unmistakable, the young tramp persisted, his big
glass eye pressed against the window pane. It had been a
great shock all the way around.

The two healthy mates could see the American film
student now, alone at a table across the room, shoveling
food into his mouth with no finesse at all. They pretended
not to note him. He couldn't harm them now, not in the
dining room, not without his monster weapon.

Besides, dinner transformed everything! Dinner was a
lovely time, especially at the end of a rainy day full of dull
card games or the pretense of reading the inferior literature of the Swiss that tumbled from the hotel's shelves,
the dreary Hesse, Gottfried Keller, Johanna Spyri (!) . . .
deprived of one's amphitheatre of lawn and lawn chairs
. . . frightened out of one's wits by a crude interloper . . .
all of it getting too close to what one *could* imagine, if
pressed. . . .

Dinner! Wrapped in one's best shawl, folded hand-
somely into one's best suit, viewing it all in the dark win-

218

dows that ran floor-length along most of the room, giving
the overly exotic Turkish waiter the more familiar appearance of the Portuguese servants they themselves employed at home—

Dinner! The wonderful food so thoughtfully prepared
for easy digestion, the soup like smooth cream, the lake-
fish a triumph of flakiness, the pink little slices of baby
cows or baby sheep or the soft breasts of young chickens
coming up, the softer desserts sure to follow—

Dinner under the gold and crystal chandelier, bright as
a glacier at noon! So grand and so ornate that someone of
crude sensibility might consider it an incongruous item in
the otherwise prim dining room, but most would be
blinded to such a possibiity by the beautiful light—and
happy for it!

And how fortunate was their little group, to have the
fixture descend from its great coin-like medallion plastered on the ceiling (white on white, barely visible but
reassuring nevertheless) to a spot directly over them.
From a corner of the eye the cognoscenti would note,
tucked discreetly into a corner, one or two of the hotel's
chairs in subdued and rich upholstery. All these touches
could make one forget that the rain went on in the dark
outside the dining room, could make one ignore the brash
American with his motorized monocle and bad manners,
make one see some tendril of hope, even, in a strange couple across the room. A beautiful woman in silk with complexion like the blancmange they had had for dessert the
previous evening was smiling very cordially at them, in-
clining her head in polite deference. At her side her ca-
daverous table-mate slumped against the wall, ill or
depressed or arrogant, who could tell? But there was hope,
yes: his days, casting such gloom over everything beautiful, were surely numbered. He looked half-dead, like a
miniature of Nosferatu of cinematic fame.

219

The German husband and French wife talked on with animation, dipping solicitously toward their spouses to tell a joke or to wipe a bit of food from a lip with the bright napkins of the little hotel. They summoned more wine, regaled each other in a high enthusiasm for everything around them, buoyant and frankly satisfied with themselves—though each always raised a silent toast sometime during such an evening to whatever miracle had relieved them from all that haunted their poor, dreary spouses, who when given a chance to make it to the outside and live in a way that added up, had muffed it.

But the poor French husband and the poor German wife, nearly gagging on the undercooked fish whose centers still retained lines of very red blood, fueled themselves at a slow rate. They endured the dining room and all its unpleasantness, hoping, even so late in the day, for absolution, though somewhere they knew that things had already added up, more or less.

4

The old people were very slow eaters, and each evening the waiters would need to prod them, and any guilty others, if there was to be an hour for the waiters themselves between tidying up the dining room and setting up the tables for breakfast and going to bed.

Many of the waiters, even now, were Swiss, though the staff had for some time been rounded out with Turks, Portuguese, Moluccans and more, as necessary. They were men of different ages—late adolescents, young fathers, middle-aged men of distinction, their white jackets especially crisp, their black pants neatly pleated; old men who did all these one better: shining their black-leather, steel-tapped shoes to reflect the trouser-cuffs; scrubbing their skin ruddy as a Rennet apple in season. These old men had worked in the structure even when it had been a sanitarium, back between the Wars.

As orderlies, they had shown an amazing resistance to lung disease and, when shortly before the War, the sanitarium had moved into a lucrative intermediate phase before becoming the little hotel, the old waiters had prospered along with it, laying aside something for later, and later still.

This phase had occurred in two parts. First, the building had served briefly as a stopping place for wealthy refugees from the East during the early premonitions of the Upheaval. Second, it had been a secret resort for some of the German Führer's most valued officers for several years, as they took a few days' respite in one another's company, and in the company of one another's mistresses, before returning to the taxing business of the War and administering Vichy France. During both parts of this phase, the old waiters—young men then—had gone on as usual with the redundant favors such guests demanded, and had gone on too after the War, hardly varying any of their routines as the officers' retreat metamorphosed into the little hotel without much renovation.

The upholstered chairs had come with the officers, and the chandelier had been donated by one high in the German command in 1943, to the immense delight of proprietors and staff alike. With the exception of a fresh coat of paint every second spring and some occasional replacements of lawn chairs and awnings that had suffered from the rainy seasons that came and went in the town by the lake, the family that owned the little hotel had felt no need to alter the original trappings. In fact they took some pride that the little hotel was so flexible and well-conceived that it had been able to suit sick people, rich refugees, powerful military men, sentimental lovers and tourists on a lark alike, for so many, many years, with very little extra expense to themselves.

The original owners were now dead, buried on a peaceful green knoll overlooking the lake. They had been the ones, during the first world madness, to shelter a good-looking young Italian, traveling with knapsack through the remote parts of their country. He was a conscientious objector, seeking momentary asylum in a civilized nation that well understood objections of conscience and many other objections as well. The original proprietors had received him gladly, though he had not been able to pay much and though he had created a slight havoc among the recovering young women among their clientele. He was a very compelling and masculine young man, intense and easy at once, with the shrewd eyes of a hawk and the enormous charm of all natural raconteurs. A few minutes' chat with him on the afternoon he wandered by, and the proprietors calculated in an instant, by a special sixth sense that had never failed them, that this would be a friendship that would pay off in the end. They had flung open the door of the sanitarium and welcomed him inside with no second thoughts.

And it had paid off. After the War was over, a grateful "Little Benny" sent them a gold figurine from Italy, a colossus of a man balancing the tiny orb Earth on one finger, a gift of great sentimental value all their lives, but nothing compared to the business he sent the way of the little hotel over the years. They, in turn, had sent him a pewter pocket watch engraved with characters from the story of William Tell.

They died before their secret guest rose to the zenith of his power. But their children had had cordial, if very indirect, relations with the Italian until his battered corpse was hoisted in a public square along with his innocent mistress, the work of ruffians. This second generation of

222

proprietors never failed to credit him, in their silent accounts upstairs, for taking an interest in them and being their emissary and advocate. Whether because of sentimental recollections of their parents' hospitality or a genuine knack for knowing a good thing, their Italian had been largely responsible for their lucrative shift from lung disease to refugees and officers. These last they had appreciated very much—such fine tastes, so generous in their contributions to the decor of the hotel. No, they wouldn't forget Little Benny, not on the last day of their lives.

And yet it was not always easy to remember, and in age, this generation of proprietors remembered less and less. They had been "retired" now for some years, and all the main details of the business had been passed along to their children. Now the old people had settled into a tidy sunset, still strolling the premises several times a day to insure that standards were being kept up by the younger generation, now nearing retirement themselves and turning more and more over to their own children. Such continuity was contenting to the old couple as they strolled about the lawn or up to the knoll where their parents reposed. Most of the time, though, they kept to their small cottage at the edge of the hotel grounds—a cottage that their parents had occupied before them, and which would one day be occupied by a child of their own. It was shaped like a chalet, but it had the solid facade of bank architecture.

Though others sometimes found the queer cottage remarkable, the old proprietors did not, and did not remark the remarking. The cottage suited them very well, and they saw nothing at all curious in its design or any other feature. On warm afternoons, they came out on its small side porch, which was a miniature of the hotel's verandahs, and they did not hide back in its shadows or otherwise shade themselves or wear protective hats or

223

anything of the sort. Rather, they put their plump legs, often dressed in shorts and short socks, boldly up on the balustrade or stretched them onto a comfortable stool, letting the sun do what it would, receiving the pleasure they had earned, and remembering nothing.

After this narcotic, they took a vigorous meal well before dark in the hotel dining room—consumed it at a steady, efficient pace, all alone among the doting waiters and their own solicitous children and grandchildren passing through, seeing to things. The couple would muse, silently and aloud, the whole meal long on the satisfactions of a life well-spent, personal *and* national. They never tired of recounting to each other how the Swiss had got clear of the crude business of Empire early on, had looked to its own house, declined to meddle in the business of others. They themselves had been active all their lives in Civil Defense, and how they admired the Nation's prudence in that matter! Let others involve themselves in pacts and treaties and coalitions and worse. The Swiss had prudently minded their own business, and now every alp had a dozen caverns burgeoning with all any citizen might need, with maybe a bit left for the carefully chosen guest, if it came to that. Yes, all, all safely numbered and coded and recorded, in case the worst happened. Oh, looking to one's own house, first things first, cultivating the well-spent life—these were the important things.

At the end of the meal, after they had congratulated each other a dozen times in between the soup and the fish and the baby animal parts, the old proprietor would peel the fruit with his ancient Swiss army knife, passing slices of apple or orange across the china and goblets and silver to his wife, beaming in great health and vigor at him, even now.

Afterward, drowsy from the meal, they would walk back across the lawn to their cottage in the last sun of the

224

day, glimpsing the old calves of dinner-bound guests coming in from the lawn, or the occasional smooth pale limbs
of some innocent in silky stocking beneath a ripple of
silky hem. Or in inclement weather, they would huddle,
smiling, under a great umbrella, warm and dry, taking
their time. In their cottage, they would sleep deeply until
morning, barely shifting in their bed. Beside them, as they
slept, a clock ticked cheerfully, imbedded in the belly of a
representation of the famed Lion of Lucerne, an heirloom
passed along from some long-dead relative, now unre-
membered even by name, who for one reason or another,
if for any reason, had wished to the commemorate the
massacre of 500 of the Swiss Guard in the French Revolution.

5

I'll break it off tonight, the Portuguese thought, driving
his fork into the tasteless alp of fowl and giving it a twist,
tearing flesh from bone. Once we're upstairs.

Putting the meat into his mouth, he suddenly felt that
he was suffocating—the food a barrier, his lungs flailing
helplessly somewhere on the other side. As discreetly as
he could manage, he raised his large white napkin to his
lips and dispensed the food into one of its folds. Then he
lowered it to his lap and shook the mess out on the floor,
taking care to aim it beyond his shoes, all the while feigning an undistressed interest elsewhere. This tactic unfortunately brought him, weakly smiling, face to face with
his mistress, who was scrutinizing him coolly, her knife
neatly packing meat into the tines of her fork. He felt an
unexpected shudder of excitement. How could this be?

He continued to look at the woman's face, mesmerized
as he had heard could happen to a person coming on a
snake in the wild. But there was nothing snake-like about
the woman tonight— No, he could see clearly her attrac-

225

tion and her subtleties, after all, and for the first time in a long while, felt that there was nothing to apologize for in his relations with this woman. Relations which, after all, had been profitable to both in various ways, in various times. Didn't the old guests raising their forks in a palsied orchestration all around the dining room watch her as if she were an actress or princess? Didn't she have the skin of an angel, the fragrance of a garden in spring?

His mistress continued to ingest the white meat of the fowl at a healthy rate, watching his face as she minced and swallowed, sipped from her wine and touched her immaculate napkin time and again to her lips. She seemed to grow more robust with each mouthful.

The Portuguese was flaming, deep inside himself. Oh, she was beautiful, and she had suffered loss, and he had had an enormous pleasure turning her this way and that on his sword. After all, she was English. Even as late as the previous night he had enjoyed that end of things. Even in the tedium of a tedious vacation, even after an interminable bad meal, consumed in loathing and critique, he could enjoy—could relish!—taking his sword to her. And there were other charms as well, other charms of speech or gesture or dress. What had he been thinking of in risking the loss of his association with this woman? The dip and curve of the flesh alone. . . .

Dizzy, he reached for his wine glass and drained it. In a moment, miraculously, he sobered, his sentimental feeling for the woman dispatched as mysteriously as it had come on him, thanks be to fortune. His former distaste was back properly in his mouth, and he felt a great relief. As a native of Porto, that rainy city he had fled years ago for the South, he had had his fill of the English, and their jokes (Any Port in a storm!) and their lawn tennis clubs and Toby mugs, which all the local porcelain companies had learned to turn out like money. Porto, Portugal too—

226

ravaged for 300 years: port brokers, bankers, shippers and more. Not to mention their precious Wellington, three dress rehearsals for Waterloo on Portuguese turf. Somebody should have gored the bastard in his cradle. Vasco da Gama could have turned the Corcisan eel into fish food in an hour. Three collisions: causing upheaval, massacre. Finally a civil war. Who stood for it? Who stood for it now when some What-Hawgh! Englisher slithered up on Portuguese turf and opened the "Wellington Publick House" or the "Wellington Bed and Breakfast"—?

As a boy in Porto, that wet city, where tuberculosis was and was still endemic, he would play a game as he went about on his father's business, carrying messages back and forth between the English and his father's import house, specializing in Brazilian coffee, but having arrangements with the English in Port as well. Carrying the messages, he would traverse the great *Praça* with its black and white mosaic of bulls and birds, and he would make a game out of counting the red "coins" of sputum that left trails among the banks and important government and business buildings edging the square. Sometimes he would get hot on a trail of fresh ones—flaming scarlet, not the purple marks of old sorrows. Forgetting the message, he would pursue the coins across the square to the tobacconist or the newsstand, up a narrow street reeking of dampness, where the buildings crumbled slightly from foundation to roof. Tracing the coins, the red ones cutting through the purple and black ones like a legend on a map, through the leaves and debris on the cobbles, through the cigarette butts and ticket stubs, past the legs of the bread women hurrying with heavy baskets on their heads, the legs with veins that clumped on their yellow skin like mountains on a *papier-mâché* map.

Sometimes the trail led to a dank doorway and disappeared, sometimes to a tired figure sunk at a table in the

227

littered garden of some nameless bistro, coughing over a glass of brandy or *aquardente*. Sometimes a pigeon would be pecking in the fresh ones, sometimes a dog lapping. He would be suddenly sick at heart, crumpling the message and setting out for the refreshing rocks and sand of the beach at the end of the trolleyline, then lying back against a boulder and drinking up the thin sun, if there happened to be any sun. Later, he would take his punishment from his father with no complaint, biting his lip against a tirade of invective, and weeping.

Finally, he broke the habit, put the childish game behind him, learned to play the real game by the agreed-upon rules, developed a keen eye for the moves of others and a keener eye in looking out for himself. Still, it had been a bad time, and it still worked on him from time to time in a very different way.

Was any of this the fault of the English? He didn't know, and yet felt it to be, felt it in his bones.

Yes, port brokers, bad-jokers, tennis and cricket players, bankers and more, and now retirees rolling in every day of the year, snapping up land on the cheap, taking houses that could have been used by the country's own Displaced Persons, so rudely ejected from Mozambique and Angola— Oh, yes: He took some delight *indeed* in her naked English buttocks raised toward his sword! Enjoyed her thoroughly at the tip, at the rip of his mighty sword.

But even that could be a bore. Even last night, impossible to recollect in any detail, now seemed to have been a bore.

He nipped at the watery vintage that the old Swiss waiter had just sloshed into his goblet and watched the grand table under the chandelier, enjoying the return of his former envy. It was a relief after the recent stroke of fascination with his mistress, an incomprehensible and repugnant accident. Absorbed entirely into her meal now,

228

she was as distant from him as the faceless woman in the gray shawl whose head shone brightly under the magnificent light fixture. That old party's face was bent into her chest, and he thought for a moment that she dozed. Suddenly, the woman raised her head, and he could see a great Vee of black eyebrow and, underneath, eyes that had traveled a universe beyond despair, a face exactly like her husband's.

The poor old things, he thought, not without irritation. They seemed little more than the husks of something. Why didn't somebody just drug their water, give them whatever their boisterous companions were taking?

He had, unfortunately, had a chance to examine these old folks up close earlier in the day.

It had happened when he and the English were in one of the common rooms, reading—he in a private chair, not the settee where she had settled and, clearly, expected him to join her. And then what? Move up close as a turtle-dove?

No, he had settled in a comfortable-enough chair under a good lamp on the opposite side of the room, and after opening a few business letters with his clever new knife, just purchased, and after scanning, unsuccessfully, the outdated newspapers for word of his neighbor, King Umberto, he had settled himself to have another go at the monster-tome on Vasco da Gama.

As a schoolboy he had naturally read the *Lusiads* of Camões, but that was a verse narrative on his hero, not quite to be trusted. Who knew what license might have been taken with man or deed in pursuit of a cunning rhyme scheme? He wanted the facts.

But sometimes a biography or a history could be slow going. After these many months of reading and re-reading at the book, he had begun to long for an expeditious film

229

on the subject, to tell the truth. But one as true to the facts as the interests of commerce and *"auteurs"* would allow. . . . He imagined the American film student venturing into such a project and found himself smiling in spite of the task at hand.

Actually, he had done quite well with the biography during these dreary days, if he thought about it. He had now reached once again the passages involved with da Gama's odyssey to the Malabar Coast in India, and he read again, with a sharp thrill, a favorite part: the raising of the famous marble pillar, claiming the discovery of the Indian sub-continent for the Portuguese.

He paused, backed up, and read it again, thrilling as if it were new information. The author had a way of infusing what must have been a lonely and exhausting operation with the natural pageantry that would have been, of course, absent at the original, but very necessary at such a distance. Well, this passage alone was worth the price of the book.

He was irritated to find his pleasure draining away as the annoying image of his mistress kept bidding for his eye. She sat primly, he thought, on the settee, indulging her troublesome habit of reading two books at once. At first she had been reading something on Queen Victoria, but then she had switched to what looked like, if he could make out the script on the binding, a biography of Mahatma Gandhi. He had every reason to believe that this was an act full of spite, though how she knew that he was reading about the Malabar Coast at that very moment, he couldn't imagine. Nevertheless, the book raised in front of her now seemed like a clear challenge to any Portuguese claims on India. He had an intense urge to call her on it: to recall for her just how things had turned out for the English in India, though surely such memories could not have lapsed! He felt almost bound for a moment

230

to call it all outloud for her and all the little hotel's guests as well: embellishing the worst humiliations and defeats with his special talent.

I must be crazy, he thought, putting a cap on it and forcing himself back to his book and becoming reabsorbed instantly, having hit on another favored part. So absorbed was he that he didn't even notice that a few rays of sun were breaking through the gloom out the window behind his lamp, nor did he notice when several old persons assembled on the verandah evenly with his chair. He read on and on—of the fortuitous miscalculation of Cabral, da Gama's arch-rival, who sailed off-course and nevertheless managed to follow his fine Portuguese nose and discover Brazil. And then it was to da Gama again, and his final *assumption* of India! The bombardment of Calcutta in all its clash and clang and boom of heroic terror. The account trailed off insensitively, the author suddenly coy and distasteful, declining to detail further the taking of Calcutta and closing with a condescending remark, "savagery too horrible to be described. . . ." Well.

Suddenly, a clamor arose at the door to the verandah, breaking his concentration. The old folks from the round table were scurrying into the room through the French doors, all of them thoroughly shaken, he could tell at a glance. The infirm half of things were hurried along to a settee, the twin of his mistress's, and the stronger two quickly swaddled the old limbs in afghans, then arranged themselves in front of the settee like shields, their terrified and defiant eyes on the window behind his back. The Portuguese turned to look behind him and saw the American, his lens pushed against the glass like a Cyclope's eye—brutally, stupidly ranging the common room, then moving down the wall of windows for a better vantage, apparently aiming for the poor wrecks huddled on the settee.

231

The Portuguese watched with remove, interested in seeing how it would turn out, and a bit put-out with the English, who was still sunk into her Gandhi and hadn't even looked up.

Suddenly, with no warning, the large eye of the camera swung away from the old foursome and moved in his own direction, causing him to start. The crude bastard!

The only thing to do was to pretend to reabsorb himself in his book and ignore everything. What could you do with the Americans anyway? They acted like they owned the universe. Why didn't they ever look to their own house, he wondered, nailing his eyes to the blurry text in his palms. Look to their own house in some kind of way that added up?

The print was irretrievably out of focus, but he didn't look up again until very much later, when the silence told him that the old folks and his mistress were gone, when some sort of sixth sense let him know that the American had left the verandah. Then he rose, laid his overlarge book on the table, and went up to dress for dinner.

6

That the little hotel was outside Montreux on Lake Geneva and not far from the famed Castle of Chillon, site of a martyrdom, was a fact that excited the English woman's imagination. She had already made two pilgrimages to the Castle. She had descended to the dungeon, in spite of the unpleasant dampness and moldy reek which worked on her asthma, a condition that she often thought of in an image she had from an American movie: a tornado, but in reverse, sucking the air from her lungs in great violence and then traveling with it to a point on the distant horizon where it disappeared. It was a terrifying thing.

Nevertheless, she was *compelled* to the dungeon. She

had made both trips alone, one in the previous week and one lately while the Portuguese played his vicious version of solitaire and stewed over his pirate's history or haunted the papers for a word on the deposed Italian King Humbert. (She would absolutely break it off tonight!) Unfortunately, on both days the site had been over-run with boarding school girls, mostly American, who chattered incessantly, battering poor English further with bits of pidgin French. They cliqued together, giggling and telling secrets, their shoes on the stones adding to the racket. They took something from the atmosphere, no doubt of it. But she had got into the mood of things, nevertheless— trudged around the dungeon's columns, brooding. She had inspected the chinks, imagining the sunbeam, pathetic and rosy at once, that had been invented for the last martyr by Byron, the dreamy rake. In spite of the girls, she had managed to brood on the men who had been imprisoned there, and on the narrator of the interminable verse narrative that she'd been forced to learn in school . . . back in dear, rainy old England. . . .

For didn't it rain in Sunny Portugal, rain more than one would have imagined? And didn't it now rain in the town by the lake, and hadn't she found more rain, all around, than she had bargained for or deserved? Bane for her asthma. And more and more, didn't it seem likely that it would be raining everywhere she might be likely to go? Wasn't it likely that it was raining even now in Sunny Missolonghi, where Byron had been martyred, after saving these martyred Swiss to torture English school-children. . . . Who could remember their names, even?

She felt cold and warm at once—cold with the vague recollection of Byron's restless pilgrimages, one even to "sunny" Portugal; warm with the memory of those terrible, dear, old school-days. "If thou regret'st thy youth, *why live?*" Byron had asked. The American boarding

233

school girls even touched her for a moment as she watched the last of their shoes and knee-socks exiting on the dungeon stairs.

There had been a time when the sun never set on England, she remembered as the voices of the girls died away. Never set, or so she had heard in school, again and again. Musing on this and enjoying the fabulous image it had never failed to produce, she had stood for a moment in a thread of pale light coming in through a crevice in the dungeon wall and marvelled like a believing pupil: an enormous green map of the world beaming with great English suns, golden and robust, sea to sea to sea. . . .

Well, at least no Kings or Queens "deposed" yet.

Suddenly overtaken by a static in the bronchi, she had come back into the dank present with a wheeze, the flush of her sunny vision disappearing as quickly as it had come, her head crackling with other noise from the beautiful club-footed poet, every school-girl's demon lover: ". . . look around, and choose thy ground, And take thy Rest."

Oh, there had been nights when the resurrected Byron had limped into her bedroom and climbed between the sheets!

She looked at the Portuguese, who was looking at the ceiling as if it were heaven. Byron's ghost was less deathy by comparison. Yes, break it off tonight and head . . . somewhere . . . in the morning.

Well, she certainly didn't trust the tale of martyrdom as told by Byron, a dissolute Romantic that only a school-girl of a certain age could trust, she thought, as the old wisteria-cheeked Swiss waiter removed the remnants of the lake-fish, and welcome to it: a hillock of overtortured flesh that had dismantled in bits that floated in the general silt of the cooking broth at the bottom of the dish.

No, she was leery of Romance, she thought, focusing on

234

the table linen, immaculate even after the rolls and the two courses. With pleasure she noted that her companion's area of linen was slightly besmirched with soup and fish and littered with crumbs where he had tested the rolls with his probing fingers. No, she preferred a nice Victorian novel, the Victorian decency and balance—all that rot about sexual distaste and hyperdeveloped sentiment was a vicious rumor. Decency and balance. And yet in the last few days, as she had been reading a biography of Indira Gandhi among several other books, she had felt a sudden fierce passion after all for the martyrs of the Castle, punished because they were symbols of something, no more. Indira, cooped up in a dungeon, hated because of something hard to detect, her comforting English sun sucked into the horizon. . . .

Well, noble deaths for *Lord* Byron, maybe.

The idea of martyrdom was exciting, but she, for one, failed to see the nobility, truly. She wished she could. It would be something of a comfort in the face of her lover's use of her, wouldn't it? And maybe a tale could be fabricated that made something noble out of the clearly ignoble. When she told him tonight, for instance: Wouldn't it be necessary to lay things out for him so that they were much more flattering to herself? Wouldn't it be very necessary for him to believe that he had misinterpreted quite a bit, quite a bit indeed? Perhaps the repressed old lover back in dear England would have to be resuscitated and revised for the narrative, her uncle and aunt with interests in the port trade and so much else pressed into service as misguided Capulets, impeding a natural affair of the heart with a trade barrier . . . yes, Auntie and Uncle Nigel: traitorous traders, never mind all Uncle's puff about "some spot that is Forever England"—!

Oh, no: She didn't think she would go back to Lisbon or England. She'd figure it out later. Right now, the impor-

tant thing was to get shut of this little, little man shrinking against the wall like a wounded animal—managing,
nevertheless, to jostle her with his elbow every time she
lifted her wine, as if jealous of her immaculate linen!

She weakly broke a roll in half and reached for her butter knife, heavy as some Sword of Damocles. The lover
was draining her dry, and for the moment she was taking
it, nothing noble about it. But it wasn't as if the martyrs
of Chillon had had any choice but to be "noble," was it?
Chained to columns and pillars. What could they do but
suffer it? The ennobling that came later in the telling of
things was curious, in Byron and in all Romantics—settling mostly on the One, the survivor. Who knew what
had been lost? Repressed? Lived down? That was the trouble with it.

She would hate to think of her lover rising up as the
One who would dominate a tale she hadn't survived to
tell. Her mind played across several faces that might be
plastered on their relations and she felt a terrible cringing
in her chest.

But the unRomantic way of telling things was curious
too: favoring no one, covering up this, slipping in an apology for that, exonerating and spreading out the blame, ig-
nobling those who'd died and those who'd survived alike.
Nobody clearly responsible, nobody clearly hurt more
than another, all having a point, the maligned mistress
and the bad-tempered lover alike, the rake and his sister,
the Brahmins and the blackest castes, the English and the
Portuguese and Indians and Americans, the sick and the
well, the alive and the dead—all equal in a vast Universal
Human Nature.

Well, she thought, her bronchi suddenly clearing as she
inhaled a very subtly seasoned bird breast, set more or
less in front of her by the incompetent old waiter—well:
what did it matter, really? All too much was made of sur-

236

viving anyway. What was one to do, when given the luck to survive, but survive?

Tossing off the whole web as unfathomable, she breathed in the fowl breast again, clearing her head as well as her lungs. Such brooding was good from time to time.

Restored by the proof, yet again, of her remarkable ability to delve into the murkiest depths of the insoluble and to rise to the surface intact, she smiled at her lover in profile. He was no threat to her just now, and she might have more fun in breaking it off than she'd thought, turning him this way and that on her sharp English wit, skewering him on her devastating *épée* without his quite realizing it. She centered her plate with good humor in front of her, looking down on it from above a chest that rose and fell in a smooth, sure rhythm, and she took up her knife and fork with new purpose.

7

He didn't need her, the Portuguese thought for the hundredth time, mashing and remashing two small boiled potatoes near a dish of puréed vegetables the color of ashes, drunk on an amazingly seductive whiff of her fragrance that had come in on a devious zephyr from somewhere, though all the windows were shut, the room tight as a crypt. Didn't need her at all, none of her Any-Port-in-a-Storm—Hawgh!

To stave off the seduction of her perfume, his mind struggled to render a grotesque kind of Toby mug composed of her matter. He imagined her face collapsing into a squashed version of itself, forcing the teeth onto a flattened lip. He imagined her breasts bulging out and sagging onto a girth of abdomen and hip that dissolved into a skirt

237

squared off broadly and flat, so you'd have some way to set the damn thing on the table—

His nostrils bloomed with camellias and flowering oranges like those that grew in her aunt's "English garden" in Lisbon. Fragrant as a mortuary, he tried to think, resisting.

He'd done all right, without the humiliation of being anyone's Port-in-a-storm! Done pretty well, in fact, once he was away from the rainy Douro Valley and the more immediate forms of English domination. Done pretty well, in spite of an inexplicable lapse into sexual and romantic madness, that had had him spreading out his business and property for the English woman's sampling, as if from an old habit.

Then one night he had seen the light, in a dream like the parables of old: a silly sheeted ghost in the shape of a Toby mug brimming with Port, who sloshed and clumped across the dungeon where he slumped against a column in chains.

And that had been that, he thought, almost satisfied with the Toby mug forming in his own head, half-balanced on a table of foggy perfume there. That had been almost that, and tonight, upstairs, That would be all that. Though things could still come on him, like a disease that went in and out of remission.

Yes, he had done pretty well, all the way around: some good business interests all his own, some lucrative hobbies, a house only a block from Umberto.

How he loved to see the old man's Italian flag rise up its pole every morning and unfurl glorious and undaunted into the sky of Cascais! It was no offense whatsoever, not a British flag or the oppressive stars-and-stripes that flew all over the universe: It was the heroic gesture of the Undaunted, refusing the petty political circumstances of any one era and rising above the facts. He admired the old

238

man more than he could say, admired how he took "Italy" with him, rather than leaving it for vandals and latter-day Visigoths, any "Duce" who might happen by. The Portuguese Court had once set itself up competently In Exile, in faraway Brazil. It could be done. You could take things with you, for a time. Arrange yourself at a discreet distance and raise your flag! Things weren't done till they were done.

How different from Portugal's own Displaced Persons. You never saw anyone flying the flag of Angola or Mozambique on a lawn, more was the pity. They had just rolled over on their backs and floated "home" like dead fish, put things behind them.

Meantime, "home" had gone to Hell—this "Revolution" and that. Someone changing the name of the Bridge of Salazar to something he could never remember. He still called it the Bridge of Salazar and would, whatever happened. Just as he would always insist, when traveling over the mighty bridge, that the great statue of Christ in Majesty that waited with its arms outspread on a mountain at the end was the equal in every way of the more noted Christ colossus on a mountain in Brazil, a fetish in the American cinema. Sometimes it was even possible to imagine oneself driving across the Bridge of Salazar directly into the arms of the Brazilian Christ.

Well, say what you would about the late President, he had managed that magnificent bridge, managed matters in Mozambique, Angola, Macau, etc. very admirably, until things went awry in a way nobody could have managed, and he had made the trains run on time. The schedule of the trains that carried help out to Cascais these days was anybody's guess, sometimes on time, just as often not.

Yes, he admired the Italian, and hoped he would make it back to Cascais to raise his flag another day. In his own old age, unless things didn't go as planned, he hoped to

rise to such exciting mornings himself—send his bright
Portuguese flag into the balmy air of a resort near Rio,
then spend his day in leisurely putter on his green estate
beneath it: among his native Indian gardeners, soothed by
the songs of parrots from deep in a jungle fragrant with
orchids and passion flowers.

The woman's perfume remained strong in his head,
creating an ache but not releasing him from the more destructive aspect of the scent. Umberto . . . who—one
heard—would (for a price) dispense a title. . . .

In despair, he looked around the room. Things could go
so that he ended up not among the frangipani and parrots
of his dreams, but in a place like this, day after rainy day,
eating one bad meal after the next, night after dreary
night. Against the long windows, he was surprised to see
the old people's heads reflecting like lilies on a swamp.
The windows were undraped.

That was a surprise. The little hotel had certainly given
him the impression that those windows were draped. Perhaps draped and shuttered too.

8

The old proprietors were sleeping deeply by their clock,
even as the waiters prodded the old guests to spoon up the
dregs of fish-juice, and deeper still when the purple breast-
bones of the birds were scooped into a waiting receptacle
and a salad was offered in words that the waiters hoped
would make it clear that a salad really would not be a
good idea this late in the day. Most of the old diners did
decline the salad this evening, the waiters noted with relief, going off to the pantry for the small servings of
charlotte russe in *crème anglais*, a few local white chocolates, and the parsimonious plates of Swiss cheese—small
wedges of Emmenthal, Gruyere, Neuchâtel—and every-

one's favorite: Petit suisse, pure white cream cheese almost innocent of the rennet's bite. Imported from France, and a bargain nonetheless.

The pudding would be ingested quickly, no problem there, and the old waiters' special sense of such things told them that most guests would have courage neither for the chocolate nor the cheese this turbulent evening. Things were too delicately balanced for that. They rarely took coffee, and should they decide to risk a small *kirschwasser*, chances were good that they would go into the common room where they could snooze over it in more comfortable chairs, leaving the waiters free at last.

The four at their generous table spooned the charlotte, the strong two occasionally reaching over to wipe a dollop of custard from a lip or shirt front. None took coffee, and once dinner was over, all four rose and went directly upstairs. It had been an unusually trying day—a disaster for the infirm, barely saved-by-dinner for their jovial mates. The sick spouses had begun to complain toward the end of the meal, intolerable to the other two. The memory of the deranged man with the camera had intruded, as well as the memory that the rain had returned after only a few tantalizing minutes of sun. And was still returning, with a vengeance. They could hear it now as they made their way up the stairs and to their respective rooms. All in all, best to turn in early.

The Portuguese and the English played with the charlotte, which was too sweet for both tastes, moved the chocolates here and there on the plate, ingested a bit or smear of cheese, even the petit suisse unappetizing for once. Then they ordered coffee and, much to the old Swiss waiter's distress, two tawny ports to be taken at table. Both lingered, watching the last guests leave the dining room—the American with his camera balanced on one shoulder, several generic older guests. Watched the

241

waiters begin the rush of cleaning up. At a sideboard, the Turkish waiter hacked at someone's leftover bird with his pocket knife, chewing rapidly, his service towel dancing on his arm like a veil. All around the couple, linen was being flung through the air, the room resounding with the clash and clatter of cutlery against china. Having nothing to say to each other, and yet not wanting to accede too readily to the waiter's obvious desire after all, each made an activity of regarding the ceiling, its stark white paint and laurel leaves in bas-relief soothing in a way. They were too far from the coin-like medallion above the chandelier to make it out, but each squinted in that direction from time to time.

But finally the activity bored them. The English woman was finding it impossible to concentrate. The Turk had finished his chicken and begun to clear the table right next to them with a terrific clamor, reminding her of certain Indian waiters in Soho after all. Why was it, if Empire was such an evil as those in charge of telling things were always insisting—why had all the Indians, West, East, and otherwise, flocked to London at the first opportunity? Bringing disease, making the streets unsafe to walk at night, firebombing whole neighborhoods, rioting like the Northern Irish, American Negroes—? She felt a swift and painful nostalgia for Merry Old England, and grew sad that she had been deprived of it long before she was born.

If only the ceiling were a deep, deep blue, and shining with a hundred red English suns. She imagined herself beneath such a ceiling, sunk into a great pink cushion of Indian silk, musing on just such a ceiling.

Pity they hadn't painted a bacchanal, her lover thought, imagining apple-cheeked nymphs in transparent robes that drooped from the shoulder, exposing a tiny nipple, seeing for the moment himself: a rugged piper with cloven hooves. He had managed to free himself of neither the woman's succulent odor nor his exasperation with her and himself, and he lingered in an intermediate emotional state, susceptible to love or hate, lust or repulsion. What . . . Well. There. Boredom always aroused him in the end, he observed, depressed.

Finally, the old Swiss waiter yanked even the vase of white lilies off the table, upsetting the woman's port in the process, and quickly turned his back, refusing to notice it. The couple, unwilling to push their luck further, got up and went gloomily toward the stairs. But at the last minute, they veered off, as if of a single mind, and hurried into the reading room where they had spent the afternoon.

The Portuguese quickly reclaimed his same reading chair, where his book waited exactly where he had left it. Though he was enormously irritated with the waiter, he was grateful that the Swiss had proven, once again, that this was one spot in the world where you could leave your property unattended and be sure that it would be there when you got back. He opened the book and located the passage of his hero's final voyage to Calicut.

Across the room, his mistress was moving along the wall, fingering the Swiss volumes. He remarked with satisfaction that she had entirely misunderstood the Swiss and had taken her own books upstairs. Raising his large biography in case he needed a hiding place, he watched covertly as she took down an oversized book with an illustrated cover: *Heidi!* Well, what could you do? He felt a wavelet of amused tenderness. And what would her inevitable second selection be? He watched sleepily over the top of his own book, his great tangled eyebrows poised and ready to shift his gaze downward—which was necessary as she selected her second volume and headed toward her settee, making an unnecessary detour by his chair.

243

He watched her sylph-like bottom-half from beneath the subterfuge of his lowered lids, caught the title of the "mystery book" held at her waist. The small white fist knotted on the book obscured the nails of her fingers— and how he longed to see that rosy pentad just now. He fought an urge to reach out, detain the little hand, an urge to caress the drape of skirt over the flank. No, better wait to see how things go upstairs. Can't be too sentimental in these things. But: a history, he noted, amused again. The woman had selected a book on the famous mercenaries, the Swiss Guard.

The poor bastards, the Portuguese thought, running his eyes down the page of his own book, searching for entry. Imagine, to be so outside the controlling of things that your service in arms could be leased to anybody by the State. It was good to live in more civilized times.

With the usual mixture of anticipation and foreboding he settled into the last pages of the text before him. You couldn't hold off the inevitable forever, and that would be something to remember upstairs as well. Might as well get it over.

He plunged into da Gama's triumphant return to India near the end of his life. They called him "Viceroy," and it was true that he set about in a princely fashion to right old wrongs, correct a hundred excesses of government and commerce. Oh, it was a splendid accounting, the author holding back nothing. Here was an heroic ancestor for her Mohandas Gandhi.

Reinvigorated and totally alert now, aware that he would be able to bring off, yet again, the most uplifting reading of the story (one never knew), he ravaged the text—consumed it heartily to the end: the symbolic death of his hero on Christmas Eve, irony of pathetic ironies, at a place called Cochin.

Relieved that he had been able to bring his hero once

again to a hero's end, the Portuguese watched his mistress fondly for several moments. She looked sleepy, very desirable, even decent. For a moment he saw her wrapped in a long white dress, reposing on some sort of settee on a verandah of his plantation in Brazil, a pitcher of exotic flowers on a nearby table, a bright parrot perching on a balustrade, as he approached her in his wide-brimmed planter's hat.

His mind wandered desultorily as the parrots and toucans cackled and cawed in the jungle. Perhaps her white, white wrists should be bound and tethered to one of his columns there, he thought with mounting excitement. Perhaps one of his Indians or Negroes should be standing over her with a whip. . . .

"Cochin." The word leapt from nowhere, buzzed into his brain like a malaria-carrying mosquito. What an unpleasant sound it had, so close to something worrisome that—

Fortunately it eluded him. And yet he could almost swear he heard a mosquito at his head, and that he had heard it even as he had shifted from the triumphant death in Calicut to his great white verandah in Brazil, and it was buzzing him right back into the common room of the little hotel. What. . . ? Looking quickly over his shoulder, he saw the great insect's eye of the American's camera, the whole mechanism whirring busily as the little shit filmed the half-dozing woman on the settee. The Portuguese quickly re-regarded her, her pale skin blooming like a gardenia, her dress transformed by the more subtle light of the room into a becoming rose tone, not feverish at all, and he was consumed with desire. He turned angrily on the student, dropping his book with a dangerous noise, which, he sensed, stirred the woman across the room. He raised his threatening finger of protest and un-

245

furled his horrific brows, preparing to leap emphatically from his chair.

Lowering his finger and allowing the brows to droop in defeat, he froze on the image: The monster bug-eye of the camera, the bearded goat behind it, and behind him the Portuguese waiter, lounging entirely out of his place in the doorway of the room, with great leisure munching a handful of chocolate; and behind him, the old fool of a Swiss waiter appeared to be paring his fingernails—giving himself a full manicure—with several of the implements on a Swiss army knife that anyone could see was fully equipped, top-of-the-line.

Sheltering his frightened mistress with his small frame, the Portuguese hurried her toward the staircase, the protectiveness the moment required dispelling his wrath and tempering the humiliation of this minor defeat. Warm with his protectionist's role, flaming anew in other regions as he watched her tiny buttocks grind together as she ascended the staircase, he felt that they would be able to work everything out upstairs. Let tomorrow bring what tomorrows bring.

9

As the English woman went about her toilet in the private bath, the spare furnishings and the spartan aspect of the bedroom took their toll on the Portuguese. They depressed his ardor and allowed the troublesome business downstairs to take over, and then the more troublesome details of his relations with the woman now disrobing in the other room . . . down to her corpse-like whiteness. . . . And then the troublesome business of the English in general, and then the troublesome business of business. . . . He would need help after all.

Slipping out onto the verandah from the large French doors of their bedroom, he stole along the wet wall in the

246

dark. He would see what he could see. Sometimes, an image, a quick glimpse, really, of strangers coupling in the shadows of their bedroom—even a glimpse of agitating sheets—would do nicely, save the day. Up ahead he could see a square of light and he increased his speed: Any port in a storm. Even these old lechers.

He felt a thud of disappointment on discovering that the French doors did not look into any private room at all, only a common hallway. But wait a minute. . . .

Concealing himself to the side of the screen, he watched the more robust old couple from dinner approach each other from opposite ends of the corridor, wearing bathrobes, each carrying a towel and a soap dish. Their skin gave off a ruddy glow, as if they had just scrubbed themselves. They paused and stared into each other's eyes in a strange way, he thought, given how many years they must have been at it. Yes, this was pretty unpromising after all.

He watched them stalled there a few minutes, vowing to return momentarily to his room and not risk any damage to lungs or other vitals from this insufferable damp, rain and lake-mist at once. The old man was stuffing the soapdish into his bathrobe pocket, never breaking his gaze on the woman's face. Well, what now?

As if on signal, the two embraced swiftly, passionately it seemed, and then pulled apart, almost as if guilty, each looking over a shoulder. Strange business. He drew back from the light and hovered at the window's edge, risking only one eye, one ear.

The woman smiled with longing, clearly, and then turned toward the door. The old goat stepped up behind her and, with his freed hand, grabbed a clump of buttock and gave a quick squeeze.

The woman giggled, the coquette now, her hand on the doorknob. Turning an amazingly elastic face to the man, she extended an almost prehensile kiss, grotesque in the extreme. Then she cooed, *"Mon petit cochon. . . ."*

The word drifted by the Portuguese at the door, snagging briefly on his ear and then traveling on, lost to him, as he watched, absorbed in the woman's coy salute, soap dish still in hand, as she twirled into the bedroom and shut the door. The old satyr, ramrod-stiff and grinning, marched off down the hallway, saying *"Ja, Schwein, ja, ja,"* chuckling toward the end.

Absolutely puzzling, the Portuguese decided. If so enamoured, why take separate rooms? These curious old goats. . . .

He turned back toward his own room, smiling, but disappointed nevertheless. He wished he could have seen . . . something. He walked slowly, hugging the dark wall of the little hotel and lightly insisting his member against the roughness of his trouser zipper. Sharpening his sword, he thought, amused, but half-distracted, trying to roll some "footage" of several unspeakable scenarios.

"Oops," said a voice, its breath hot in his face, as he collided with a damp bulk in the dark, giving him a terrific fright. "Careful," the American said. "Let me get a hold on the camera. Hang on. It's the South American, isn't it? What're you doing out here in the rain, Man?"

What was he doing, indeed? the Portuguese fumed, not answering. Wasn't it the verandah to his own French doors? What was this idiot doing out here?

"Blood Money," the American said.

What did he mean? Maybe one was in danger, trapped up here in the dark with this maniac. . . .

"What do you think?" the American asked. "I got pictures of this dump, right? The spa footage. One of those old waiters said if I just go some place not too far from here I can get peasants, muddy little farms. . . . Of course it might be another wild goose chase. I never heard of any

248

peasants and muddy little farms in Switzerland, but he swore it was true. Ignorance, poverty, skinny goats, disease, the whole shot, right up one of the mountains. But he looked guilty as hell, probably lying."

What the hell is he talking about? the Portuguese thought, impatient for his mistress's bed. He tried to push by the American and felt his chest impeded by a heavy arm.

"Then, I'm going to fly back home and head down to Florida. Do you know they've still got slaves working down there for the sugar companies, right in the USA? Illegals. I saw them on TV, chained up at night. Then I'm going to head down your way, get some jungle footage, *nouvelle vague*, some Indian exploitation, maybe an interview with those guys that hunted down some Indians like deer a few years back, a little *cinéma vérité*, some urban shots, slums of Rio, that kind of stuff, kind of *film noir* atmosphere, but a lot of rack-focus. Rub their noses in it. Some *cinema nôvo* too. Nobody's getting off the hook. Then I'm going to splice in Spa and Montreux, and some shots of your wife, looking like the last rose of summer— no offense, Man. She's beautiful. Really. Then I'll cut to the old folks, then back to her, and back to them, and then close-up to your face looking like it's gonna explode any minute. Deep-focus the old birds from this afternoon, the books. A little Schüfftan. Call it *Blood Money*. What do you think? Some jump-cuts to me with the camera, a little *kino-glaz*. Maybe dress up somebody like a conquistador and just have him ride through some scenes, or maybe just cut in stock. Or both. Or maybe zoom in on your book: *Vasco da Gama*. I remember that dude, discovered the Pacific Ocean. Anyway, the conquistador degenerating, getting more sweaty and gritty and desperate all the time. Did you see *Fitzcarraldo*—"

"Shut up," the Portuguese said in a phrase and a deadly

249

tone that he had learned from the American cinema.
Pushing past the dark bulk, he hurried down the verandah
toward his room. Americans, and their crude connections!
And Umberto: would he make it, make it all the way
back to Cascais? And would the Portuguese waiter be in
evidence tomorrow? And would one have to take it per-
sonally and pay the tab as well? Try to bribe the wretch
home with promise of a job? Why couldn't a person just
check out of the little hotel, tonight?

The rain blasted his face with tropical intensity. He
shouldn't have let her threaten him into this trip. It was
all her fault.

Inside the bedroom, while the Portuguese endured the
American in the rain, the English woman lay in the dark,
naked in the over-crisp sheets, wondering where her lover
had gone. She could have sworn something was on. If he
didn't come soon, it would be truly an annoyance. Sometimes that was how he did it: rousing her out of sleep
with no apology. She could feel how it infused him with
false power. And yet downstairs, and on the way up the
stairs, he had behaved in a fetching way, living up to her
expectation of him on the best day of his life.

Before turning out the light, she had been reading the
books brought up from below—the *Heidi*, a childhood
favourite, what nonsense! Where, ever, in Switzerland did
you see poor old uncles, goatherds in rags? And an utterly
poignant history of the Swiss Guard. Martyred for centuries. Mostly serving the French, even that black par-
venu Napoleon. No survivors. No stories of the One, only
the valiant, if faceless, many. But then springing up anew,
like Dragon's Teeth. Now guards to the Pope. Such deeds
spoke for themselves, did not require a poet.

Did not really require more history, and so she had
turned off the lamp, a shade perched on a bulb, perched in

250

turn on a tiny earth poised on the finger of an absurdly Romantic masculine figure. Not a decoration characteristic of the little hotel at all. In fact, somewhat cheap, wasn't it? The figure was cast in an undistinguished metal whose gold paint was badly scarred, as if someone had been scraping at it with a knife.

Meandering toward sleep now, she thought how strange it was that somebody would call up an army and then rent it out, indiscriminately, if indeed to Napoleon. That was a different order of martyrdom altogether, no glory of dungeon for a cause, no Missolonghi there. She was exhausted. She wished she'd never let him prevail on her to come here. The mattress was too soft, the sheets raking her with their angles. . . .

The rain misted her face as her lover threw open the doors from the verandah and came into the room. She could see him outlined like a colossus in the doorway, black on black. Well, too late tonight, wet Romeo. She shut her eyes, feigning. Her head did truly ache. Her brain was drained of connections. She felt weak as water, truly ill. She knew everything was on his terms now, but maybe she could put off till tomorrow what she was in no mood for tonight. She hadn't bargained for the rain, dungeons, starched sheets. . . . She drifted off reciting from Byron: "We were six who now are one. . . ."

The Portuguese stumbled in the dark, disheartened by his mistress's asthmatic wheeze, telling him she was asleep. He put on a small light across the room which would not interfere, honoring the vestiges of his earlier nostalgia for her, now gone for good.

Ah, the newspaper at last, only one day late. He began to unbutton his damp shirt, fumbling with the paper, searching—

Well. There it was.

Poor Umberto, dead in Geneva. His illness still "undisclosed." No more flags in the morning, alas. His generous titles beyond reach now. . . . Left the Shroud of Turin to the Pope, did he? Well. Well.

Sitting on a chair and pulling off his shoes and socks, he gazed again at the woman slumbering in his rented bed. She was beautiful. He was always forgetting. There was something so—commanding! Sometimes. Even in her sleep. He would never be able to give her up entirely. Yes, she had shaped him in some crucial way, no escaping it.

He was suddenly ravenous, a great bubble of acid rumbling in his belly. He reached for his jacket and riffled the contents of its pockets, bringing forth several tidbits from the dining room that he'd stashed there on a previous evening against such an emergency: a few niblets of the special cheese hardened in a paper, some chocolates furred over with pocket lint. Slowly and contemplatively, he ate them, his palate swirling between the excessive sugar of the candy and the bite that the cheese had acquired as it aged in his pocket. The hunger more in control, he studied the sleeping woman.

Really, who drained whom?

He turned slightly to regard an image of himself in the tiny mirror over the dresser: a man pale as a corpse? Or hale as the woman blooming against the white, white sheets? Even in this neutral light it was impossible to tell much.

Across the black lawn outside, in their little cottage, soothed by the regular ticking of their absolutely accurate clock, the aged Swiss proprietors lay rump to rump in their bed, smiling in the dark and gently snoring.

Woman Waiting for Train at Dusk

*

I⊤ is almost dusk on a perfectly normal evening. Across the rocky field, beyond the milkweed and Queen Anne's lace, the many bungalows and the few larger structures of the town have settled into a cluster of squares and triangles against a lavender sky. Here and there a telephone pole rises in a cruciform, here and there a parabola of elm or maple, and the steeple of a small church pricks at the evening like the point of a very sharp pencil. In the immediate foreground, the train station stands deserted behind its concrete platform, where down at the end, just before it drops off into the rubble of paper and tin and gravel, a woman sits alone on a green slatted bench.

The woman has settled a large purse on her lap and an old-fashioned wicker suitcase near her feet. She is in profile: a small straight nose and round chin thrust up slightly against the light, an erect and motionless posture. Her dress, a mauve silk with a high neck and long sleeves, reaches down to her feet, which are neatly crossed in their quaint shoes and tucked beneath the bench. Over the dress she wears a dark jacket, cropped at the waist. There is enough light to see that her hair, rolled back into a bun pinned low on her neck, is chestnut and that her eyes are dark and unblinking, fixed on the air above the train tracks in front of her almost as if she were a mannequin. But the skin on her face looks real enough, like lavender cream. Since the light is falling further, much must be imagined: the tracings of vein in the cheek, the creases in the furl of underlip, the small blue shadow that clefts the space beneath it. No, she is real all right, but she has a very fetching Other look, is the conclusion.

Inside the hair (and this is where you come in): you think you can see a pearly ear, curled nautilus-like around the opening to a long black tunnel that seems to go on and on, subsuming the station, the town, the sky beyond. Within that tunnel, a dim light slowly spreads to a sepia glow, revealing a bedroom with flowered wallpaper and the heavy carved furniture of the most indulgent phase of the last century. The high-backed bed rises in a swirl of ebony roses from a tangle of sheets and pillows, and to the side, the woman, dressed in a thin gown, seems to be protesting something. Her hands are raised in front of her, the fingers bent not very gracefully at all to repel something or someone, and her hair has fallen out of its bun and travels in loose frantic waves about her shoulders. The face seems to have knotted up to protect itself, the eyes squinting, the cheeks tight and contorted. The lips move, but there is no sound.

Suddenly a man steps sideways into view, his huge back toward you. He is dressed in some kind of uniform, but very old-fashioned, with epaulets and thick fringe. You cannot see his face, but the rigid posture tells you he is angry. He looms against your eye, and further away the woman, still protesting, has backed up and settled against the bed's wooden roses. She looks very small, compressed between the bulk of the man and the bulk of the furniture. Her eyes are still frightened, but you think you see a suggestion of resignation. As the man moves toward her, for a moment you want to step forward and identify yourself, struggle with the brute, save the day. But beyond his shoulder, the long window reveals you slipping out a side door and scuttling across the garden (you coward!), breaking into a sprint as you cross the street.

While you were occupied, the train has arrived without a sound, a series of dark windows segmented by bands of steel, something like a strip of film. Turning to look at it more closely, you are fascinated by these immense frames and the impressions they are generating from even the dim light remaining. Forgetting the woman, you watch these and follow the long segmented tail as it stretches back into the dark, only vaguely aware of the metallic rumble of doors opening and closing nearby. Then the windows begin to roll by, and you turn again to watch the train go, curving up to the right of the town, shrinking lower and lower until it hardly makes a bump on the wide, wide plain.

Back on the platform, the woman is gone. You feel a mild disappointment and unease, though you are unsure why you should, and since it is so mild, you are not inclined to pursue it to its source. The green of the bench has disappeared into the dark, and when you squat to tie your shoes, you glance between the slats and see, in the last wisp of light, the little town across the field, a solid geometry against the night.